D1281760

To Jim and Cindy Mosley,
Best wishes —
Bill Harris

NO SURRENDER!
A Battle Plan for Creating Safer Communities

NO SURRENDER!

A Battle Plan for Creating
Safer Communities

Bill Gibbons

Published in 2009 in the United States of America
by Top Shelf Press, Inc.
9 Kenilworth Knoll, Suite 311
Asheville, North Carolina, 28805

Cover and book layout by
Allegra Print and Imaging, Asheville, NC

Gibbons, Bill

Library of Congress Cataloging-in-Publication Data
Gibbons, Bill, 1950-
No Surrender! A Battle Plan for Safer Communities / Bill Gibbons
LOC number 2009903434
Includes bibliographical references and index
ISBN 978-0-692-00305-3
1. Politics, government. 2. Urban renewal. 3. Inner cities.
4. City development. 5. Urban policy. 6. Community planning.
7. Social conditions. 8. Environmental conditions.
9. Crime reduction

I. Gibbons/Bill. II.Title.

The paper used in this publication meets the requirements
of the American National Standard for Permanence of Paper
for Printed Library Materials Z39.48-1984.

The real threat of crime is what it does
    to us and our communities.

No nation hiding behind locked doors is free,
    for it is imprisoned by its own fear.

No nation whose citizens fear to walk their
    streets is healthy, for in isolation lies
    the poisoning of public participation.

A nation which surrenders to crime…
    is a society which has resigned itself
    to failure.…

—— *Senator Robert F. Kennedy, 1968*

CONTENTS

ACKNOWLEDGEMENTS

I could not have written this book without the help, encouragement, and assistance of others.

First, I am grateful to the encouragement of my wife, Julia, who insisted that I set aside time at night and on weekends to see this project through to its conclusion, even when it meant some interruption in our personal lives together. I thank her for her patience and understanding.

Second, Jennifer Donnals' hands-on assistance was critical to the completion of this project. Without her help in pulling together all the data and other information, interviewing people, and organizing it all in a coherent fashion, this would have been an impossible task to undertake.

Third, many thanks to Dr. Cheryl McClary, who guided me through all the necessary steps and served as a liaison with the publishing world, which is totally unknown to me. Absent her assistance, I would still be trying to figure out how to get this book published.

Finally, I thank Guardsmark, LLC, and its founder and chairman, Ira A. Lipman, for their support of the National District Attorneys Association (NDAA), which made this endeavor possible. Ira Lipman is a leader in the field of security services and a strong promoter of best practices in the fight against crime. Proceeds from the sale of this book will benefit American Prosecutors Research Institute, a think tank operated by NDAA to promote best practices among America's prosecutors.

Bill Gibbons
Memphis, Tennessee

INTRODUCTION

A compelling image made the front pages of newspapers around the world. It grabbed my attention right away. Several days after Hurricane Katrina hit New Orleans, Nita LaGarde, an 89-year-old white woman seated in a wheelchair, clutched the hand of Tanisha Belvin, a five-year-old black girl, as the two were led away from the Superdome. Both had been trapped for days. In that scene of chaos and confusion, the unlikely pair captured the attention of an Associated Press photographer. That photo hangs on the wall of my office. During that moment of crisis in New Orleans, the picture symbolizes how black and white, young and old, pulled together to survive.

Post-Katrina New Orleans faced another crisis very quickly. The city had a breakdown in the ability of its criminal justice system to cope with the level of lawlessness occurring in the city. In the 2006 recovery period, New Orleans was deemed the bloodiest city in America, only to see things get worse in 2007. The city had an increase in homicides of almost 30 percent compared to 2006. Police attributed most of the violence to drug trafficking and retaliations.

To a large degree, the underlying problems of violence and drug trafficking pre-dated Katrina, but the situation after the hurricane brought the problems to the forefront.

A pivotal player in coming to grips with crime in New Orleans was the Orleans Parish District Attorney's (D.A.'s) office, which was suffering a meltdown. The D.A.'s office was buried in pre-Katrina cases, with evidence lost or destroyed by the hurricane and witnesses no longer available. The court dockets were filled with cases the D.A. had no chance of winning. The relationship with the New Orleans Police Department had deteriorated. The office was operating out of make-shift space. Prosecutors and staff worked on folding tables. Access to computers and telephones was difficult if not impossible to find. To make matters worse, former employees had sued District Attorney Eddie Jordan for discrimination. The court had awarded them a multi-million dollar judgment. The federal court ruled that the office's assets could be seized to satisfy the judgment!

In the midst of this crisis, the New Orleans Police and Justice Foundation asked the National District Attorneys Association to assemble a team of prosecutors from across the country to develop a plan of action to get the Orleans Parish D.A.'s office back on track in maximizing its resources to reduce crime in New Orleans. I became part of that team, along with four other elected prosecutors: Paul Howard from Atlanta; Peter Gilchrist from Charlotte; Bob Meggs, Willie from St. Louis County, Missouri; and Kamala Harris from San Francisco.

We arrived in post-Katrina New Orleans in the eye of a new storm. District Attorney Jordan had resigned from office just days before our arrival. The new interim D.A., Keva Landrum-Johnson, had assumed the helm of an office in a state of disarray.

My first and biggest concern was that five elected prosecutors from different parts of the country would never be able to agree upon a course of action. However, it quickly became apparent to all of us what the immediate priorities were, what would and would not work, and which best practices needed to be put in place. Along with addressing basic operational needs, there was the need to focus the office's limited resources on the priorities of violent crime and drug trafficking. Moving toward community-driven prosecution that met the needs of specific parts of the community and more effectively addressing treatment of drug addiction were essential. It soon became obvious that we were in general agreement about what tools prosecutors needed and the policies and practices they should implement to make communities safer.

Much of our crime problem requires long-term solutions. We have an alarming number of births to out-of-wedlock teenagers that create an entire new generation of juveniles who far too often make bad choices due to the lack of adequate role models and stability in their lives. We have an engrained culture of poverty in which many have no hope for any meaningful future, resulting in a don't care or I'll get what I can now approach to life. We must begin to tackle these factors aggressively but realize that there are no quick fixes to such cultural influences on crime.

At the same time, there are approaches prosecutors and communities can take to produce safer communities within a short time. This book focuses on the tools, resources, policies, and practices that can help us start winning the war against crime now. They include effective steps to hold those who make the choice of committing crimes fully accountable. They include actions that can turn lives around before it's too late. And they include steps we can take to reduce the number in our midst who would ever be inclined to commit a crime in the first place.

This book is not an effort to put on the table every good prosecutor-driven idea to make our neighborhoods, homes, streets, and schools safer. There are hundreds of good ideas. The purpose is to identify a number of ideas that, together, point a path to victory in our fight for safer communities. Prosecutors, other law enforcement officials, political leaders, and citizens who care about their communities must not surrender. Every community needs a battle plan for victory.

PART 1

Get the Thugs Off Our Streets

It was July 3, around dusk. I had been waiting for the temperature to go down a bit (a relative thing in Memphis in July) before going for a run. My five-year-old daughter Carey wanted to ride her bicycle to the end of the block first, so we headed down the sidewalk together.

We had gotten about four houses down from our own home when a car pulled over and a voice asked, Do you know where Alaska Street is? I looked to my right at the car to see four guns drawn. The driver stayed in the car while the others piled out and approached us. Give us your money, or we'll kill you, one of the thugs demanded, with the guns pointed right at me. My daughter straddled her bike, not quite understanding what was happening.

My first reaction was a combination of fear and anger. I worried that one of them might pull the trigger but also asked myself why we had been singled out. And it crossed my mind that these guys, all appearing to be in their late teens or early twenties, were not the brightest bulbs in town. I was wearing running clothes with no pocket for a wallet! Did it look like I was someone with money on me? After hearing the demand for cash, and the consequence of being killed if I didn't meet the demand, I had to tell them I didn't have any money! One of them demanded my wedding band. Now, I can remove it with a slight twist but can't just pull it off. At this point, I was irritated enough to just say, It won't come off! Then, he demanded my $18 digital running watch, which I readily handed over. As they drove off, I managed to get the license plate number, and then ran home to call 911. It turned out that, a few hours earlier, these thugs had stolen the car they were using.

At the time of the robbery, with the adrenaline flowing, I was perturbed as much as frightened. My fear level actually went up after the event just thinking about what could have happened. With four gunmen, all it would have taken was one trigger-happy guy to follow through on the threat to kill me, my daughter, or both of us, maybe out of anger, or for no real reason at all.

Or they could have attempted to kidnap one or both of us. I'm just glad my daughter was young enough to not fully comprehend the situation and suffer the trauma that could have gone with it.

No one was ever charged with robbing me at gunpoint. They got away with that crime. But it's pretty safe to say I wasn't their only victim, and it's probable they were convicted for one or more other crimes. My guess is their lives have ended up like a revolving door, in and out of prison. No telling how many people have been their victims.

❄ ❄ ❄

I did not know Mark Pilgrim well. I knew him well enough to say a good morning to him at Sunday worship and to sit at the same table with him on occasion at our church's luncheon once a month after Sunday morning services.

Mark was what we commonly refer to as a street person. He attended Idlewild Presbyterian Church, where my family and I are members. He was a regular at our More Than a Meal outreach effort each Thursday evening. Eventually, Mark joined the church. He was always courteous and respectful to others.

Mark's life ended tragically and violently. Police found his body in an abandoned building. He had been stabbed to death. I attended his memorial service along with hundreds of others, both church members and friends of Mark's from the streets. There were many family members in attendance. It was obvious they loved and cared for him greatly. The testimonials of Mark's life were gripping. He had an artistic talent, with some of his work on display at our church. He volunteered to help disabled people learn the craft of ceramics at a city community center. He had a sense of humor. He didn't always have a place to go during bad weather. He jokingly referred to lightening accompanying a storm as God's way of taking my photo. He was a gentle man who consistently sought to avoid violence on the streets.

I don't know how Mark ended up in the streets. It may have been an addiction problem, and there was probably a darker side to Mark's life. But his death is another tragic example of senseless violence we must stop. As of this writing, we don't know who killed Mark. There is nothing we can do to bring him back. Was his killer someone whose drug addiction was never adequately addressed before it was too late? Could we have stopped Mark's death if his killer had been behind bars for prior serious crimes? We must have a battle plan to get the dangerous offenders off the streets and stop the senseless killings!

CHAPTER 1

Put Violent Criminals Where They Belong

Shuntell Maxine Taylor really thought she was going places. In the summer of 2004, at just 19-years-old, the Memphis college student had just moved into her first apartment. She was so proud about this milestone in her life. Shuntell was using the summer break from school to earn some money at a local print shop.

Excited and ready to put her own special touch on her new place, she headed out shopping for the annual Independence Day sales on July 4, just one day after moving in. She found the perfect pair of new curtains for her apartment. After she made the purchase, she raced home and hung the curtains that same day. Then she headed to her folks' home for a holiday cookout.

A week later, Shuntell would spend Sunday afternoon visiting with her parents at their home after church. Even though she was out on her own, she still enjoyed spending time with her family. She even called them on the phone from her apartment later that night.

Little did her parents know that would be the last day they would see Shuntell alive. Her young life was cut short by a convicted felon released from prison on parole just six weeks earlier.

Germaine Whitley pleaded guilty in 2001 to three counts of aggravated burglary and one count of theft of property. He was sentenced to eight years in prison but released on parole under Tennessee law on June 3, 2004 after serving just three years of that sentence. After Whitley was released on parole, he had moved into the apartment complex Shuntell would eventually call home. Shuntell did not know her killer.

According to the evidence in the case, on July 12, 2004, in the middle of the night, Whitley pried open a window in Shuntell's apartment, slashed her hands with a knife as Shuntell tried to fight him off, then carved up one side of her neck before plunging the knife into the other side, killing her.

Memphis police officers were called to the scene and found Shuntell lying face down on her blood-soaked bed. The case remained unsolved for almost a year. Homicide detectives followed up on many leads, but each turned up no suspects. That was until DNA evidence found at Shuntell's apartment matched the DNA of someone who was already in the justice system and on parole. Ironically, the evidence that sealed Whitley's conviction for first degree murder was a blood sample found on the brand new curtains Shuntell proudly hung in her new apartment one week before she was killed.

If Tennessee didn't have a parole system allowing early release of many felons convicted of serious crimes, Whitley would have still been serving his eight year sentence for the aggravated burglaries and theft. He would not have been able to get out of prison after just three years, move into Shuntell's apartment complex, invade her home, and stab her to death. Shuntell would very likely be alive today. She likely would have graduated from college and started a career. We will never know what the future would have held for this bright, young woman. If there was ever a good example of why there should be tougher sentencing with no parole for serious offenders, it is the story of Shuntell Taylor.

❋ ❋ ❋

From time to time, a well-intentioned person will make the argument to me that tougher sentences won't have any impact on the crime rate and will only put a burden on the taxpayers who will have to foot the bill to house prisoners for longer periods. It's an argument that is absurd on its face. If violent offenders are serving longer sentences, then they have less opportunity to become repeat offenders! It's an argument that assumes no one will be deterred by the prospect of a lengthy time in prison and that no potential criminal weighs the risk involved. A number of states have tackled the problem head on by taking such steps as greatly increasing the percentage of time a serious offender has to serve before becoming parole-eligible, simply eliminating parole for serious violent crimes, and providing enhanced sentences for crimes committed with guns. They've given prosecutors and judges the tools they need to hold violent offenders accountable. Not surprisingly, they've experienced reductions in crime and, in some cases, the number of inmates housed.

In 1994, Virginia state lawmakers passed a sentencing reform act drastically reducing the gap between the sentence pronounced in the courtroom and the prison time actually served. The reform, advocated by then Governor George Allen, eliminated parole and instituted truth-in-sentencing for all felony offenders. No longer would the sentence given to a violent criminal be a legal fiction, but rather a true length of time in prison. (Inmates would still earn credit for up to 15 percent of sentences for good behavior in prison.) Prior to this change in Virginia's law, many violent inmates were being released after serving as little as one-fifth of their sentences. The legislation also increased the length of sentences for violent, repeat offenders. Prison stays for violent offenders became significantly longer than prior to reform, and sentences handed down in Virginia became some of the toughest in the nation.[1]

Virginia created more bed space for violent criminals by safely punishing lower-risk non-violent felons through alternative punishments. After a decade on the books, Virginia's focus on tougher sentences for dangerous felons resulted in a dramatic shift in prison population, with the percentage of prison beds occupied by violent offenders jumping from about 59 percent to about 69 percent.[2]

The law worked to reduce crime in Virginia. From 1994 to 2000, Virginia experienced a 26 percent reduction in crime. During that same time period, Virginia's incarceration rate grew by only 6 percent, while the national average incarceration rate increased almost four-times that level by 22 percent.[3] In 2002, the overall serious crime rate in Virginia was lower than at any point since 1970. By 2003, murders had dropped 28 percent compared to 1994, and reported robberies had dropped 23 percent.

It's interesting that the action by Virginia's lawmakers in 1994 enacting tougher sentences for violent criminals and moving toward more of a truth-in-sentencing system was not in response to an alarming violent crime rate in that state, although there were certainly pockets of high violent crime, such as the city of Richmond.

The national violent crime rate was almost double Virginia's crime rate with 684.5 incidents per 100,000. From 1995 through 2007, the national violent crime rate dropped an impressive 31.8 percent, while the rate in Virginia dropped 25.4 percent. But it's important to remember that the significant drop in violent crime in Virginia was from a starting point that was relatively low. In 1995, the first full year the new law was in effect, there were 361.5 reported incidents per 100,000 residents. As of 2007, Virginia's violent crime rate remained more than 40 percent below the national rate!

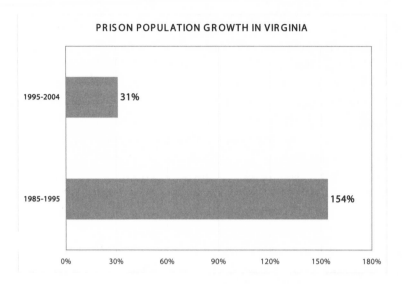

PRISON POPULATION GROWTH IN VIRGINIA

The rate of prison population growth in Virginia dropped drastically after tougher sentences were enacted. In the decade from 1985 to 1995, the number of inmates housed in Virginia's prisons grew 154 percent. After enactment of the tougher sentencing laws for violent offenders, coupled with more alternative punishments for less serious offenders, from 1995 to 2004, the prison population grew just 31 percent. Something was clearly working in Virginia.

New York is another state that has taken effective steps to keep violent criminals off the streets. Between 1995 and 2000, not only did the New York State Assembly eliminate parole for violent felons. It also reinstated the death penalty, passed laws to protect children from sexual predators, imposed tough penalties for violent assaults, and reformed domestic violence laws.

Two key pieces of historic legislation proved that holding violent offenders in New York accountable was a top priority of lawmakers. The Sentencing Reform Act of 1995 ended parole for second-time violent felony offenders. Three years later, the State Assembly went a step further by eliminating parole and requiring fixed sentences for first time violent offenders (Jenna's Law). Under this law, a criminal convicted of armed robbery or burglary can now be sentenced up to 25 years in prison. Importantly, the law also mandates five years of post-release supervision of all serious violent felons to help insure they do not repeat their crimes. The sentencing judge may reduce the post-release supervision period down to two and a half years for first time violent offenders. The Board of Parole is responsible for imposing conditions of post-release just as it would for a paroled inmate. Violations of post-release supervision conditions can result in further incarceration.[5]

While there were other factors at work as well, ten years after the tough-on-crime legislation was enacted, New York was the safest large state in the nation. In fact, in 2005, New York's overall crime rate of 2,554 per 100,000 residents fell way below the national average of 3,899.[6] While the population of New York increased by more than one million people from 1996 to 2005, there were some 260,000 fewer reported crimes![7]

More importantly, in addition to the overall downward trend in crime, New York witnessed a downward trend in violent crime. In 1996, the first year after enactment of the first round of tougher sentencing laws, New York's violent crime rate was above the national average. It was 727 incidents per 100,000 residents compared to 636.6 incidents per 100,000 residents nationally.[8] By 2007, New York's violent crime rate had dropped 46.5 percent, compared to a 26.7 percent drop nationally.[9] New York's violent crime rate officially dropped below the national average in 2002 and remained that way through 2007.

In the ten years from 1995 to 2005, the homicide rate fell 45.3 percent. That's nearly cut in half! The robbery rate dropped 46.3 percent, and the overall crime rate in New York declined 38.7 percent.[10]

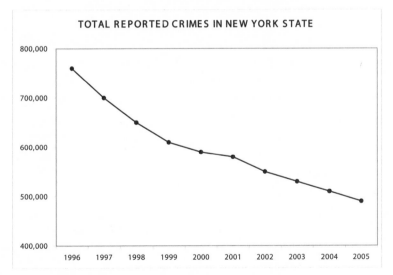

TOTAL REPORTED CRIMES IN NEW YORK STATE

New York experienced a reduction in the prison population after the enactment of tougher violent crime legislation. It created more alternatives for handling non-violent offenders in order to insure adequate prison space for the violent offenders. From 1997 to 2006, the number of inmates in the custody of the New York Department of Correctional Services dropped from around 69,000 to just more than 63,000.[11]

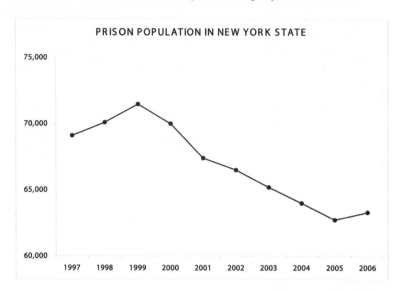

The rate of repeat offenders in New York decreased as well. The percentage of offenders who returned to prison after two years for a new felony conviction fell from 12.4 percent in 1995 to 7.7 in 2004.[12]

Jenna's Law has had a significant impact on victims. In 1997, Jenna Grieshaber was a 22-year-old nursing school student, about to graduate from Russell Sage College in Albany. She was murdered in her apartment by Nicholas Pryor, a paroled violent felon who had been released from prison after serving just two-thirds of his sentence. A parole board granted Pryor's early release in spite of a 14-year criminal record of violence that included felony convictions for robbery and stabbing a person. Jenna's murder was the beginning of a crusade led by her parents to end parole for violent felons in New York.

The new provisions provide certainty to victims and make it much easier to give victims accurate and clear information about the meaning of sentences, said Monroe County (Rochester) District Attorney Mike Green. Saratoga County (Saratoga Springs) District Attorney James A. Murphey agrees. One of the liabilities of indeterminate sentencing is the lack of closure it provides victims of crime, he stressed.

Other factors have contributed to New York's drop in crime. New York City's strong commitment to data-driven policing under Mayors Rudy Giuliani and Michael Bloomberg is a big factor. And increased law enforcement/security funding in New York City since 9/11 has certainly had an impact. But New York's lawmakers deserve credit for taking steps to get violent offenders off the streets and keep them off the streets for longer periods of time, along with insuring post-release supervision once they do get out.

Gun crime in Florida had been steadily decreasing since peaking in 1990.

This included the number of reported aggravated assaults, robberies, and murders committed with firearms. However, in the mid 1990s, Florida still ranked as the most violent state in the nation.[13]

Jerry Blair served as the Leon County, Florida state attorney (Florida's equivalent to district attorney) for 30 years, culminating in his decision in 2008 to retire. He noted that, beginning in 1995, Florida began a multi-stage process of strengthening its sentencing structure, while at the same time making a commitment to provide adequate prison space.

In 1995, Florida began the process of significant changes in its sentencing structure with enactment of the:

- Habitual Felony Offender Act;
- Habitual Violent Felony Offender Act;
- Violent Career Criminal Act; and
- Stop Turning Out Prisoners (STOP) Act.

As the names indicate, the first three measures provided enhanced sentences for repeat offenders. The fourth measure had an even more significant impact on the overall sentencing structure in Florida by essentially eliminating parole and requiring all convicted felons to serve at least 85 percent of their sentences.

Florida's legislature followed with enactment of the Prison Release Reoffender Act in 1997. It provided that, if a convicted violent offender committed another felony within three years of release, the sentence upon conviction for the new offense would be the maximum sentence allowable.

While the violent crime rate was decreasing in 1998, state lawmakers were still concerned with the high number of violent gun crimes committed in Florida. That year, criminals used guns to commit 31,643 violent felonies, including nearly 14,000 armed robberies. The violent crime rate in 1998 in Florida was 938.7 per 100,000 residents, far above the national violent crime rate of 567.6.[14] With the backing of then Governor Jeb Bush, Florida legislators in 1998 enacted the 10-20-LIFE legislation providing enhanced minimum mandatory prison terms for offenders who commit crimes with guns.

Under the no-nonsense law, there is a mandatory minimum 10-year sentence for pulling a gun while committing a crime, such as armed robbery; a mandatory minimum 20-year sentence for firing a gun during the commission of a crime; and 25 years to life if the bullet fired causes death or injury. Additionally, there is a mandatory minimum additional sentence of three years if the offender is a convicted felon.[15]

As part of the effort to curb gun violence, legislators also appropriated funding to communicate the message to the street level. They spread the word of tougher crime laws. The Florida Department of Corrections provided printed materials from the panhandle to the Keys. Through schools and businesses they distributed bumper stickers, posters in English and Spanish, and brochures in English, Spanish, and Haitian Creole.

A 2006 study by the University of Florida questions the impact of the 10-20-LIFE law, noting that Florida's violent crime rate had started to decrease prior to enactment of the law. Yet, after the law was enacted, Florida's violent crime rate continued to drop and at a faster rate than the national decline.

From 1995, when Florida began its sentencing restructuring, through 2007, the violent gun crime rate in the state plummeted 30 percent. During that same time period, Florida's population grew by more than 2.5 million. By 2004, Florida had its lowest violent crime rate in 34 years, with just more than 700 incidents occurring per 100,000 residents. Florida remains one of our most violent states, ranking fifth among the fifty states in 2007. Prior to enactment of its tougher sentencing laws, though, it ranked first.

The Florida Department of Corrections estimates that since the enactment of 10-20-LIFE, some 10,000 fewer victims have been robbed at gunpoint and 380 lives have been saved, individuals who would have probably been killed by armed criminals had crime numbers remained at 1998 levels.[16]

A combination of all the measures taken together has had a significant, positive impact, observed Blair. Commenting on the 10-20-LIFE law in particular, State Attorney Willie Meggs of Tallahassee said, Simply put, it's a tool that's helping us keep violent criminals off the streets for longer periods of time. He noted that use of the enhanced penalty under 10-20-LIFE is discretionary. Even if I decide not to use it in, say, a case involving a first offender, the threat of using it gives me the ability to negotiate a tough sentence that gets the offender's attention.

Meggs added a word of caution. He observed that the series of tough laws enacted in Florida means a higher rate of cases would actually be tried. But prosecutors in Florida had been facing serious budget cuts, resulting in reductions in staff and significant turnovers due to non-competitive salaries. Legislators have given us valuable tools to hold serious offenders accountable, but we need a significant number of good prosecutors to use those tools as well, he said.

Fed up with the violence in their state, Florida's legislators acted to hold those threatening the safety of its citizens more accountable. And, in the case of the 10-20-LIFE law, they coupled it with a clear communications campaign to get out the message. Florida's approach reduced the number of thugs on the streets of its communities.

✻   ✻   ✻

He pleaded guilty to killing someone in the 1980s. But Memphis M.O.B. gang member Ronnie Henry served only a fraction of his 20 year sentence, and by the early 1990s he was back on the streets. He was charged and convicted of theft and other felonies. He was sentenced to prison, but again released early on parole. His third and final time back in the community, he picked up more charges and was convicted of four aggravated robberies and a federal firearms violation. He's finally behind bars for good, but it took nine felony convictions to get it done.

Henry's not the only member of the Memphis M.O.B. who as a convicted felon was released early from prison to terrorize our streets because of a broken parole system. Eddie Partee was on parole for an attempted murder in which he had been accused of firing an AK-47 assault rifle into an occupied residence wounding two people, including a four-year-old boy. While on parole for that violent crime, Partee was charged and convicted of shooting and killing someone inside a well-known Memphis barbecue spot.

Ronnie Henry and Eddie Partee are prime indicators of a broken system that far too often fails to keep dangerous offenders off the streets so they cannot continue their reign of terror.

My own state of Tennessee lags far behind such states as Virginia, New York and Florida in getting the thugs out of our neighborhoods through tougher sentences. Many other states do too. Comparing crime rates among different jurisdictions is far from an exact science. Some jurisdictions do a better job of collecting and reporting data than others. But it does give a generally valid indication of where a state or community stands.

With that word of caution, it's safe to say that, as a result of not learning our lesson and not implementing some common sense solutions, Tennessee has suffered through a serious crime problem. Out of more than 300 metropolitan areas, the FBI crime data for 2006 showed the Memphis metropolitan area, which includes Tennessee's Shelby, Fayette and Tipton Counties, Crittenden County in Arkansas, DeSoto County in Mississippi and three other counties in northwest Mississippi[17], had the highest violent crime rate per 100,000 residents in the entire country. But that's not the only bad news. The Jackson, Tennessee metropolitan area ranked 13th worst for violent crime. The Nashville metropolitan area came in at 20th, followed by the Chattanooga metropolitan area at 59th.[18] Tennessee had three metropolitan areas in the top 20, four in the top 60. Even worse, comparing the 2007 FBI crime data by state, Tennessee had the second highest violent crime rate in the country.[19] In the ten year period 1998 through 2007, while the national violent crime rate was dropping 32.2 percent, Tennessee's violent crime rate rose 11.7 percent. In 2007, we had 753.3 violent crime incidents per 100,000 residents compared to 466.9 nationally.[20]

Simply put, Tennessee was not sharing in the national drop in violent crime. We were going against the national trend.

TRACKING VIOLENT CRIME RATES		
STATE	**STATE RATE CHANGE**	**NATIONAL RATE CHANGE**
Virginia*	-25.4%	-31.8%
New York**	-46.5%	-26.7%
Florida***	-31.2%	-26.7%
Tennessee****	+11.7%	-32.2%

*   From 1995 (year after enactment of new law) through 2007.
**   From 1996 (year after enactment of new law) through 2007.
*** From 1996 (year after enactment of first new law) through 2007.
**** From 1998 through 2007.

Prosecutors, police chiefs and sheriffs in Tennessee have tried to persuade the Tennessee General Assembly to pass tougher crime legislation. We've asked for mandatory minimum sentences for violent crimes. We've asked for greater punishments for gang-related crimes. Year after year, we get the same answer: there's not enough money. Those who calculate the projected fiscal impact fail to adequately consider the savings from less crime or the fact that many serious crimes are being committed by individuals released from prison early simply to become repeat offenders.

Finally, in 2007, our General Assembly passed a scaled-down version of what we had been pushing. The so-called Crooks with Guns law increased the penalties for criminals convicted of certain violent crimes committed with guns by adding an additional charge of employing or possessing a firearm. Crimes covered by the legislation included attempted second degree murder and voluntary manslaughter, among other violent acts, and the additional penalty can be up to ten years consecutive to the sentence for the underlying charge. And it eliminated parole for second and subsequent aggravated (armed) robberies. In 2009, legislators amended the law to include attempted first degree murder as one of the crimes covered by enhanced punishments for employing or possessing a gun. But, the Crooks with Guns law still affects a fairly small percentage of the violent crime cases in Tennessee. The law still omits first offense aggravated (armed) robbery, as well as the most common violent crime, aggravated assault. (In 2007, the Tennessee Bureau of Investigation reported 11,090 charges of robbery in Tennessee.)

Enactment of the Crooks with Guns law was an important step in the right direction, but it doesn't get us where we need to be to effectively reduce crime in Tennessee. After the law's passage, one of my chief assistants summed it up best. We asked for a hammer, and they gave us a screwdriver. Nonetheless, we are now using the tools given to us to hold violent criminals accountable. The Crooks with Guns law for which we fought so long finally took effect on January 1, 2008. And during 2008, more than 120 indictments applying the new law had been returned against defendants in Memphis by a state grand jury.

One of the first defendants in the state to be indicted for attempted second degree murder under the new law was charged with shooting and injuring two victims, one of whom was a Memphis police officer attempting to serve a search warrant during a drug investigation. The Memphis Police Department's Organized Crime Unit for weeks had been conducting an investigation into drug sales and prostitution at a local motel located on a heavily-traveled U.S. highway which runs right through the city. When officers knocked on the door of the motel room and announced who they were, the defendant grabbed a woman inside the room and held her between himself and the police, using the woman as a human shield. The police ordered him to drop his weapon. Instead, the defendant fired his gun which he was holding behind the woman. The bullet of his handgun sliced through her before striking an officer.

We're doing what we can with the laws we have, but there are thousands of defendants in Tennessee charged with robbing citizens at gunpoint or firing shots at someone to end a dispute still not covered by tough, mandatory sentences. I refer to them as the street terrorists who are a threatening our neighborhoods. These individuals are more than just neighborhood nuisances, but it is as if we have created a legal loophole enabling them to tiptoe around tough penalties.

Along with other states that inadequately hold serious offenders accountable, I hope my own state of Tennessee will show a willingness to fix our broken system by enacting significant changes so that serious offenders are truly held accountable.

It's frustrating. The very first sentence of the very first section of Tennessee's constitution notes that free governments are founded to insure the peace and safety of the people. Other states have similar constitutional provisions. All states need laws that hold serious criminals accountable and protect the public. Where such laws don't exist, legislators need to make it a priority so their constituents can experience the same sense of safety and security that citizens in Virginia, New York, Florida, and many other states have experienced.

I wish I could say the tragic deaths of Shuntell Taylor and Mark Pilgrim that I mentioned earlier were rarities. Regrettably, they are not. And in my community, there are many victims of violent criminals like Ronnie Henry and Eddie Partee. There's three-year-old Jessica Borner, who lost her life due to a drug deal gone bad. Jessica lived in a tough area of Memphis called Nutbush. Jessica lost her life when three individuals attacked the home in which she lived, two of them using assault rifles. They fired about 50 shots at her home. Six other people were injured, including Jessica's grandmother who was struck seven times. It's hard to imagine, but the three perpetrators were retaliating against one of Jessica's relatives. He had complained about the quality of marijuana he had purchased from one of the gunmen.

Damien Woodard was just 11-years-old when he walked through the courtyard of an apartment complex in Memphis as gang members started shooting at each other. Damien was caught in the crossfire and lost his life.

Marquette Mason was tossing a football in the air near his home in Memphis. A drug dealer saw another drug dealer with whom he was having a dispute and fired at him. He wasn't a very good aim. He hit and killed nine-year-old Marquette instead.

And there's 64-year-old Brenda Rogers who was shot in the head while sitting inside her car at a stop light. She was delivering a cake she had just baked to a friend. I could give hundreds of other examples of victims of senseless violence in my own community.

There is nothing anyone can do to bring back Shuntell Taylor, Mark Pilgrim, Jessica Borner, Damien Woodard, Marquette Mason, or Brenda Rogers. We need to think about these and the other innocent victims who have been senselessly killed or assaulted in so many communities. We need to think about the citizens who are afraid to go out at night, afraid to go anywhere alone, afraid to walk to school. **Any realistic battle plan must include tough laws that get the thugs off our streets.**

CHAPTER 2

Go With Custom Made Prosecution vs. Assembly Line Prosecution

The popular crime drama Law & Order entered its 18th season on network television in 2008. Fans can catch reruns nearly every day on various cable channels. Virtually every adult I know has watched the program. This show is how most Americans perceive our criminal justice system operates. Although the program is far from reality, there is some accuracy in what the writers and producers portray in each episode. In some offices, you can count on one team of homicide prosecutors being assigned to a case from the very beginning, sometimes even before a suspect is charged. Those same prosecutors stay with that case through arraignment, take it to a grand jury, and, ultimately, to trial. They work with homicide detectives along the way. They ask them to follow-up on information or work on developing additional proof.

In reality, this is how criminal felony cases are handled in the Manhattan District Attorney's office. As it's portrayed on TV, the same prosecutors handle the case from beginning to end. This is called vertical prosecution. It's the best way to ensure justice and the best possible outcome in a criminal case.

However, what the American public does not realize is that many prosecutors' offices across the country do not use a vertical system to prosecute most cases, even those involving serious crimes. Many use a horizontal method. When a case comes in, it is assigned to one prosecutor to handle preliminary matters. It is then given to a prosecutor at the grand jury level, who then hands it off to a prosecutor at the trial level. Sometimes, more than one prosecutor handles the case at any given step in the process. This can create frustration for the victims and confusion for the witnesses. However, due to resource restraints and the need to move a high number of cases through the system in an efficient manner, many prosecutors' offices across the country do not have a choice.

Some refer to this as an assembly line vs. custom made approach. For example, a chair that is mass produced by a company in the furniture business is going to use an assembly line method to make the most products possible for the least expense. One employee will build the frame, another employee will sand the wood, another employee will attach the legs, and so on. The chair will still work. Someone can still sit on it. But a custom made chair is going to be created by one individual. That chair builder will hand select the wood, cut it precisely to specifications, then intricately carve a design on the chair back. This process leaves that person's own personal mark. He or she will decide if it is better to use one-inch screws or two-inch screws as well as the best stain to use after thoughtful consideration of the type of wood and the purpose of the chair. This particular chair will cost the buyer much more money than one that could be bought for a fraction of the cost at any big-box retailer. But it will be a better quality product that will last for many years.

Now apply that analogy to prosecuting cases. The way many offices, including my own, prosecute most cases is to do it assembly line-style. This is the most practical way to get the job done. But the end product would be better if we had the resources to support vertical prosecution.

The prosecutor assigned to handle the case would have a better understanding and knowledge of all the facts surrounding that case. He or she would have personal contact with the victims and witnesses from beginning to end. This same person would know the history of the case, information from a preliminary hearing, or things a police officer had noted while investigating the case. All this makes the prosecutor better prepared to handle the case and requires less preparation at each individual stage of the judicial process.

Vertical prosecution provides better accountability on the part of each prosecutor. If there is a problem with the case, only one prosecutor, or possibly a team of two, is responsible for the prosecution. The case cannot be dumped off and become someone else's problem.

Vertical prosecution encourages realistic charging decisions and practical plea offers. The decisions on whether to charge someone for a crime and which offense to charge are often difficult to make. If the same person making those decisions is handling the case from beginning to end, greater care will go into making that decision. The same applies to offering plea agreements. It is important that the person making the offer knows all of the ins and outs of the case. The more familiar a prosecutor is with a case, the more likely he or she will be to make the best, most appropriate offer.

Most importantly, vertical prosecution enables victims, families, witnesses, and law enforcement officers to always know who is handling a certain case. We are able to better service the public by creating situations where victims and witnesses are not bounced around from person to person. The justice system is confusing enough without the added factor of not knowing who to ask for help or assistance.

In the Manhattan District Attorney's office, one of the largest prosecutors' offices in the country based on caseload and number of prosecutors, every felony case is handled in a vertical manner.

It makes everybody more responsible, said District Attorney Robert M. Morgenthau, who has led the Manhattan D.A.'s office in New York City for more than 30 years. When he first took office, Morgenthau insisted that his office adopt a vertical style of prosecuting all felony cases and misdemeanor domestic violence cases. Having one assistant handle a case from beginning to end is so much better, he told me during a visit to his office.

I wanted to see first hand how an office of that size, with the magnitude of criminal cases handled each day, executes such a plan. When I entered the office, I immediately knew all work moved quickly. Prosecutors were hustling about, carting files and legal pads. There was an order about the place. Everyone knew exactly where to go and when to be there. The office was a well run machine. Prosecution teams formed into six large trial bureaus that rotated responsibility for screening cases and drafting complaints seven days a week. The arrests made that day were handled by that day's designated team. The prosecutor who wrote the actual complaint normally handled the case from arraignment to indictment, and through the final disposition, whether that was a guilty plea or a trial. Each bureau was led by a veteran prosecutor who not only kept the machine moving, but mentored the less experienced prosecutors assigned to the team. You've got to be good at spinning lots of plates, one veteran assistant admitted. But you get a better result. I can't imagine prosecuting cases any other way, he added.

When Morgenthau's office went vertical, he said dismissals of indictments dropped and the number of guilty pleas jumped in Manhattan. We send more people to state prison. Some people criticize that, but all I know is if you're in prison, you're not out committing more crime, and that's because of vertical prosecution.

Jim Backstrom has served as county attorney, the county's chief prosecutor, for Dakota County, Minnesota since 1987. It's a growing jurisdiction just outside Minneapolis-St. Paul. He's been able to implement a vertical prosecution system for all of his cases. As part of the process, he's worked it out with local law enforcement agencies so that a prosecutor must approve on the front end any charge resulting in a physical arrest. With the exception of homicides, which are specially assigned, the prosecutor approving the charge initially will keep the case.

We're not reinventing the wheel by new assistant county attorneys having to become familiar with the facts of a case as it moves through the system. One assistant county attorney will know the case from top to bottom, said Chief Deputy County Attorney Phil Prokopowicz.

About 700 felony drug cases per year are handled by three prosecutors in a special Drug Prosecution Unit. Otherwise, prosecutors in the Dakota County Attorney's Office end up vertically prosecuting a variety of cases. Overall, it results in a better quality staff because every assistant county attorney has to know all areas of our state's criminal laws. It's an opportunity to become better lawyers, argued Backstrom.

Unfortunately, the reality is that caseloads and lack of resources do not make it prudent for many prosecutors' offices to handle the majority of cases in a vertical manner. However, I believe vertical prosecution maximizes our ability to successfully go after the thugs we need to get off the streets. My own office has taken steps to vertically prosecute all first degree murders, domestic violence cases, major gang-related crimes, crimes committed by convicted criminals with serious criminal histories, cases of severe physical or sexual child abuse, and certain white collar crime cases. These cases are the most difficult to handle and require more time than other types of criminal cases. The prosecutors assigned to these various cases approve all charges on the front end and handle the cases through disposition. Employing some out-of-the-box thinking and creative use of resources, we have been able to make it work.

Critics of the theory of vertical prosecution are few. However, there are some obvious disadvantages. The drawbacks involve court scheduling. In order to implement a complete vertical prosecution model, the judiciary must be on board. But this factor can be overcome if there is the will to make quality prosecution a priority. **Vertical prosecution is essential to build the strongest cases possible against serious offenders who threaten the very lives of citizens in our communities.**

CHAPTER 3

Use A Team Approach

The lights on the squad car flashed brightly just as Jerry Morrison's vehicle cruised by. It was a routine traffic stop that resulted in a misdemeanor citation for Morrison who was driving and packing a pistol. But the case didn't end with a slap on the wrist for the convicted felon in possession of a firearm. The Project Safe Neighborhoods (PSN) team reviewed the case in its weekly meeting, and because of Morrison's previous felony convictions (for aggravated robbery, aggravated burglary, and two counts of aggravated assault), the case was taken directly into the federal system for prosecution. Morrison was convicted at trial and sentenced to 200 months in prison followed by three years of supervised release. This 16 year and eight month federal sentence (from which he cannot be released early on parole) was more than double the time of his previous state sentences. His most lengthy was an eight year sentence for aggravated robbery. Morrison was paroled after serving 30 percent of the time. In federal court, Morrison was convicted for just possessing a firearm.

This tough sentence would have been unheard of prior to 2002, when we initiated the PSN model in our community. Tennessee has very weak laws covering felons in possession of guns. But through the PSN cooperative effort, local, state, and federal law enforcement officials are working together to put away convicted felons in possession of firearms for much longer sentences, primarily through the federal system.

Each week a team of state and federal prosecutors and local law enforcement officers meets to discuss every gun crime arrest made during the prior seven days. When Morrison's arrest ticket came up, prosecutors knew they had a strong case at the federal level.

PSN has been a nationwide effort administered by the United States Department of Justice to significantly reduce gun crime by bringing about more coordination among law enforcement agencies in tackling such crime and providing them with the resources to be successful. Since its inception in 2001, the Department of Justice has spent about $1.5 billion on hiring new federal and state prosecutors, supporting investigators and other law enforcement officials, distributing gun lock safety kits, deterring juvenile gun crime, and developing communications efforts regarding the consequences to convicted felons of carrying firearms. The beauty of PSN has been the ability of each community to shape it to suit its needs. PSN was not designed as a one-size-fits-all approach. It was created to encourage custom made approaches to address gun crime at the local level.

PSN grew out of Project Exile in Richmond, Virginia. In 1996, the city was in a violent crime crisis. That year, Richmond reported 140 murders. Guns were used in 122 of these murders. Richmond police reported that someone was shot or killed every 40 to 45 hours. The city had the second highest per capita murder rate in the country.[21] The Richmond Police Department and the U.S. Attorney for the Eastern District of Virginia met to determine how to combat the crime epidemic sweeping their community. They developed a unique way to address the increase in violent gun crime. They used existing federal laws to aggressively target and prosecute convicted felons who terrorized the community with firearms. They joined forces with the Virginia Attorney General's office; the Richmond Commonwealth Attorney's office (Virginia's equivalent to district attorney); the Bureau of Alcohol, Tobacco and Firearms; and the Virginia state police. This team approach to gun crime resulted in mandatory federal sentences for gun criminals. Every gun crime arrest was evaluated by a team that decided whether to prosecute the case in federal court, state court, or both. The results were head-turning. Richmond reported 94 homicides in 1998. Homicides dropped to 72 in 1999 which was about half the number that occurred in 1996.[22]

The Department of Justice soon seized the momentum of Project Exile and encouraged similar initiatives in other jurisdictions. Shortly after taking office, one of President George W. Bush's top priorities was fighting gun crime. The administration knew there were successful programs like Project Exile. This encouraged other communities to build upon what was working and provided the resources needed to get these efforts off the ground.

Former U.S. Attorney Terry Harris and I visited Richmond to get a first-hand look at its program. The Shelby County D.A.'s office teamed up with the U.S. Attorney's office for the Western District of Tennessee to begin our own local crackdown on felons in possession of firearms. The PSN Task Force in Memphis is comprised of 11 Memphis police detectives, a lieutenant, a Shelby County Sheriff's deputy, a deputy U.S. marshal and an ATF special agent, as well as federal and state prosecutors. Through mid-2008, the Task Force had reviewed more than 11,500 arrests at weekly PSN meetings. This is where the team approach really comes into play. Everyone involved is at the table. Potential problems with each case are addressed. Details are worked out right then and there.

As of mid-2008, this effort had resulted in more than 1,000 federal indictments and 400 state court guilty pleas to above-range offers in felon in possession of gun cases.[23] Most defendants who plead guilty to the state charges are trying to avoid the higher federal penalties. Usually, for defendants with one prior felony conviction, prosecutors give them the option of a state guilty plea, or taking their chances of a tougher sentence in federal court. They understand they can't ask for probation in state court if they plead guilty. Defendants with more than one prior felony conviction usually go to the federal system with no state offer put on the table. As in Jerry Morrison's case, this process works to single out the most serious career criminals for federal prosecution with tough sentences upon conviction. These are the most dangerous offenders who pose the greatest danger to our community.

Jasper Temple is another one of those offenders. During an early summer morning in Memphis, the sun was just starting to rise. Benigno Amaro had just left his apartment and was walking to his car when Temple, armed with a handgun, approached him. With the barrel of the weapon pointing right at Amaro, Temple demanded money. The gun-wielding thug made off with $900 from the victim, probably thinking he'd never be caught. Just a few nights later in the same apartment complex, Temple and one of his cohorts spotted Ramon Aguino walking to his unit. They ordered Aguino to turn over his money. Aguino thought quickly and eluded Temple and the other suspect. He immediately notified an on-site security guard. The guard apprehended Temple and detained him until Memphis police could arrive. When officers got to the scene they arrested Temple and put him in the back of a squad car. Not happy with the situation, Temple kicked out the back window and physically assaulted one of the officers. Both victims positively identified Temple as the man who aimed a gun at them and demanded their cash. Both of these were far too common instances of criminals preying on Hispanic victims. The criminals target them in the belief they are more likely to carry cash and less likely to report the crime. But that is not what happened in this case. Because of the victims' willingness to come forward, Temple was hammered in court. The reason was not for the robbery and attempted robbery, but for being a previously convicted felon in possession of a firearm. As an armed career criminal, his case was taken directly to federal court. Temple was convicted, and a U.S. district court judge sentenced him to 27 years in federal prison, without parole.

In its first year alone, the PSN effort resulted in an increase in the number of federal firearms prosecutions in the Western District of Tennessee by more than 400 percent. By 2004, homicides in Memphis reached the lowest rate in more than a decade. The overall number of reported gun crimes was down almost 27 percent. Sadly, the number of gun crimes slowly crept back up over the following three years. A University of Memphis criminologist, Professor Richard Janikowski, attributed some of that turning tide to the lack in funds to communicate the gun crime message.

The PSN initiative in the Memphis area is the best example in my community of a law enforcement team effort focused on getting real results. All of the cases that end up getting tried are in federal court. Only guilty pleas with agreement to out-of-range sentences and no probation are handled in state court. To help handle the federal trial caseload, I've dedicated two state prosecutors to serve as special assistants in the U.S. Attorney's office firearms unit. This important partnership and the coordination of all the agencies involved has made PSN work in our community. It has made our approach a national, award-winning model. Officials from Nashville and as far away as Detroit have visited Memphis to see the PSN unit in action and learn how we have worked together to become so successful. Other jurisdictions look to Memphis and wonder how all of these different agencies, from the local, state, and federal levels, can come together, sit around one table to review cases, and make group decisions on how to handle each and every case. This truly is an amazing show of collaboration and team work in tackling violent crime. This willingness to work together has not gone unnoticed. The Memphis area PSN effort has received many honors at national PSN conferences. These include the Most Significant Individual Contribution (Memphis Police Department Colonel Jeff Clark), Top Training Program, Most Significant Local Police Contribution (Memphis Police Department), and Most Significant Community Involvement.

The team approach to fighting crime is not limited to the crackdown on illegal gun possession by convicted felons. For years, this same process has been applied to crimes of sexual and serious physical abuse against children. When children are victims of crime, several different law enforcement, government, and social service agencies are usually involved in investigating the crimes and making sure the victims get the services they need. But, with a multitude of agencies involved in a single case, children can easily fall into the black hole of bureaucracy.

In Shelby County, we have followed a national multidisciplinary model and created a team of multiple law enforcement and child welfare agencies to better address these types of crimes. The goal of the Memphis Child Advocacy Center (CAC), a non-profit organization independent of any law enforcement officials, is to ensure that children who are victims of sexual and serious physical abuse are not intimidated or mishandled by the systems designed to protect them. A children's advocacy center is a child-focused, community-oriented, facility-based program in which team representatives meet to discuss and make decisions about investigation, treatment and prosecution of child abuse cases. Centers also work to prevent the further victimization of children.[24]

In addition to its own staff of social service providers, the Memphis CAC houses personnel from the Tennessee Department of Children's Services, the Memphis Police Department and the D.A.'s office to enable more effective and efficient investigations of child abuse. Child victims are brought to the CAC. Forensic interviews and physical exams are performed in a kid-friendly and safe environment.

In the mid 1980s, the Tennessee General Assembly passed a law to improve the response to sexually abused children. The Covington Bill was passed in 1985 mandating that a multidisciplinary team work together to investigate child sexual abuse cases [25]. The multidisciplinary teams in Tennessee are called the Child Protection Investigation Teams (CPITs). The law specifically mandates which agencies shall be members of the CPITs and which may be members of the teams. An amendment to the law added child advocacy centers to the shall be category. In 1997, our Child Protection Investigation Team became housed at the Memphis CAC to better serve the children of Shelby County.

We have found that the team approach to investigations of sexual and severe physical abuse is the best approach for children, said Nancy Williams, executive director of the Memphis Child Advocacy Center. Tennessee is now a model for other states where multidisciplinary teams are considered best practices but are not mandated by law.

In Shelby County, various law enforcement agencies make up the team, and the CPIT is chaired by an assistant D.A. The team meets weekly to review all reports of child physical or sexual abuse. State law requires that information about allegations and evidence collected be openly shared among the team members as needed without the need for subpoenas.[26] All identifying information on a child is confidential among the team members and is not released to the general community.

The goals of the weekly CPIT meetings are as follow:

- Information sharing;
- Clear lines of communication between agencies;
- The safety of the child;
- The needs of the child and family;
- A forum to discuss the appropriateness of prosecution (although the final decision concerning prosecution rests with the D.A.'s office); and
- Assistance in the eventual prosecution of the case.

The prosecutors who serve on the CPIT and approve criminal charges handle the case from beginning to end. This is crucial to building trust and a relationship with the child victim. Vertical prosecution and vertical case review result in the best outcomes for the children who have already experienced trauma no children should ever have to face, stressed Williams.

The case of Marktrail Lee is a sad example. A jury convicted the Memphis man for physically abusing his two-month-old son. Lee inflicted injuries so severe that the young victim narrowly escaped dying and will forever be disabled. The infant suffered bleeding on his brain, blood behind both his eyes, bruises on his neck, a burn on his hand, and a fracture of his leg. Lack of oxygen to the victim's brain caused irreparable and extensive brain damage. He will live with a shunt in his head to drain fluid from his brain for the rest of his life. The victim's pediatrician testified at trial that what happened was no accident. The combination of injuries and the amount of force caused to inflict those injuries meant they were done intentionally. Proof would show that Lee was the only adult alone with the victim.

This case was initially investigated by the Memphis Police Department. They were called to the scene of LeBonheur Children's Medical Center the night of the incident. But the coordinated efforts of the CPIT resulted in immediate action by the Tennessee Department of Children's Services and the District Attorney's office. The thorough, coordinated efforts of the CPIT in gathering evidence in a quick and efficient manner resulted in a guilty verdict at trial. A judge sentenced Lee to 23 year in prison for this brutal crime. This outcome may not have been possible had the coordination of agencies not happened.

The safety and welfare of the public is the common goal of everyone who works in law enforcement. We are all on the same team, with different positions to play. Just as a football team wouldn't win with a field full of quarterbacks, or a baseball team would surely lose if it had all pitchers and no hitters, each agency plays a different role to create a successful case. **It takes a team approach to fight crime and make our communities safer.**

CHAPTER 4

Hold Violent Crime Offenders Accountable

Police are called to the scene of a murder. Homicide detectives arrive and interview witnesses. They gather evidence and put the pieces of the investigative puzzle together. A suspect is charged. The case goes to court. During the trial, dozens of witnesses are called. Usually there is a dramatic moment in court that invokes a long pause. The judge even peers down from the bench, intensely looking at the witness waiting to hear the bombshell information he is about to tell the jury. Most of the time, the defendant is convicted. All of this happens in 60 minutes.

The above is not reality. The public has this misconception of the criminal justice system because of television shows such as Law & Order. Most law-abiding citizens have had no contact with the criminal justice system. They believe every case goes to trial. Someone is charged with a crime, and he'll get his day in court. Every individual charged with breaking the law has this constitutional right. In reality, though, only a fraction of all criminal court cases actually go to trial in our country. A study of the nation's 75 largest counties showed that 97 percent of all felony convictions occurring within one year of arrest were obtained by guilty pleas.[27] Only three percent of the felony criminal cases resulting in conviction in these large communities went to trial! A quarter of the three percent that actually did go to trial were defendants charged with murder.[28]

This is where plea-bargaining or negotiating enters the judicial process. The prosecution and the defense work out an agreement in which the defendant pleads guilty. The defendant usually pleads to lesser charges or only one of several charges in order to avoid the risks of the case going to trial. Sometimes the defendant pleads guilty as charged and the prosecutor agrees to recommend a shorter sentence. However, in most jurisdictions, a judge may reject this agreement.

Many citizens view plea-bargaining to be soft on crime. The judicial system makes it impossible to take every case to trial. Memphis has ten divisions of criminal court. In 2007, the grand jury returned nearly 10,000 criminal indictments. This is about our yearly average.[29] Every court is assigned approximately 1,000 new cases every year! There are just not enough days on the calendar for every case to make it to the trial stage. Negotiating agreements is essential to the judicial process.

When I became D.A., I felt we needed to find some middle ground. We needed to effectively and efficiently move cases through the system but at the same time hold violent offenders accountable under our state laws. Also, I believed in deterring potential violent criminals by sending the message that a negotiated plea to a lesser charge was not to be expected. Many of our laws in Tennessee are not as tough as they should be. I thought we should do our best with the laws we had to hold violent criminals accountable and deter would-be violent criminals.

One office that has seen its fair share of criminal cases implemented a version of a no-plea bargaining policy in 1992. In New York City, Robert T. Johnson has served as the Bronx district attorney since 1989. In 1992, he directed his staff to no longer negotiate plea agreements to anything less than the top charge in any case that had been indicted by a grand jury. Exceptions would be made when a drug-addicted defendant wanted and needed treatment, a defendant was willing and able to cooperate with a current investigation, or truly exceptional circumstances existed (such as a change in proof making the case not provable). New York law requires that cases in which a defendant remains incarcerated be presented to a grand jury within 120 hours (5 days) from the time of arrest, unless the arrest occurs on a weekend day or holiday. The time limit for this period is a little more than six days from time of arrest.[30] The grand jury determines whether there is probable cause to send the case to court. In many states, including Tennessee, this is what takes place initially during a preliminary hearing. The end result of the Bronx D.A.'s policy is that more defendants are pleading guilty to the top charge before indictment. The office is experiencing a higher felony conviction rate. Prosecutors are freed up to spend more time preparing for the cases that do go to trial. Because of this policy, the number of cases submitted to the grand jury and placed on court dockets after indictment is significantly less than it otherwise would be. In addition to helping reduce the docket, though, the policy seems to be producing good results in terms of convictions.

As the new D.A., I wanted to implement some form of a no-plea bargaining policy that would work in Memphis. My main concern was maximizing accountability for committing violent crimes. So in 1997, our office started applying a No Deals policy on violent crimes. I modeled it slightly after what was being done in the Bronx. The Memphis No Deals policy states that once an alleged criminal is indicted, the case will not be plea-bargained absent the presence of an ethical or legal basis. Initially, our No Deals policy applied to the violent crimes of first degree murder, second degree murder, especially aggravated robbery, aggravated robbery and aggravated rape (committed with a weapon). In 2005, we decided to expand the policy to carjacking and attempted first degree murder charges. The policy was broadened because Memphis was experiencing an increase in the number of reported carjacking incidents and violent shootings. The expansion of the No Deals policy was done in conjunction with the Memphis Police Department's creation of a Felony Assault Unit to more effectively investigate those types of cases.

If the No Deals policy was to serve as a deterrent, we needed to get the word out to the public. Shortly after the policy took effect, the county sheriff provided drug forfeiture funds to help communicate the message that we would not negotiate deals with violent criminals. The word spread like wildfire! A full communication effort, complete with billboards, bumper stickers, print ads, and television commercials, got the public's attention. The sheriff told me that inmates in the county jail were warning each other about the consequences of committing a violent crime. The building which houses the D.A.'s office also houses the criminal courts. I heard defendants talking about the No Deals policy in the elevators of our office building. That told me the No Deals policy was working.

The policy has been in effect since 1997. As of 2007, our grand juries had returned 9,761 indictments covered by the policy. During that time period, we disposed of 6,934 cases either through guilty pleas to the indicted offenses or by going to trial. Most of the trials were murder cases. For ethical or legal reasons, we made exceptions to the policy in 1,307 cases. Most of those cases were reduced to guilty pleas for lesser charges. Some were dismissed due to the cases simply falling apart on us. However, prior to the policy being adopted, about 35 percent of the types of cases covered by the policy were being plea bargained.

As a result of the No Deals policy, we no longer plea bargain certain types of cases as a way of simply reducing the docket. We have worked very hard to enforce the policy in a consistent manner. Exceptions to no-plea bargaining policies sometimes have to be made even when the decisions are extremely unpopular. Attorneys are bound by a professional code of responsibility. If we know we cannot prove beyond a reasonable doubt that someone is guilty of a crime, it is unethical for us to proceed with the case. Sometimes new information or evidence emerges years after the crime. This alters our ability to meet our burden of proof. These difficult decisions are made with the utmost concern for the victims and their families. Sometime, they are extremely saddened and upset by the change in circumstances and by the sense of failure of the justice system.

Dale Mardis was a Memphis auto repair business owner. Police charged Mardis for the first degree murder of 46-year-old code enforcement officer Mickey Wright. The victim was last seen in early 2001 when he made a call to Mardis' car lot. Three years passed and Wright's body was never found. Eventually, the D.A.'s office had enough evidence to approve charges. The grand jury indicted Mardis for premeditated first degree murder. During the three years it took to go through pre-trial motions and preparations, new information surfaced that made it impossible to prove beyond a reasonable doubt the murder was a premeditated act.

We had two options. The first one was to go into court and tell the judge that we would have to try Mardis for second degree murder. The problem with this option was the possibility a jury could find Mardis guilty of a lesser crime, such as voluntary manslaughter or criminally negligent homicide. Or, the jury could have returned a verdict of total acquittal. Therefore, the best and most ethical option was to work out an agreement which would allow Mardis to plead guilty to second degree murder with a sentence of at least 15 years as opposed to the maximum 25 years. This option was conditioned on Mardis' agreement to tell us where he disposed of the body. We hoped to provide some closure for Mickey Wright's family.

The victim's family was not supportive of this second option we ultimately felt obligated to make. Mardis pleaded guilty to second degree murder. He was sentenced to 15 years in prison for the crime. Much of the public was outraged, including members of Mickey Wright's family. I admit we did not do a great job in communicating why we made the decision to allow the exception to our No Deals policy, but it is a decision I still stand by as the ethical thing to have done.

One of our biggest challenges in avoiding the necessity of making exceptions to the policy is the growing number of robberies involving Hispanic workers as victims. Most Hispanic laborers in our community don't have credit cards or checking accounts. They operate in cash. Many are undocumented or come from cultures where law enforcement is not trusted. Crimes in which they are victims are not always reported. Soon the gangs in our community figured out that Hispanic laborers were good robbery targets.

Even with reluctance on the part of many to report crimes, about a third of all the current aggravated robbery indictments I sign involve Hispanic victims. That's a big change from the 1990s when there were very few. These cases are covered by our No Deals policy. However, many Hispanic laborers are transient. Delays in getting the cases to trial can result in the unavailability of victims and an inability to proceed. We've responded with a designated staff member whose sole job is to work and stay in contact with Hispanic victims. He makes a special effort to move these cases through the system as quickly as possible. Still, we end up sometimes losing contact with Hispanic laborers who are victims of serious crimes.

We have taken some criticism for our No Deals policy by some who feel a plea bargain is somehow a right. Several other prosecutors across the country, though, have implemented similar policies for their offices. In early 2005, a newly elected prosecutor from Arizona traveled to Memphis to learn about some of our programs and procedures in a search of best practices to apply to his office. Andrew Thomas was the prosecutor for Maricopa County (Phoenix). He had only been in office for a few months when he came to see me. I discussed how we put into practice our No Deals policy, the challenges we faced at the time, and the results we had experienced over the years. Thomas went back to Phoenix armed with information. He initiated a No Deals policy in his own office. He titled the plan Plead to the Lead.

The Plead to the Lead policy in the Maricopa County Attorney's Office requires defendants charged with an array of serious offenses to plead to the most serious charge or go to trial. Lesser offenses related to the same incident or set of facts may be dismissed. The offenses included in the policy are first and second degree murder, manslaughter, aggravated assault, sexual assault, arson of an occupied structure, armed robbery, burglary in the first degree, and kidnapping. In addition to these charges, prosecutors make no plea offers to defendants charged with aggravated assault of a police officer when a firearm is pointed or discharged at an officer in the line of duty. Thomas didn't stop there. He mandated that repeat offenders charged with crimes not covered by Plead to the Lead not be given probation-eligible plea offers. Of course, deviations to the policy are made for legal or ethical reasons that may arise as a case proceeds.

The effects of these policies, along with the hard work of our law enforcement officers, have been evident, said Maricopa County Chief Deputy County Attorney Philip J. MacDonnell. He also noted that while there has been an increase in the number of inmates from Maricopa County housed in the Arizona Department of Corrections since these policies have been implemented, there has also been a reduction in the number of offenses reported by the law enforcement agencies in the county. In 2007, the FBI unified crime reports noted the violent crime rate for the Phoenix metropolitan area decreased to 490.8 per 100,000 residents compared to 509.9 in 2006.[31]

From Memphis to New York City to Phoenix, and across the country, we all want the same result. We want safe communities. Approaches may have to be adjusted to meet variations in state laws and the dynamics of an individual community. But the message is clear. **Violent offenders aren't automatically entitled to plea bargains and must be held accountable.**

CHAPTER 5

Get the Word Out On the Street

Convicted felon Jerry Morrison persisted in carrying a gun. His future is written on the wall, or actually, the billboards, bumper stickers, buses and bus shelters, posters, even television and radio stations, throughout Memphis: Gun Crime IS Jail Time. The message is clear. If you are a convicted felon, it's illegal to use or possess a firearm. It's too late for Jerry Morrrison. He didn't get the message. But by getting the word out on the street, others will get the message and change their behavior.

We had just started our local crackdown on gun crime using the Project Safe Neighborhoods (PSN) national model of prosecuting felon in possession of firearm cases in federal court. The laws were tougher and penalties stiffer. I knew from our efforts to communicate our no plea bargaining policy on violent crime that it was critical to communicate at the street level what we were doing and the consequences of committing such a crime. If our plan to reduce gun crime was going to work, we had to make sure the public knew we were serious about enforcing gun crime laws. We could not just depend on stories in the newspaper written about our efforts. We needed to get the message to the public and, specifically to our primary target audience of convicted felons.

Nearly a year after our PSN efforts got off the ground, the U.S. Department of Justice awarded a $250,000 grant to the Shelby County D.A.'s office and a separate $170,000 grant to the Memphis-Shelby Crime Commission to reinforce our endeavor. Some of these grant funds were awarded to cover personnel costs and general supplies for the PSN unit. Another portion of that federal money was exclusively earmarked for marketing and communication purposes. With those funds and additional contributions from the private sector, we were able to secure an advertising agency to help us craft our message: Gun Crime IS Jail Time. The message was uncomplicated and straightforward. We kept the artwork for the campaign clean and simple. We used red and black words on a stark white background. It was bold. It was strong. It meant what it said.

The fight against gun crime in the Memphis area did not fall solely on the shoulders of law enforcement. This battle was a community effort. We were able to get the ad agency to do the work at cost. We approached our local media outlets. They graciously gave us matching air time or ad space so we could double or triple the scope of the campaign. We mass produced bumper stickers and inserted them into the Sunday edition of the local daily newspaper. We encouraged citizens to display the bumper stickers on their vehicles. Police officers helped hang posters in mom and pop shops, diners, and local businesses that would let them. We even used guerilla marketing by printing the Gun Crime IS Jail Time message on the back of court appointment cards that are presented to defendants as a reminder of when to return to court. Soon, the Memphis market was blanketed with the Gun Crime IS Jail Time message!

The initial campaign began in 2003 and included a blitz of television and radio commercials supplemented by billboards and bus signs. The television ads, radio spots, billboards, and bus signs ran through 2004. We targeted our TV spots for the maximum impact. For example, we targeted certain television sports events, such as the Memphis Grizzlies NBA playoff games. I don't know much about marketing, but the marketing executives and I agreed that our primary target audience of potential and convicted criminals, as well as the whole community, would tune in to watch sports. Eventually, the money allocated for marketing was spent. The campaign came to an end by mid-2004, although posters and bumper stickers can still be seen.

Professor Richard Janikowski at The University of Memphis Center for Community Criminology and Research analyzed the impact of the PSN media campaign and issued a report with encouraging conclusions. There was a substantial drop in the number of criminal cases involving firearms in 2004. Memphis experienced its lowest number of homicides in 25 years! The number of murders fell 138 to 118 in just one year. In 2004, 82 of the homicides were committed with firearms. This was down from 106 in 2003. The report concluded that the decrease in violent gun crime ended following the end of the media campaign. The results of the study suggested that the media campaign portion of the PSN effort played a critical role in the downward trend in firearms offenses. By being proactive, PSN changed the behavior of those exposed to the message. The study found that without an ongoing public relations media campaign reinforcing tough sentences for gun possessing convicted felons, reports of crimes committed with guns quickly increased.[32]

I believe the campaign against use of guns in committing crimes in our community worked for two fundamental reasons. First, the message was succinct, direct, and easy to grasp. Second, the campaign had enough funding and media company matching donations of time and space to build a high degree of awareness on the street through billboards and transit signs, and in living rooms through TV ads, said advertising executive David Wayne Brown. Brown, along with his former partner Dan Conaway and Trust Marketing executive, Howard Robertson created the Gun Crime IS Jail Time campaign.

Nine months after the marketing effort began in 2004, Professor Jankowski and his staff conducted a survey of 1,013 adults to test their knowledge of the PSN initiative. They found that more than half of all respondents (55.6 percent) had heard of the Gun Crime IS Jail Time message. Comparatively, only a quarter (25.7 percent) had heard of Project Safe Neighborhoods. This proved that the marketing effort combined with swift and stiff prosecution was more effective than the PSN program alone.[33] We know the ads worked because crime went down measurably following the advertising periods, Brown said. We learned anecdotally that the 'bad guys' were warning each other to stop carrying guns. Word-of-mouth advertising is always the best form!

The studies and the stats both show that a strong communications effort is an essential part of the mix. The billboards, bumper stickers and TV ads were very effective at the street level to spread the message that you don't want to be caught with a gun. If you are, you can be prosecuted federally, stated David Kustoff, former U.S. attorney for the Western District of Tennessee. [34]

Similar marketing efforts have been made in jurisdictions across the country. In reference to Metro Nashville's PSN initiative, Craig Morford said it best. Offenders need to know that violence will not be tolerated in our neighborhoods. They need to know that felons will not be allowed to carry and possess guns with impunity. And they need to know that violators will be held accountable and severely punished. Morford was the U.S. attorney for the Middle District of Tennessee at the time. He would later become acting deputy U.S. Attorney General. He posted billboards across Nashville warning convicted felons with the Carry a Gun and You're Done message. While we are fully committed to aggressively prosecuting felons who possess firearms, we realize that we will never prosecute our way to safe neighborhoods. Reducing gun violence requires an 'all hands on deck approach,' he added about the need to communicate the penalties of gun crime. Morford warned that the message is not enough. Law enforcement and prosecutors must be willing to back it up with tough action.[35]

When Florida lawmakers enacted the state's tough 10-20-LIFE law in 1998, the state Department of Corrections produced a marketing campaign to communicate the stiffer consequences to the public. The new law added ten years to the sentence of someone convicted of using a gun to commit a crime, 20 years if convicted for firing a gun during a crime, and up to 25 years to life if convicted for injuring or killing someone by gunfire. Governor Jeb Bush even enlisted the help of Hollywood to spread the message: Use a gun, and you're done! Actor Chuck Norris was the primary spokesperson for the television campaign. Thousands of spots aired on television stations across Florida. The state-wide campaign also included radio spots, billboards, posters, and brochures that were given to inmates under community supervision.

Former state attorney Jerry Blair of Leon County, Florida noted that the 10-20-LIFE marketing effort …did raise expectations of citizens, but in addition, it helped get the word out to the criminals that there is a heavy price to pay. Willie Meggs, the state attorney for Tallahassee agreed. The marketing has helped. We've seen an increase in robberies with criminals using fake guns in an effort to avoid application of '10-20-LIFE', Meggs stated.

When creating our battle plans to make our communities safer, we must be smart and creative. The word must spread to citizens in the community about what we are doing. That includes effectively communicating our message to past and potentially future criminals. One way to keep thugs off our streets is to reduce their numbers by changing their behavior through communication of a clear message. Some will calculate the risk and decide it's not worth it. However, they must first understand the risk in clear street-wise terms. Communication is a vital step that should not be overlooked when executing a successful crime-reduction plan. To keep violent crime down long-term, communicating the message must be constantly sustained. Short-term marketing saturations have short-term temporary results. **Long-term changes in behavior require a long-term commitment to influencing that behavior by communicating the consequences of engaging in crime.**

CHAPTER 6

Remember That Most Convicted Felons Will Come Back Home

You hear it time and time again. The most heinous crimes are committed by previously convicted felons. Felons who were behind bars are released from prison only to offend again.

Repeat offenders account for many of the criminal court cases that go through the justice system. I refer to it as a revolving door. A national study of recidivism showed that more than two-thirds (67 percent) of the convicts released from prison are rearrested within three years.[36] Most former convicts were rearrested shortly after getting out of prison: 30 percent within six months, 44 percent within a year, 59 percent within two years.[37] Law enforcement officials cannot ignore those statistics.

We need to get the thugs in prison where they belong. But except for the most violent offenders, even most serious offenders will get released back into our communities at some point. We need to do what we can to make sure they don't go right back to the same life of crime and being a thug. To put it simply, another way to get the thugs off our streets is to permanently reduce the number of thugs.

Part of the answer is making sure those returning to our communities from prison understand the consequences of going down the same wrong path. In Memphis, we conduct a monthly Project Ceasefire meeting. We want to make sure that newly released convicted felons hear straight from the prosecutors and the police about the risks of carrying a gun. Some are on parole, and others are on probation. But all are under court supervision and ordered to attend the Project Ceasefire meetings. These meetings are organized by the Tennessee Board of Probation and Parole and the partnering agencies in Memphis' Project Safe Neighborhoods effort.

You tellin' me I can't have a gun? How am I supposed to protect myself, and my family? asked one parolee at a Ceasefire meeting held in the dark auditorium of Shelby County's Criminal Justice Center.

If you're going to carry a weapon, you might as well give me your name right now, a federal prosecutor answered. That will save me the time of having to find you in the system when you're picked up, she warned.

The straight talk about gun laws and the stiff penalties they will face if caught with a gun or even just a bullet gets through to most in the audience. Police officers describe their efforts to crack down on gun crime and enforce gun laws. Parole officers explain what is expected of the newly released prisoners now that they are back in society. But the meeting isn't solely focused on what the newly released prisoners cannot do. A representative from a non-profit organization called Hope Works explains how to get jobs and offers assistance with training, creating resumes, and interviewing. He or she encourages the convicted felons to sign up for help and describes the opportunities for individuals who have been released from prison. The face-to-face Project Ceasefire meetings are a non-traditional approach that we have been taking in our community to reach out and help those who are re-entering our neighborhoods.

A prosecutor willing to take a novel, proactive approach to reduce the number of repeat offenders in his community is Brooklyn District Attorney Charles Joe Hynes. Hynes recognized the need to tackle the problem of recidivism in Brooklyn. He realized that if re-entry into society for convicts was smoother, it would also be safer for the individual and the entire community. If convicted felons released from prison had help finding jobs, securing a place to live, treating a drug or alcohol addiction, and re-establishing relationships with the right friends and family members, they might not be as likely to return to prison.

The fact is, former convicts are coming back to live in our neighborhoods, stated Hynes. In 1999, he created a prosecution-based re-entry program to act as a bridge between prison and the community. ComALERT (Community and Law Enforcement Resources Together) is a coalition of community-based organizations, religious institutions, and social service providers helping released prisoners make a safer return into society in Brooklyn. ComALERT members provide clients with services such as drug treatment, counseling, physical and mental health treatment, GED preparation, transitional housing, and employment.

The effort began when ex-offenders in three specific areas of Brooklyn were invited to community meetings where they learned of the different services offered free of charge from ComALERT partners. From these meetings, nearly 300 ex-offenders took advantage of the services. But Hynes believed the ComALERT program could have even more potential. In 2000 his office hired a licensed social worker to work specifically for the ComALERT program. His program started as a community meeting-based model for ex-offenders. It grew into a model of direct assessment and referral. Because of networking with supervised release officers, more clients began entering the program. As the ex-offenders came in, counselors specifically referred them to one or more of the partner agencies.

In 2001, ComALERT partnered with the Doe Fund, a non-profit organization that had been providing transitional employment and housing for the homeless. The Doe Fund had already established the Ready, Willing and Able (RWA) program that offered the homeless, some with criminal histories, a place to live while holding a transitional job and receiving counseling. But many ex-offenders already had places to live. Therefore, the Doe Fund created the Ready, Willing and Able-Day program to meet the transitional employment needs of ex-offenders who were not homeless but could benefit from the counseling services RWA provided.

In 2006, the Brooklyn D.A.'s office received a state grant that funded another expansion of the ComALERT program. This program focused on the areas of Brooklyn in which the largest percentage of ex-offenders lived. With the grant money, an entire ComALERT staff was hired to run the program. This allowed ex-offenders from all precincts in Brooklyn to participate.

ComALERT clients include those convicted of petty to violent crimes. Most are on parole for a drug crime, but others have previously been convicted of robbery, assault, and even homicide.[38]

ComALERT has shown positive results. Participants in the program are 15 percent less likely to be re-arrested after two years from release from prison than those with similar criminal histories who do not participate. Those who graduate from the ComALERT program are more than 30 percent less likely to be arrested than the comparison group.[39] If a ComALERT client is re-arrested for a new offense, the staff counselors act as liaisons between the prosecuting attorneys and the supervised release officers.

The bottom line is that ComALERT reduces crime in Brooklyn, Hynes stated. It also saves taxpayer dollars. The cost of housing an inmate in jail in New York is $175 per day.[40] Medical costs are not included. In contrast, the Doe Fund spends just $43 per day per client it helps find and keep transitional employment.[41] Keeping prior offenders from becoming repeat offenders and helping them live and work as productive citizens pays off. In 1999, six in 10 Brooklyn ex-offenders were back in prison within two years. As of early 2008, two out of 10 ex-offenders were back behind bars within the same amount of time.[42] While saving money by re-arresting fewer ex-offenders was not the goal of ComALERT, the savings have been a tremendous bonus.

Prosecutors and law enforcement officials who simply wait for crime to occur aren't having the maximum impact. This reactive approach makes it way too easy for those who have been imprisoned to return to lives of crime. We must be proactive. We must be aggressive. **By turning around the lives of offenders who ultimately return to our communities, we can reduce the number of repeat offenders.**

PART 2

Take Back Our Neighborhoods

My wife Julia and I were sitting in a restaurant one Friday evening having dinner. This is a weekend ritual we look forward to after what has usually been an eventful, sometimes stressful, week for both of us. The waitress handed me a business card and pointed to a man sitting at a table in the corner. On the back he'd written a property address and a plea for help to get rid of drug dealers doing business on that property.

That incident is not unusual. People give me addresses when I'm in the grocery store or at my neighborhood laundry. I get calls and letters from ministers, lawyers, and elected officials with tips about drug trafficking and related activities such as prostitution at specific locations from all areas of Memphis. I get more calls and letters on this issue than any other. When I'm appearing before groups, it's almost always the number one topic. It's followed closely by the related problem of rundown properties. We have been working with law enforcement to shut down drug houses and gang dens for several years. The more positive the results, the more additional tips we get. It gives hope to the entire community. Citizens are empowered to step forward when they learn that residents across the city are working with law enforcement to get the criminals out of their neighborhoods.

❋ ❋ ❋

The events that were about to occur were the last things Memphis Detective Paul Sherman expected. The veteran undercover officer had made hundreds of arrests throughout his career as a police officer. He was an intimidating man. He stood taller than most of his fellow officers. It was clear that he worked out on a regular basis. He was used to dealing with the worst of the worst. He had taken down the most violent gang members and unscrupulous thugs on the streets. But after Detective Sherman led a hand-cuffed drug dealer out of a crack house in the Normal Station neighborhood to a waiting squad car, he was shocked when a woman grabbed him around the shoulders and embraced him in a bear hug. In fact, Melissa Pearce was so happy the police were arresting the neighborhood menace and boarding up his house as a result of a court order obtained by the D.A.'s office, the neighborhood watch leader planted a kiss on Detective Sherman's cheek. It was enough to make the burly detective blush.

The Normal Station neighborhood sits just south of the University of Memphis campus. The neighborhood is in transition. It has long-time residents coupled with younger new residents, both married and single. Melissa Pearce and other law-abiding residents of the neighborhood know it takes just one rotten apple to spoil the entire neighborhood. One criminal act can tip the scales toward a downward trend, resulting in declining property values. Neighborhood residents had been working with law enforcement on the problem of the crack house in Normal Station. On that spring afternoon, Melissa Pearce's despair and frustration were replaced with hope for the future of her neighborhood.

Each year, we prosecute thousands of drug dealers who threaten our neighborhoods. But many get out on bond awaiting trial. They may get probation upon conviction or early release from prison through our unfortunate parole system. We get frustrated and understand why it leads to lack of confidence by the public in our criminal justice system. Far too often the drug traffickers and gang members can end up right back in the same neighborhoods with predictably bad results.

The gang members and drug traffickers seem to be getting craftier. All of us must fight back! Prosecutors, police, lawmakers, and citizens who care about their neighborhoods must be innovative and creative to develop the means to protect their lives and their property. No one should have to live with a sense of hopelessness. By working together, we can use our resources in creative, sometimes inspired, ways to take back and protect our communities from the gangs, gun-toting felons, and drug traffickers that plague them.

Every state has different laws. Each community is unique. We must learn from each other and celebrate other communities' successes. We can apply some of the same methods or ideas used elsewhere to our own unique crime circumstances. There is no need to re-invent the wheel. Sharing our best practices with each other will help us win the war on crime and take back our neighborhoods.

For example, I discussed in previous chapters coupling tough sentencing laws with policies and practices that take maximum advantage of those laws through such efforts as vertical prosecution, Project Safe Neighborhoods, and effectively marketing at the street level the consequences of engaging in violent crime. Another method is to creatively use other legal remedies and approaches.

To do that, more and more communities are turning to various forms of civil actions. These include civil public nuisance actions, eviction proceedings, and injunctive relief to go after the places where the drug traffickers and violent gang members hang out. This means when they are out on bond, probation, or parole they can't go right back to the same neighborhoods doing the same things. We must disrupt their activities. In such civil actions, the burden of proof is a preponderance of the evidence, rather than proof beyond a reasonable doubt required in criminal prosecutions.

Many communities are turning to innovative approaches designed to disrupt the flow of drugs and curtail the surrounding criminal activities. Along with criminally prosecuting individuals, we must use as many creative ways as possible to take back and keep control of our neighborhoods.

CHAPTER 7

Shut Down The Drug Houses

Prosecutors rely upon a frontline law enforcement investigative agency to take the first step against drug trafficking. In many cases, this means an undercover operation. For me, that frontline agency is usually the Memphis Police Department. We are frequently able to make a case as a result of a police investigation. Sometimes, we can't.

Our drug cases have skyrocketed as a result of Memphis Police Department undercover operations aimed at drug trafficking in many of our neighborhoods. For the three years ending in 2006, the total number of drug charges coming into the system jumped about 87 percent. The number of drug offenses that went to criminal court for jury trial increased 50 percent.

This isn't because of a sudden increase in drug use in the Memphis community. It is the result of a concerted effort by the police department and the D.A.'s office to go after drug trafficking in our neighborhoods. As a result of special undercover operations beginning in 2004, numerous roundups of indicted drug dealers have occurred. These often involve more than a hundred drug dealers each time.

We monitor our conviction rate on roundup cases. It is approximately 93 percent. But because of weak state laws, many of these drug traffickers get probation once convicted. This means they're still in our midst. Even when incarcerated, they are usually eligible for parole after serving 30 percent or less of their sentences. Additionally, they have a constitutional right to a reasonable bond. This puts many drug traffickers right back in the community while awaiting trial.

We are determined to disrupt their ability to return to the same neighborhoods and engage in the same activities. Through our use of some creative approaches, we hope drug traffickers will get the message that Memphis is a tough town in which to be a drug dealer and decide to go elsewhere. That's what's happened in New York City. During the last decade the city has witnessed a virtual turnaround in living conditions because of a sharp reduction in the number of crimes. Thugs and drug dealers decided it just was not worth the risk.

That bear hug that Memphis Detective Sherman got was the culmination of a lot of work and proactive brainstorming by the neighborhood, the police, and the D.A.'s office. The Memphis police had been working with the Normal Station Neighborhood Association. They were concerned about the drug traffic going in and out of a run-down, dilapidated crack house in the center of a middle-class neighborhood near the University of Memphis. Young families with children, students attending the university, and retired citizens made up the neighborhood. A Catholic church and elementary school were just down the street. Children played behind the church every afternoon just a half block away from the crack house.

The crack house stood out like a sore thumb among the other nice homes with well-kept yards. But it wasn't just the physical appearance of the house that made neighbors suspicious of what was going on inside its walls. Morning, noon, and night, there was constant traffic of people and cars. The noise, the smell, and the repeated visits by police were incessant. Fringe crime, such as car break-ins, thefts, and trash in the street, were daily events. Law-abiding neighborhood residents finally had enough. They were not going to let one house bring down their property values and make their neighborhood unsafe!

The citizens in the Normal Station neighborhood of Memphis decided to take action. They began documenting every strange occurrence at the suspected crack house in their neighborhood. They noted the comings and goings of individuals. Some were strangers, others had familiar faces. The frequent visitors to the house created too much traffic up and down the street. The neighbors eventually started calling the police a lot more often to report what they believed to be drug activity. Their suspicions were correct.

The constant calls and reports from residents prompted the Memphis Police Department to conduct an undercover investigation at the house. The neighbors didn't realize they were sometimes calling the police on the police. For weeks, deep undercover officers purchased crack cocaine from inside the house. Every sale was documented. There was enough evidence built to present the case to the state grand jury. This jury returned several indictments against the homeowner and his cohorts for felony drug violations. But that's not all. There was also enough evidence for the D.A.'s office to proceed with one of the strongest weapons in our arsenal against crime: a civil nuisance action that would permanently disrupt drug activities from that location.

Nearly 100 years ago, state lawmakers had the foresight to enact a public nuisance law that gives the district attorney the authority to file a civil petition against someone for creating or maintaining a public nuisance.[43] The law was created in response to citizens making, selling, and imbibing in moonshine during the days of prohibition. It was the tool used by law enforcement to shut down bootleggers' shacks and seize their stills. Little did our ancestors in the state legislature know that in the 21st century we would use that law not only to stop the trafficking of crack cocaine and other illegal drugs like methamphetamine and heroin but also to help go after bastions of gang violence. We shifted from busting black market booze to curbing the deadly combination of gangs, guns, and drugs.

Tennessee's nuisance law covers certain types of criminal activity. These include prostitution, patronizing or promoting prostitution, unlawfully selling alcohol and illegal drugs, unlawful gambling, and acts of violence.[44] If we can prove to the court that there is a continued pattern of any of these illegal violations occurring on a property, the court can take action to abate the nuisance. This holds true for either a business or a residential location.

In Tennessee, we've used our old nuisance law in Memphis and Nashville to close motels, nightclubs, bars, convenience stores, and most recently, residential properties. This law has given us the ability to shut down those crack houses that had once put neighborhoods at risk.

Back on that spring afternoon in the Normal Station neighborhood, the police officers on the scene were not only armed with guns. They also carried drills, hammers, and plywood. Most importantly, they had a court order to close and padlock the property as a public nuisance.

It was a great day for taking back Memphis, not just for our neighborhood but for the city. We made it clear that we were taking a stand for the streets, the neighborhoods, the community, Melissa Pearce explained as she recalled the day she and her neighbors regained their street and their overall security.

Before we decorate this city, we must make it safe, smart, livable, and strong, she argued, referring to new construction projects around the community.

And that's exactly what happened on neighborhood leader Melissa Pearce's street. With the homeowner in jail awaiting trial for possession of cocaine, prosecutors worked with his family to sell the property to a neighbor. Although code enforcement officers had deemed the house unlivable in its current state, the neighbor agreed to refurbish the house. He changed it from the eyesore and haven for crime it had been and turned it into a viable, safe, and appealing residential property. Citizens, their homes, and their neighborhood all benefited.

Prosecutors and police were able to build a criminal case against the previous homeowner. Using an out-of-the-box approach to crime fighting, they cleaned up a neighborhood and made it safer for the residents. The street and the house from which most of the problems on the block started were literally given back to the concerned and proactive citizens of the neighborhood.

That kind of community-based prosecution has spread to many other cities across the country. Similar to the way Tennessee prosecutors can close properties found by a court to be public nuisances, the city attorney's office in Milwaukee is actively using a Wisconsin public nuisance law to close drug houses there.[45] And, like in Memphis, these nuisance actions are routinely brought after complaints from neighbors.

It's a holistic approach to fighting crime, said Assistant City Attorney Adam B. Stephens, who is assigned to the Milwaukee office's Community Prosecution Unit. On one occasion, Stephens went to court to obtain an order to close a drug house one block away from a redeveloped neighborhood of relatively new homes. Over a two-year period, Milwaukee police had made several drug seizures at the property. Officers had also been called to the address when a man was shot in the chest. A year later, a woman was slashed with a knife at the same property. The judge issued the order. The house was boarded up. Stephens said that even though court action is always the last step, this house was a threat to a challenged neighborhood in the midst of revitalization.

The Milwaukee city attorney had occasionally used civil remedies to fight crime since the mid 1990s. But in 2005, the office refocused its efforts to more actively go after public nuisances. Local leaders provided the resources needed to make it a priority. The Milwaukee Common Council passed a resolution to fund two positions in the city attorney's office to solely handle community prosecution. The result was the creation of the Community Prosecution Unit. Stephens and his unit work closely with the Milwaukee County District Attorney's office, which handles the criminal prosecution of individuals at the locations the city shuts down. The D.A. prosecutes people, the city prosecutes properties, Stephens explained.

Since 2004, we've closed more than 150 drug houses in Memphis under our state's old, almost forgotten, nuisance law. Many of the houses have been sheer hellholes with ghastly living conditions. Many don't have operating bathroom facilities. Many don't have electricity, although some drug traffickers have learned to hook up to electricity on their own. The stench and filth can be overwhelming.

Who lives in such squalor? Drug traffickers at the bottom of the distribution ladder who usually are supplied enough drugs to support their own habits in return for also selling to others.

In addition to a lot of stolen property, one house we closed had a live duck in it! The stench was overpowering. When we entered, we were amazed to find a very elderly woman living in the midst of the filth! It was an unanticipated development. Luckily, a priest from a nearby church agreed to take responsibility for getting her to decent shelter. Not only did we close a drug house that day but we also rescued an elderly woman from a living hell.

Just like one rotten apple can eventually spoil an entire bushel of apples, a drug house left alone can eventually spoil an entire neighborhood. **By identifying and shutting down the drug houses, law enforcement and law-abiding citizens can salvage entire neighborhoods and give residents hope for the future.**

CHAPTER 8

Throw Out The Drug Dealers

The concept of using civil court actions to curb crime is not new. In New York, civil actions have been used as a unique way to help fight crime for almost 20 years.

Just a week or so before I was sworn in as D.A., my predecessor, John Pierotti, said he had referred an apartment building owner named Danny Quinn to me. He said Danny had some ideas about getting drug dealers out of rental properties based on what the District Attorney's office in Manhattan had been doing.

A day or so later, Danny showed up at my law firm as I was packing to begin my new life as the state's top law enforcement officer for my community. I could tell that Danny was frustrated. I could also see his determination to wage war on drug dealers and win. He had been on the front line. He had already had his share of close encounters in his effort to keep his properties free of drug trafficking. He was tough. He really cared about maintaining a safe environment for his law-abiding tenants, many of whom were single mothers struggling to raise families and make ends meet.

Danny handed me some information about the Narcotics Eviction Program operated by the Manhattan D.A.'s office. I immediately decided it was worth pursuing. To his credit, Danny Quinn didn't let up. After I took office, Danny kept pushing me to take a chapter from New York City's fight against crime and implement something along the lines of what Manhattan had initiated.

One of the first trips I took as D.A. was to the Manhattan D.A.'s office to get a first hand look at its efforts to curb drug trafficking. I managed a meeting with long-time Manhattan District Attorney Robert Morgenthau. He takes great pride in the Narcotics Eviction Program and its results.

Morgenthau developed the Narcotics Eviction Program in 1988 to get drug dealers, and the crime-related problems they often create, out of commercial and residential properties. With more than 30,000 arrests for narcotics each year in Manhattan, the D.A. uses the Real Property Actions and Proceedings Law, a New York civil law, to help target drug dealers for eviction.[46] It's also been used to go after prostitution, gambling, and gun trafficking.

Citizens are encouraged to report to police drug dealings in their neighborhoods or in their apartment buildings, with the guarantee they can remain anonymous and not have to testify in court. Then, based on a police investigation, if there's reason to believe drugs are being bought and sold at a certain rental property, the D.A.'s office asks the landlord to begin eviction proceedings against the tenant. If the landlord doesn't cooperate, the D.A.'s office has the authority under the New York Real Property Actions and Proceedings Law to bring an eviction action in court.[47]

The New York law does not require the D.A. to actually prove that the tenant committed a specific crime. Eviction can happen based on evidence that the rental property is being used for illegal purposes. Most of the cases come from the review of evidence obtained by search warrants executed by the New York Police Department.

Similar to the Tennessee public nuisance law, New York's law was enacted more than 140 years ago, in 1868, to shut down bawdy houses.[48] The law was expanded in 1947 to include any illegal business.[49] There are some mid 20th century legislators looking down at us today, smiling at how this long standing law is currently being used to bring peace and justice to the citizens of New York.

Since the program's inception, drug dealers and others involved in criminal activity have been evicted from more than 6,200 locations in Manhattan. Law-abiding citizens are the beneficiaries of the efforts by prosecutors and police to clean up the borough's neighborhoods. Calvin Solomon, director of the Manhattan D.A.'s Community Affairs Unit, said just one drug-dealing occupant can bring down the quality of life in an entire building. Dealing drugs obviously makes someone an undesirable tenant. He recalled one elderly woman who was extremely grateful. She was the only tenant in an entire five-story Harlem brownstone not dealing drugs. She witnessed people coming and going at all hours of the day and night. When police raided the building, they also entered her apartment. They soon realized she was the victim of the drug dealers' behavior. That inconvenience didn't deter her one bit. She called to say what a great job we had done, Solomon said.

Tenants have vacated the rental properties before any formal court action became necessary in more than half the cases initiated by the Manhattan D.A.'s office. In the cases that have actually gone to trial, over half have been uncontested by the tenants. The D.A.'s office has been able to remove drug traffickers in 98 percent of the cases that have gone to court.

The eviction program has withstood legal challenges that it constitutes double jeopardy on the basis that a tenant who is also criminally prosecuted faces double punishment. Removing the tenant from the rental property is an administrative remedy designed to remove a public nuisance, and only the separate criminal case results in actual punishment for the illegal activity.[50]

After launching the Narcotics Eviction Program in 1988, Robert Morgenthau went a step further in 1991 with the Trespass Affidavit Program (TAP). While the Narcotics Eviction Program was proving to be a an effective tool in going after drug trafficking out of specific apartments, law enforcement was being confronted with drug dealers taking control of public areas of apartment buildings and using them as their retail markets. They were using threats of violence as a means of intimidating law-abiding tenants into remaining silent and not working with law enforcement to stop the marketing of drugs in their apartment buildings. The law-abiding tenants and their landlords felt powerless to do anything about the drug trafficking in the public areas.

Manhattan created TAP in response to this problem. TAP is a common sense, straight-forward approach. Concerned citizens can make confidential complaints to the D.A.'s office about drug trafficking in a particular apartment building. The D.A.'s office contacts the landlord about signing up for TAP. This allows the landlord to give law enforcement the express authority to arrest anyone for trespassing if that person is not a tenant or a tenant's guest. Once signed on, landlords post signs throughout their buildings proclaiming Tenants and Their Guests ONLY. Landlords provide the police with a regular list of tenants and keys to their buildings. Police are permitted to conduct patrols on the premises and make arrests for criminal trespassing. The bottom line is that it gives the police easy access and a reason to be in the buildings.

More than 3,200 buildings are now enrolled in TAP. It has become a valuable tool for law enforcement in Manhattan to not only go after drug trafficking but also prostitution, burglaries, assaults in apartment building public areas, and trespassing on vacant properties.

Working with apartment managers and the Memphis Police Department, the D.A.'s office in Memphis has started using a similar approach to address drug trafficking and other problems in apartment complexes. We are enacting a more comprehensive approach that involves instillation of surveillance cameras and background checks on potential tenants. Our Anti-Trespass Abatement Program (ATAP) began with a major apartment complex in the Hickory Hill area of Memphis, with plans to expand it to other apartment complexes.

My trip to New York and visit with Robert Morgenthau convinced me early on to think out-of-the-box and not be tied to the status quo. In order to implement a program in Memphis similar to Manhattan's Narcotics Eviction

Program, I knew we were going to have to convince the Tennessee General Assembly to change our law and give Tennessee D.A.s the kind of authority D.A.s in New York have to file civil eviction actions based on drug activity.

Some state legislators were a little skeptical at first about giving D.A.s such authority. But we stayed focused on the New York success story. Ultimately, the legislation became so popular that legislators were rushing to sign on as co-sponsors. The bill passed unanimously in the 1997 legislative session.[51] That summer, we launched our Drug Dealer Eviction Program.

Each morning, Monday through Friday, an investigator in the D.A.'s office reviews all drug arrests involving possession with the intent to sell to determine which ones occurred at rental properties. The program has enabled us to remove more than 2,600 drug dealers from rental property as well as prosecute them for their underlying drug offenses. We've disrupted their business by making sure they can't go right back to the same apartment in the same neighborhood while out on bond awaiting trial, while on probation, or after they've served their sentences.

Rarely do we or the landlord have to file a formal eviction action. Normally, after giving written notice to the landlord that a tenant is facing drug trafficking charges and is subject to eviction, the landlord is very cooperative in confronting the tenant with the notice. The tenant is usually packing his bags rather quickly. A letter from the D.A.'s office usually gets a drug dealer's attention.

Some argue that we're merely displacing drug dealers from certain neighborhoods to other neighborhoods in the city. I'm sure there's some truth to that. But it requires them to re-establish their operation in a new location, often in competition with other drug dealers who may have well-established turfs. The key is to continue aggressive use of the Drug Dealer Eviction Program, constantly send a clear message that Memphis is not friendly territory for drug dealers, and make it clear that we will pursue them wherever they are.

The success of the program depends upon the active support of citizens and their willingness to report drug activities in rental properties. Such reports are usually what initiate police action and subsequent prosecution and eviction. For those citizens who are reluctant to give their names, we've arranged for anonymous tips through our Crime Stoppers program, with monetary rewards available when someone is arrested and removed from rental property.

The Drug Dealer Eviction Program in Memphis owes its existence in large part to Danny Quinn, an apartment owner fed up with drug trafficking and willing to share his ideas. We knew Manhattan's program worked. We were not hesitant to apply the same approach to our community. **Prosecutors must have the necessary tools under the law to root out illegal activity occurring in rental properties.**

CHAPTER 9

Close The Drug Markets

The furniture industry may have put High Point, North Carolina on the map, but another type of market, one that law enforcement and concerned citizens were able to shut down, was giving the home furnishings capital of the world unwanted attention.

High Point is home to around 90,000 residents and more than 50 retail furniture outlets. Unfortunately, this beautiful city was also falling victim to overt, open-air drug markets. Parts of High Point, located between and just to the south of Winston-Salem and Greensboro, were known as locations where drugs were readily available for purchase. Drugs were sold out in the open at all hours of the day and night. These drug markets, most of which were concentrated in the city's West End neighborhood, created spill-over crimes, such as prostitution, burglaries, thefts, robberies, shootings, and even murder. The crime problems made property values plummet. Many residents were afraid to go outside of their homes. Parents would not let their children out to play. Neighborhood playgrounds sat empty and quiet. There was little community involvement. The crime problem peaked in 2003, when three young, street level drug dealers were charged with a home-invasion robbery and murder of a West End resident.

Police reacted to the violence with drug sweeps and enforcement crack downs. We'd make arrest after arrest, but the drug dealers would always return, Major Marty Sumner of the High Point Police Department told a group of prosecutors and law enforcement officials at a national conference on alternative ways to reduce crime in communities. We thought no one in the community cared.

But the community did care. It just did not believe police alone could solve the problem. Also, the additional sweeps and arrests in their neighborhood were creating distrust between the residents and law enforcement. Clearly, traditional law enforcement methods weren't working to stop the drug sales and the ancillary crimes in this community.

Not one to give up easily, High Point Police Chief Jim Fealy contacted David Kennedy to discuss ways to break the cycle of drugs and violence in the West End neighborhood. Kennedy at the time was a criminal justice professor and researcher at Harvard University. He would become the director of the Center for Crime Prevention and Control at John Jay College of Criminal Justice in New York City. Kennedy developed a very unconventional plan that required a lot of faith, not only from the community, but also from police who were used to long-established methods for stopping drug traffickers.

Kennedy's approach was to focus on the street level dealers, make undercover buys as leverage, put the dealers on notice, and give them alternatives.[52] He believed that even though dealers engage in dangerous criminal activity, they are not irrational. Most low-level dealers get picked up, plead guilty, and are back out on the streets in little to no time. They feel there are no real consequences to dealing drugs. Kennedy, however, thought differently. He believed that if the police, the community, and the dealers' families could join together to tell the dealers their behavior was not acceptable, it would have a powerful impact.[53] High Point police officials put their faith in Kennedy's plan. The success of this plan completely depended on the two components of enforcement and community support.

Part one of the plan was the enforcement component. The enforcement component was more conventional and data-driven. It was easier for the police to wrap their hands around this part. Police gathered statistical, crime-mapping information to target drug dealers, drug suppliers, and street-level drug sales. This was done by plotting all calls to 911 for police service, contacts made by officers in the field, and locations of arrests for violence and/or drug crimes for an entire year (2003).[54] Five hot spots, including the West End neighborhood, were identified in High Point. However, the police wanted to choose one location to pilot this plan. To achieve success, a strong community-based network of residents and established groups was needed. Police believed the area that needed the most help and had the most to contribute was West End. Thus, the High Point West End Initiative was born.

Once the crime-mapping and area selection was complete, the High Point Police Department's vice and narcotics unit identified a target list of low-level drug traffickers who worked the neighborhood. These were street-level dealers who conducted the most business in the West End's open air drug market. Working with probation and parole officials, the police determined that some of the individuals identified needed to be immediately apprehended. The mid-level and high-level dealers and those who committed violent offenses were arrested. Police identified 12 other offenders as appropriate targets for part two, the new approach of community support. Using undercover tactics, investigators built cases against the 12 offenders. Once the investigations were completed and the cases were put together, it was time to rely on the community and begin the second component.

High Point police officials called on several community and faith-based groups to implement the second phase of the initiative. Law enforcement and volunteers from these groups formed small, non-threatening groups which made contact with immediate members of the offenders' families. During these visits, the teams explained the goals of the initiative and invited the families to join them in asking the offenders to quit engaging in illegal activity. In most cases the family members were receptive.[55]

The next step to the effort was dubbed the face-to-face call-in. This was the most critical step. Before the community volunteers left the family meetings, they delivered letters from the police chief to the offenders. The letters asked the offenders to come to call-in meetings, with the promise to each offender that he or she would not be arrested at that meeting. Nine of the 12 targeted offenders showed for this step in the High Point West End Initiative. Most of those who came arrived with family members by their sides. Each meeting had two parts. First, members of the community offered help, but also voiced their concerns about the offender's activity. One offender admitted to the crowd, I've never really been embarrassed about what I was doing until you all held that mirror up to my face. Second, law enforcement delivered a two-pronged message that stated street drug dealing and violence would no longer be tolerated and offenders were being put on official notice. The police showed the offenders the evidence they had built up against them (the hammer to hold them accountable) and gave the offenders very short deadlines to quit. The strategy was to warn, allow escape, and prevent the return. Officers and the community then carefully watched for the first sign of drug dealing.

Some criticized the plan as soft on crime. Others dubbed it hug-a-thug. But, working with the Department of Justice's Bureau of Justice Assistance and a multi-agency team of local and federal law enforcement officials, neighborhood leaders, social service providers, and local government officials, the High Point Police were willing to give it a try. The results spoke for themselves.

Analysts tracked a 13-week period of crime statistics from the West End neighborhood. They started six weeks prior to the week of call-in meetings and ended six weeks later. Following the initiative, burglaries, drug sales, assaults, and robberies all declined.[56] Prior to the initiative, these four crimes accounted for two-thirds of the total number of crimes in that area. Six weeks following the first set of call-in meetings, these crimes accounted for less than one-fifth of total crimes in the West End.[57]

While the statistics are impressive, it's the neighbors who tell the real story of success. One area minister admitted that before the High Point West End Initiative, the neighborhood was evidently and visibly known as a drug-infested haven where drugs could be obtained rather freely.[58] After the initiative, neighbors noticed a dramatic reduction in drug trafficking. The open air drug sales seemed to almost disappear. Abandoned houses were no longer being invaded by drug addicts and prostitutes. Another minister rejoiced that citizens were starting to come out of their homes because they felt safer. Later that summer, one neighborhood church reported 35 children attended its vacation Bible school. This was the same church where only a handful of kids attended the previous year. Children and parents were not afraid to walk down the street to church since there were no drug dealers or prostitutes to intimidate them. The targeted offenders benefited too. Those who were called in for the meetings with police and the community during the pilot phase of the initiative received assistance in finding jobs and help with lack of education. Some received substance abuse counseling, housing assistance, and other aid.

The West End High Point Initiative earned the city of High Point an Innovations in Government Award from the Ash Institute for Democratic Governance and Innovation in 2007. It has become a model for other communities across North Carolina and the country.

In fact, we have implemented a version of the High Point model in my hometown of Memphis. Called the Memphis Drug Market Initiative, it's a team approach by the Memphis Police Department, the D.A.'s office, the U.S. Attorney's office, and neighborhood leaders to close down the open air drug activity in a targeted area and suppress the violent crime that goes with it. **Communities can curtail low-level drug dealers by building good cases, then relying upon the influence of neighborhood leaders and family members to help change behavior.**

CHAPTER 10

Never Give In To Gang Activity

How do you fight a public nuisance that is not limited to a particular property or physical structure such as a crack house? Gangs have been around for years. They create chaos and turmoil for lawful citizens who live in the areas the gangs control. While it is unique to think of a gang of individuals as a public nuisance, it is not that far fetched, said Los Angeles Deputy City Attorney Max Shiner. We don't usually think of the harms caused by gangs, which normally include murders, assaults, robberies, threats, and drug dealing, to be a nuisance, but they fit the description, Shiner wrote in an article for the National District Attorneys Association.[59]

California law defines a public nuisance as anything that is injurious to health, indecent, offensive to the senses, or an obstruction to the free use of property in a way that interferes with the comfortable enjoyment of life or property by an entire community or neighborhood.[60] Numerous communities in California have used this definition of a public nuisance to go after gang activity threatening the safety and well-being of citizens.

The Los Angeles City Attorney's office first filed for injunctive relief against gang members as a way to reduce violent crime in 1993. They have done so regularly since 1997 when the California Supreme Court upheld the constitutionality of the approach. In its ruling, the Court stated, Liberty unrestrained is an invitation to anarchy. Freedom and responsibility are joined at the hip.[61] Since 1993, the L.A. City Attorney's office has filed more than 30 actions for injunctions against at least 50 different gangs as public nuisances. An injunction will typically prohibit members of a gang from engaging in certain activities in a certain geographic area. This ranges from associating with one another in public to possessing, or being with others who possess, certain items such as weapons and drugs.

Once a gang injunction action is filed, and a court order has been entered prohibiting certain gang members from engaging in activities in a certain target area, violation of the court order can result in contempt of court and jail time.

This has been the hammer the city attorney's office in L.A. has used as a deterrent to gang members. It is working. According to the Los Angeles Police Department, there is normally a decrease in the number of gang-related crimes in a targeted geographic area after an injunction has been granted. Shiner says that gang injunctions are typically welcomed by the community, and the comments his office receives are extremely positive. Residents in these areas have told authorities they feel safer after an injunction is in place.

The word has spread to the gang members as well. Shiner believes gangs find it increasingly difficult to conduct their business when placed under an injunction. He told what one gang member wrote in a letter from jail to one of his colleagues on the outside: the injunctions ain't no joke. Shiner also noted that some gang members have acknowledged that the injunctions are actually good. He recalled a hearing on an injunction when a judge asked a gang member if he objected to any of the provisions of the order. The gang member proclaimed, I don't object to none of them. I think that's going to be better for the community.[62]

Several other cities throughout California and other states have started to file requests for injunctions against gangs. From California to Texas, law enforcement officials have tackled crime through the use of gang injunctions. Leaders from many other cities across the country are considering the idea of using injunctions under their state laws to fight gang crime in their communities. Where gangs tend to operate in definable geographic areas of communities, injunctive relief prohibiting activities in those areas can effectively disrupt the ability of gangs to carry on business as usual.

Another out-of-the-box idea signed into law by Governor Arnold Schwarzenegger gives California authorities an additional weapon to use in their fight against gangs. As of 2008, district attorneys and city attorneys may bring damage suits against, and seize the assets of, known gang members. All proceeds recovered are to be returned to the communities damaged by the gang. The law will be used as a tool to undercut the ability of gangs to operate in California, explained Los Angeles City Attorney Rocky Delgadillo. The legislation unanimously passed the California State Assembly in 2007 with a bi-partisan vote of 77-0.[63]

Thugs should not be allowed to spoil entire neighborhoods. Law-abiding citizens and law enforcement officials don't have to sit back and surrender entire sections of a community to gangs. **Our laws must give prosecutors the means to fight back and prevent gangs from controlling any part of any neighborhood.**

CHAPTER 11

Make It More Difficult On The Suppliers

In many respects, the supply side of the illegal drug equation must be left to national and even international efforts to reduce production. But, in the case of a drug such as methamphetamine which is often produced locally, states can enact common-sense laws that can dramatically curtail production and reduce supply.

Much of the meth consumed in this country is made in super labs in Mexico. Unfortunately, we've also seen a lot of home cooking as small meth labs have sprouted up across our landscape. These local labs have become major sources of meth for many communities. In 2004, law enforcement seized 17,033 meth labs nationwide, compared to 7,438 seizures in 1999. This represents an increase of 129 percent.[64]

Tennessee was witnessing a similar jump. In fact, my state was becoming a leader for home cooked meth! From October 2003 through August 2004, law enforcement in Tennessee seized nearly 1,200 meth labs. That was almost a 400 percent increase over the number of labs seized in 2000![65] By 2004, Tennessee accounted for a whooping 75 percent of all meth lab seizures in the southeastern United States.[66] In calendar year 2004, law enforcement in Tennessee seized 1,574 meth labs, second only to Missouri among all the states.[67] Clearly, Tennessee was headed toward a meth epidemic, with the problem being especially acute in the southeastern part of the state.

Make-shift labs can be found just about anywhere. They are in homes, hotel rooms, cars, trailers, abandoned buildings, and wooded areas. They compose major cleanup headaches. Every pound of illegally manufactured meth leaves behind five to six pounds of toxic waste.[68]

Many meth users produce meth for themselves and others. Over the course of a year, the cookers typically share their knowledge, usually teaching about ten others how to make meth. The production proliferates.[69]

States and local communities can't do much about meth produced in the super labs of Mexico or other countries. But they can do something about locally produced meth. Tennessee has taken a successful chapter out of the playbook of other states, like Oklahoma, in an effort to come to grips with meth production.

In 2004, at least 11 states enacted restrictions on the sale of pseudoephedrine. This is a common decongestant found in what had previously been over-the-counter cold and sinus medicines. It had emerged as the key ingredient in the manufacture of meth.[70] Oklahoma devised one of the toughest laws. It limited pseudoephedrine products to pharmacies and required placing them behind the counter. Oklahoma enacted the law in 2004. Within less than a year, meth lab busts in Oklahoma had dropped by over 50 percent.[71]

In Tennessee, in 2004, the Governor's Task Force on Methamphetamine Abuse recommended tough laws to deal with the problem of proliferating meth production. In 2005, with the active support of the governor and prosecutors across the state, the Tennessee General Assembly enacted the Meth-Free Tennessee Act.

Now in Tennessee, those who manufacture, deliver, sell, or possess with intent to manufacture, deliver, or sell meth face tougher penalties, and the previous personal use loophole has been eliminated.[72] Legislators went a significant step further. They enacted tough penalties for conviction of initiating the process of manufacturing meth or promoting the manufacture of meth. This is defined as possessing more than a certain quantity of key ingredients used to make meth, with exceptions for possession of drugs containing pseudoephedrine by licensed pharmacists, wholesale drug distributors, and licensed drug manufacturers.[73] Legislators appropriated $2.4 million for the first year to cover the projected increased incarceration time as a result of convictions under the tougher laws.

Seeing the success in other states such as Oklahoma, Tennessee's new law also required any product containing an immediate methamphetamine precursor to be sold by a licensed pharmacy, the most common being products containing pseudoephedrine.[74] The new law prohibited the sale of more than three packages of any such product or any combination of products containing more than nine grams of pseudoephedrine to the same person over a 30-day period without a physician's prescription.[75] Items containing pseudoephedrine must be placed behind the pharmacy counter or in a locked case within view of the counter.[76] A pharmacist or someone working directly under a pharmacist's supervision must handle the sale. The purchaser must submit identification, and the pharmacy must maintain an electronic record of the sale or a written log for at least a year.[77] Violations by a pharmacy are now a crime in Tennessee. Violations are reported to the Tennessee Board of Pharmacy for appropriate action.[78]

Using the pharmacy data base, Memphis law enforcement officials noticed the purchase by certain individuals of products with pseudoephedrine from various different locations. Eleven individuals were indicted by our grand jury for promoting the manufacture of meth. The investigation resulted from a spike in lab busts in the Memphis area. Law enforcement officials knew something was up and were able to move quickly thanks to the new Meth-Free Tennessee Act.

The icing on the cake was recommended by the task force appointed by the governor. Its job was to come up with solutions to our meth problem. As a result of the task force's recommendation, Tennessee's new law set up a Meth Offender Registry Database. After March 30, 2005, anyone convicted of manufacturing meth or initiating the manufacture of meth must register with the Registry Database. This registry is maintained by the Tennessee Bureau of Investigation and available on-line to the public.[79]

After enactment of the Meth-Free Tennessee Act, the number of meth lab busts dropped significantly. May of 2005 was the first month that products with pseudoephedrine were removed from the shelves of stores in Tennessee. At least 86 meth labs were seized in the state that same month. In May of 2006, only 48 meth labs were seized. This was the lowest monthly total in more than four years.[80] By 2006, the yearly figure was down to 583 lab seizures, far fewer than the pre Meth-Free Tennessee Act figure of 1,574 seizures in 2004.[81] But, we are seeing some increases in lab seizures in our state. Law enforcement seized more than 600 labs in 2007 and over 800 labs in 2008.

Part of the increase in seizures is the result of good law enforcement. The record-keeping required under the Meth-Free Tennessee Act is helping law enforcement successfully investigate and track down meth producers.

The increase is attributable in part to the ingenuity of meth producers in finding ways to ply their trade. Many are traveling long distances to acquire the necessary products. Some are using extensive groups of people to assist them in an effort to avoid being tracked through the data base. Many have reverted to simple shake and bake labs that only require rubber tubing and two-liter soda bottles.

Clearly, the new law has made things more difficult for the home cookers to produce meth in Tennessee. By using a common sense approach, we've sharply reduced the amount of meth produced in our state. But we cannot afford to let up. Law enforcement must be vigilant. Tougher laws may eventually be needed.

Of course, we still have the problem of meth being produced by out-of-state, out-of-country super labs and shipped into local markets. And while much of the answer to the flow of drugs into this country must be addressed at the national and international levels, there's an important role for local law enforcement to play as well.

Under our state law, D.A.s in Tennessee have the authority to organize and operate drug task forces. It's the only example in our state where an elected prosecutor actually oversees a front-line police agency. In west Tennessee, D.A.s have joined forces to operate a multi-district drug task force. The elected D.A.s make up the board of directors. Through federal grant funds, the drug task force maintains a staff of its own. In addition, a number of other police agencies in west Tennessee have assigned officers to the task force as a way of creating an area-wide drug enforcement agency.

One important activity of our drug task force has been a drug interdiction unit created to intercept the flow of illegal drugs to and through west Tennessee.

Interstate 40 runs from the southwest United States all the way to the east coast. It is one of the leading drug trafficking corridors in the country, possibly the leading corridor. Frankly, I think it's the responsibility of law enforcement all along I-40 to do what it can to disrupt the constant flow of drugs along this crucial artery. We need to make it as difficult as possible.

Some interdiction units have not operated as they should. Abuses have occurred. Proper procedures must be in place to account for all drugs and drug proceeds seized. And officers responsible for interdiction need to have a good understanding of search and seizure laws. Otherwise, prosecutors will be facing cases that just will not hold up in court.

But well-run drug interdiction units with proper procedures and good legal advice are critical to disrupting the flow of cocaine, meth, marijuana, and other drugs into our communities. This is particularly important along such corridors as I-40.

I had the opportunity, along with a number of other elected D.A.s from across the country, to get a briefing on drug trafficking at the Tucson, Arizona office of the U.S. Drug Enforcement Administration. This meeting reiterated the important role of local law enforcement on the supply side of the drug problem.

As pointed out in that briefing, drug traffickers in the United States obtain almost two thirds of their drugs by sending their money and people to southern Arizona. Mexican drug cartels smuggle drugs across the border on the backs of illegal immigrants, sometimes through tunnels. Many of these illegal immigrants are forced at gunpoint into backpacking heavy bales of drugs across the border.

Violence accompanies drug deals that go awry. In Memphis, we've faced a number of high profile cases involving retaliation for unpaid money owed to drug cartels. Communities across America are faced with the violence that accompanies drug rip-offs and turf wars.

One recent example in Memphis was the trial of Mexican drug cartel enforcer Daniel Lopez for a 2005 kidnapping and double murder. Lopez had been sent to Memphis to find out what happened to about 6.6 pounds of cocaine supplied to a local dealer and for which the drug cartel didn't get paid. The cocaine had a street value of $60,000. Lopez was convicted on all charges and sentenced to 152 years in prison.

I-40 runs right through southern Arizona, and it is obvious why it is such a major drug trafficking artery. The first line of defense is of course at the border and in southern Arizona itself. Once drugs get on I-40, other states and communities, such as my own, become the front line in efforts to impact the supply of drugs.

We must be vigilant in going after the local producers of such drugs as meth. Likewise, we must not stand back and surrender to the drug traffickers. Prosecutors and other law enforcement officials along major drug trafficking corridors in particular have a major role to play. The more interdiction activity we have the more positive impact we will have on drugs produced elsewhere reaching our communities. Never think that the drug interdiction units you see on our interstates are not intertwined with the drug trafficking in your community. **The battle to take back our neighborhoods must include concerted, effective efforts to go after the local production of drugs such as meth and intercept the flow of drugs from the outside.**

PART 3

Break the Cycle of
Drug Addiction and Crime

We must get the violent thugs off the streets. We've got to get the drug traffickers and others engaged in patterns of criminal activity out of our neighborhoods. At the same time, any battle plan must include an attack on drug addiction that drives so much of our crime.

Drug or alcohol addiction is never victimless. Of course, there is the theft that goes with the urgent need for money to support drug habits. There's the violence when addictions escalate. There's the driving under the influence, which far too often results in injury or death to innocent persons. And, of course, there's the living hell it puts families through as they face the consequences of lives driven by addictions.

As I was growing up, my family knew firsthand the consequences of an addiction. In my family's case, it was alcohol. My father was a smart, gifted man. But he had an alcohol addiction. When I was four years of age, he abandoned us. The end result was that we lost virtually everything we had. First, we lost our farm in Arkansas. Eventually, my mother sold most of our personal belongings to put food on the table and keep the lights on in the house. At an early age, I was acutely aware of the poverty we faced and my father's responsibility for it.

During my pre-teen and early teen years, my father would land at home from time-to-time, usually just long enough to dry out. After my father's death, some of my siblings told me that my father had physically abused my mother during the time just before he walked out on us. If that's the case, I feel certain that was attributable to the influence of alcohol.

With the help of my older brother Gordon, who had just finished serving in the Air Force, my mother and I left rural Arkansas and moved to Memphis in 1965. The last time I saw my father in my youth was in 1966, when the police took him out of our home in Memphis in a drunken state. The next time I saw him was in 1980, when my wife Julia and I tracked him down in New Orleans. After that, I saw him several more times in New Orleans. Then, I moved him to Memphis in 1984, and got him into a nursing home, where he lived until his death several months later.

My father was a college graduate, good athlete, regional manager for a major insurance company, and farmer. After re-establishing contact, I found out some more things about my father. He had ended up desperate on the streets of New Orleans. From 1966 until 1984, his home was the Baptist Union Mission on Magazine Street in downtown New Orleans. As best I can tell, he managed his addiction successfully and served as a staff member in return for room and board. (Since Hurricane Katrina, the Baptist Union Mission has been closed. The multi-story structure will probably end up being converted to apartments or condominiums. And Magazine Street has become a trendy business district with a variety of shops and restaurants.)

My father's addiction to alcohol resulted in apparent violence against my mother, a state of poverty and sense of hopelessness for members of his family, and a skid row life for himself.

❀   ❀   ❀

Over time, I've learned that most families have experienced the impact of addiction. In many cases, especially when the addiction is alcohol, the harm is limited to the addicted individual and his or her family, which was my case. In many other cases, though, it spills over to the community. Addicted individuals steal to support their crack cocaine or heroin addictions. Or they engage in unpredictable acts of violence as a result of meth. One way or another, whether it be domestic violence, vehicular homicides, thefts, home burglaries, or senseless acts of violence, addiction is the driving force behind most of our crime.

The U.S. Department of Justice's Bureau of Justice Statistics reports on a consistent basis that about 70 percent of all inmates in local jails either committed a drug offense or use drugs on a regular basis. An American Prosecutors Research Institute study shows that about the same percentage of state felony cases involve drug offenses or are drug-related. It is those of us responsible for prosecuting offenders under state laws who handle more than 95 percent of drug cases in the United States.

Drug offenders in state prison systems fall into two basic categories: traffickers (or dealers) and users. Trafficking offenders account for about 70 percent of the inmates incarcerated for drug charges, and users account for the remaining 30 percent.[82] Accountability must be the key in tackling the large number of drug offenders.

Those who commit drug trafficking offenses, violent crimes, and significant property crimes need to be locked up. They need to be off the streets and out of our neighborhoods.

There's a second front in the war against drugs, though, that must be part of our battle plan. That second front is effective treatment for the drug users with the active involvement of judges and prosecutors, clear accountability for results, and meaningful consequences for offenders who don't stay the course.

While we must do what we can to impact the supply side of drugs into our communities, the bottom line is that prosecutors are also in a unique position to help break the cycle of drug addiction and crime by focusing on reducing demand. To reduce crime, we must not just routinely prosecute huge numbers of drug offense cases. We must also use the leverage we have to reduce demand.

.

CHAPTER 12

Don't Keep Doing the Same Thing
And Expect Different Results

He was homeless, without a job, searching for food and living on the streets. That's not how James Long envisioned his life. After all, the successful business owner operated two thriving hair salons in the suburban Memphis area. He was paid to travel the country, styling models' hair for fashion and design shows. Long was at the top of his profession. He could afford a house in Memphis and a condo in Florida. From all appearances, Long lived a great life, both professionally and personally. But, his perceived perfect life all came crashing down when an intense addiction to alcohol and drugs finally caught up with him.

Long began experimenting with alcohol and drugs when he was just eight years old. In the 1970s, Long mostly drank alcohol, smoked pot, and took Valium. By the mid eighties, he graduated to shooting morphine, Dilaudid, and heroin to feed his growing addiction. He learned the art of cosmetology and started a profitable business, but with most of his income going to support his habit, Long ultimately lost his salons. With no income, he could not afford his Florida condo and eventually lost his home.

But drugs didn't just take a financial toll on Long. Their powerful affects were also wreaking havoc on his body. A family history of heart disease did not deter Long from his drug habit. The drugs Long injected into his body only exacerbated the problem, to the point that he ultimately suffered a heart attack. Long was rushed to the hospital in critical cardiac condition. While in the ER, Long clearly heard the doctor telling his family he might not make it. Even at that moment, Long admitted he didn't think of his family or the very real possibility of losing his life. I only thought, 'good, the doctor has to give me more drugs.' James Long was definitely having a low moment, but he still had not quite hit rock bottom.

Long recovered from the heart attack, but his life continued to spiral out of control. If the heart attack did not kill him, the drugs surely would. I was going to die a dope head, confessed Long. Homeless, he spent nights with friends and family, until eventually each one kicked him out. Then one day in May 2005, Long was busted. Police caught him red-handed with his drug of choice, Dilaudid. He was arrested, but soon made bond and was back on the streets, doing anything he had to do in order to get more drugs. Later that same month police caught Long again. This time, he was shooting heroin. Like so many others, Long was just another drug addict, with dependence so great, nothing else mattered but getting high. His family, his job, his home, even his life, meant nothing. As always, drug addiction is never victimless.

In Memphis, Judge Tim Dwyer had seen too many James Longs come through the system. He describes it as a revolving door. The Shelby County general sessions criminal court judge was first elected to the bench in 1984. For more than a decade, Judge Dwyer would see the same type of defendants in and out of his courtroom: troubled individuals with obvious substance abuse problems arrested for misdemeanor drug possession or other misdemeanor crimes, such as theft of property, to support their habits. Despite locking up these offenders, Dwyer would see many of them back in court time and time again. Prison time was not a deterrent. The judge knew there had to be a better solution, one that would hold the offenders accountable yet, at the same time, provide them with the help needed to break the cycle of addiction and crime.

In 1996, under the leadership of the founder and chairman of Guardsmark, LLC, Ira Lipman, Memphis formed a Crime Commission as a local think tank to help identify best practices the community could adopt in the battle against crime. One of the Crime Commission's first recommendations was creation of a drug treatment court.

In 1997, I and several others approached Judge Dwyer about creating the Shelby County Drug Treatment Court in response to the Crime Commission's recommendation. It would be on a pilot basis with the initial help of some federal grant funds. The judge jumped at the opportunity. I just thought it was the right thing to do, he said, looking back at that day more than 10 years ago when the first drug court offender entered the substance abuse treatment program.

The pilot phase proved so successful that, in 1999, we approached the Tennessee General Assembly about creating a new division of general sessions criminal court in order to free up Judge Dwyer to be a full-time drug court judge. Legislators agreed to our proposal. Our local drug treatment court was off and running.

Non-violent offenders charged with drug-related crimes as well as some property crimes are eligible for the alternative sentencing of the drug treatment court, but it is voluntary. The program is not offered to individuals facing charges of violence or charges involving the use or possession of a firearm. Drug offenders who choose not to accept the treatment alternative or who are simply not eligible have their cases prosecuted in the normal course of business.

An offender who agrees to the treatment program must plead guilty and, in most cases, volunteer to undergo an intensive 12-month outpatient program. In some cases inpatient treatment is required. Treatment programs are available through a number of providers under contract.

During the period of treatment, the offender is mandated to report back to the judge, who personally reviews the progress being made. Judge Dwyer addresses any challenges or slip-ups that may have occurred, and there are sanctions for those in non-compliance. For many, drug addiction holds a tight grip, and getting clean does not come easily. It's not uncommon for an addict to falter during the 12-month period and have a relapse. If an offender has a positive drug screening or misses a scheduled screening, bond is usually revoked for one to three days, and for every violation the sanctions increase. Sanctions are also imposed on those offenders who miss classes they are required to attend or cause a disturbance for the treatment provider, such as threatening a counselor or disrupting a class.

In addition to the mandatory random drug testing, treatment includes assessments for chemical dependency and attendance at treatment sessions and support group meetings. Some offenders are required to undergo family, individual, or mental health counseling; participate in programs to prepare for the GED or get jobs; attend sessions that teach life-skills, parenting lessons, or anger management; or participate in other programs deemed necessary by the Drug Court Team. In addition to treatment for addiction, these programs focus on preparing the offenders for the transition back into society and futures as productive citizens.

It's clearly a period of intensive work for the offender, but the result is great: a chance at a new life and a clean record. Offenders who successfully complete treatment and meet the necessary requirements of the court have their charges cleared.

In May 2005, James Long, who was then 48, entered the Shelby County Drug Treatment Court program. He spent thirteen months at an inpatient treatment facility. It saved my life, Long declared. His experience of getting clean and sober taught him how to live again. During that time, Long enrolled in classes at Southwest Tennessee Community College to get the training he needed to counsel others. He had experienced life at its lowest point, so he knew he could help others with drug dependencies. Long didn't just graduate from the Drug Treatment Court. He holds a college degree. Now sober, Long helps other drug court participants fight their addictions. Most drug addicts aren't bad people. They just have a disease that needs to be treated, he said one day from his office at the treatment facility that primarily counsels drug court participants. You can't just keep recycling people through the system. It's just not the answer.

Memphis didn't create the drug treatment court concept, although our drug treatment court has won several awards and in 2003 was named a National Mentor Court by the National Association of Drug Court Professionals. (Between 30 and 40 drug courts in the nation have the distinction of being national models.)

The first drug court in the United States opened in 1989 in Miami-Dade County, Florida, as a direct response to the crack cocaine epidemic of the 1980s. The federal government had mandated Miami-Dade County to reduce the inmate population created by the growing number of drug offenders. If not, the state would lose federal funding. Officials observed a pattern of inmates returning to the system over and over again because of an underlying drug addiction. It was time to think outside the box. The conventional judicial system was clearly not working. Officials wondered if they could pair treatment services provided by community partners with judicial leadership, prosecutors, and others in the criminal justice system. With the theory of using alternative judicial sentencing to reform drug and alcohol addicts, the treatment-based drug court was created. Judge Stanley M. Goldstein was the first presiding drug court judge, and Janet Reno was the state attorney (Florida's equivalent to district attorney). Their ground-breaking efforts transformed the criminal justice system to help those with drug addiction, and the Miami-Dade County Drug Court became the model for all other drug treatment courts in existence today.

In New York City, Brooklyn District Attorney Charles J. Joe Hynes took notice to what was happening in Florida. Like Miami, New York City was reeling in the aftermath of the crack cocaine epidemic and facing a growing demand for heroin. The justice system there was bursting at the seams with drug offenders.

Adult felony drug arrests in Brooklyn jumped from 15,173 for the 1981-1985 period to 49,345 for the 1986-1990 period.[83] With the crack cocaine epidemic came increased turf wars among drug dealers. In 1990 alone, there were 759 murders in Brooklyn![84] New York's state prison population doubled in the 1980s. In 1982, drug felons made up 11 percent of the 12,000 new prison admissions in New York. In 1990, 48 percent of the some 34,000 new admissions into prison were drug felons.[85]

Could Miami's new strategy of breaking the addictions of drug offenders work in New York? Brooklyn's Joe Hynes was deeply concerned about what was happening to his community and frustrated at incarcerating drug users without addressing their underlying addictions. In 1990, Hynes, together with community-based treatment providers, the judiciary, the defense bar, and the probation and parole officials, initiated the Drug Treatment Alternative-to-Prison Program (DTAP). This was the first prosecution-run program in the country to divert prison-bound felony offenders to residential drug treatment.

A key to the program, one that is missing in some other well-intentioned but ill-conceived efforts, was the prospect of substantial time in prison for those who failed treatment. Hynes wanted to focus on a targeted group of offenders with obvious addiction problems and who were clearly part of the crime problem in Brooklyn. He decided to target offenders who were charged with felonies, had at least one prior felony conviction, appeared to have drug addictions, and had been motivated to commit the new offenses because of those addictions.

Under New York law, such offenders faced mandatory prison time, so the alternative of 15-24 months of inpatient treatment was a big incentive to get clean and turn their lives around. That's a pretty large hammer to hold over someone, said Brooklyn Assistant District Attorney Gerianne Abriano, who has spent part of her career as a prosecutor assigned to the Brooklyn Treatment Court.

Hynes has come up with an approach under which defendants accepted into DTAP plead guilty to a felony charge and have their sentence deferred while they undergo intensive residential drug treatment. Upon successful completion of the program, the D.A.'s office agrees to withdrawal of the guilty plea and dismissal of the charges. On the other hand, failure to complete the program results in sentencing to prison. This possibility of prison time is critical to the success of the program.

It all began on a pilot basis in 1990 with the help of funding from the Robert Wood Johnson Foundation. The findings were immediately encouraging. Of the 138 defendants accepted into DTAP in the first year, there was a one-year retention rate of 58 percent, much higher than retention rates reported in various other treatment programs.[86]

DTAP has evolved into a model program. Its success is rooted in the hands-on approach by the Brooklyn D.A.'s office and the leverage of mandatory prison time if the treatment alternative doesn't work. To determine initial eligibility, an assistant D.A. looks at the facts of a case and the defendant's criminal history. Felony drug offenses and theft cases are the types most commonly reviewed. Misdemeanors are not considered because the prosecutor doesn't have the leverage of a mandatory prison sentence as the alternative. Those with histories of major drug trafficking or violence also get weeded out.

If a defendant passes the initial screening by a prosecutor, a clinical assessment by a non-profit case management organization, Treatment Alternatives for a Safer Community, is the next step. That's followed with a review by the D.A.'s Enforcement Team, which conducts a field investigation of each defendant. The Team interviews a defendant's family members and friends to get a better feel for whether he or she is a good candidate for DTAP. Individuals with violent tendencies or who don't have roots in the community are not placed in DTAP. Public safety is the number one concern of the Team. After all the screening information is reviewed, the D.A.'s office decides whether to accept the defendant into the program.[87]

Judges who preside over the cases in Brooklyn play a key role. The presiding judge must approve a defendant's participation in the program prior to entry of the guilty plea. Once in DTAP, the judge monitors compliance with the treatment program and applies both sanctions and rewards in order to impact the defendant's behavior.

Just from talking to him, it's obvious that one of the high points of Joe Hynes' job as Brooklyn D.A. is attending and participating in a DTAP graduation ceremony. Graduates' family members and friends are usually present. Some give testimonials about their experiences. On such occasions, Joe Hynes can see some light at the end of the tunnel in the fight against crime.

Since it started in October, 1990 through 2007, a total of 2,539 felony offenders had been placed in DTAP. That represents 37 percent of the total number of defendants screened for possible participation. Of that total, 1,066 (42 percent) had graduated, and 386 (16 percent) were still in treatment.[88] Because the Brooklyn prosecutor's office has the leverage of prison time for failure to complete treatment, DTAP has a one year retention rate of 72 percent. The median length of stay for a DTAP participant is 20 months. This is a much lengthier time than the three month median length found in 19 long-term residential treatment programs surveyed by the National Institute on Drug Abuse.[89] Four years into the effort, a job developer was added to the DTAP staff to provide job counseling and placement services for graduates. An evaluation of 2007 graduates shows a dramatic increase in employment of participants. At the time of their arrest, 33 percent had been working. After graduation, 92 percent had jobs![90]

The bottom line in the battle for safer communities is the impact on crime. That's why Joe Hynes started DTAP. On that score, DTAP gets high marks. First of all, when a defendant bails out of treatment, the D.A.'s Enforcement Team swings into action, and the court handling the defendant's case is notified immediately. The Team takes pride in quick apprehension of absconders for purposes of sentencing. Accountability is the key. For those who remain in treatment, the likelihood of further criminal conduct drops significantly. A recent study compared in-treatment DTAP offenders with comparable offenders who were eligible for DTAP but did not participate. Of the DTAP participants, four percent were rearrested while undergoing treatment, while 13 percent of the non-participants were re-arrested.[91] This begs the question concerning what happens after graduation. A five-year recidivism study compared DTAP graduates with comparable non-DTAP offenders. Of the DTAP graduates, 30 percent were rearrested within five years of graduation. On the other hand, 56 percent of the offenders in the comparison group were rearrested within five years of prison release.[92] A Columbia University study evaluated more than 1,000 individuals who had graduated from DTAP and found them 87 percent less likely to return to prison than their counterparts who did not enter the program.[93]

In 1997, the U.S. Department of Justice selected DTAP as one of the six most effective programs among the some 500 programs receiving Byrne grant funding from the federal government.[94] The district attorney in Manhattan established a DTAP program in 1992, followed by the D.A.s in Queens in 1993, the Bronx in 1998, and Staten Island in 1999.[95] So, in less than ten years, Joe Hynes' idea had taken root in all the boroughs of New York City.

In 2003, then New York Governor George Pataki and New York Senate majority leader Joseph Bruno launched the Road to Recovery initiative designed to encourage D.A.s throughout New York to establish programs similar to DTAP and provide funding for them. The initiative was renamed Structured Treatment to Enhance Public Safety (STEPS), and 16 New York D.A.s outside of New York City had similar efforts underway as of the end of 2007.[96]

In 2008, the United States Congress enacted the Second Chance Act, and President Bush signed it into law. It authorized the U.S. Department of Justice to make grants to states and local prosecutors to develop, implement, or expand drug treatment programs based on the DTAP model.[97]

At a DTAP graduation, one testimonial was from a 45-year-old who was one of 12 siblings, all addicted to something. He grew up in a troubled, single-parent home. By the time he was 13, he had experimented with marijuana and alcohol. By the time he was 16, he was addicted to cocaine, selling drugs, and getting arrested. In 2005, after 25 years of drug abuse, he entered DTAP and spoke at the 2007 graduation. I graduated to more hard drugs like heroin and cocaine. I truly lost myself. I became so self-centered… and manipulated anyone I could. I spent 13 years in prison, and I was offered drug treatment after drug treatment after drug treatment after drug treatment, and I always denied it... I was a three-time loser and all my cases - all 35 of them - had to do with drugs or were drug-related. Finally, I was given DTAP... I want to thank Mr. Hynes for saving my life.... Today, I am running a small corporate contracting business.... I have my children back and have a wonderful girlfriend now who supports me in my recovery.[98]

Brooklyn didn't stop with initiating DTAP in 1990 for second-time felony offenders. Following Miami's model, in 1996, the Brooklyn Treatment Court opened its doors to first time felony drug offenders. The success of the DTAP program helped lay the groundwork for this alternative treatment court, the first drug treatment court in New York City. The D.A. didn't need to convince anyone because DTAP worked so well, said Gerianne Abriano, who has spent several years prosecuting cases in the Brooklyn Treatment Court. The court is distinctively different from DTAP. It follows the standard drug treatment court model which has been implemented in jurisdictions across the country, and most participants receive outpatient treatment. Through 2005, more than 1,000 individuals had graduated from the program. A study by The Urban Institute found that the court reduced re-offending by 30 percent over a one-year period after intake and graduates' heroin or crack cocaine use was cut by 67 percent.[99] The physical transformation of graduates was equally amazing. It's like two different people, Abriano said. By the end of treatment, there's not one person who remotely resembles his or her arrest photo.

Drug treatment courts and other judge and prosecutor-driven efforts to tackle drug addictions aren't soft on crime approaches. They're plain common sense. It's our job to stop crime and keep the streets safe. Public safety is the number one goal, and anything that helps is what you have to do, stated Abriano. She also notes the significant percentage of offenders who stop committing crimes to support their drug habits once they receive treatment. Intense treatment is a means of holding offenders accountable. It is not an easy road to travel for many drug addicts. Regrettably, some refuse to participate in such programs and prefer time behind bars to exercising the discipline it takes to complete drug treatment successfully. **An essential part of any battle plan must be an effort to break the cycle of drug addiction and crime rather than just overseeing a revolving door of drug addicts cycling through the system.**

CHAPTER 13

Reduce Addiction By Focusing On What Works

What began in Miami in 1989 has not just been picked up by Brooklyn and Memphis but by thousands of communities across America. It's an example of how a bold experiment in one community to help alcohol and drug addicts break the cycle of addiction and crime and lessen the burden on jails, prisons, and courts can turn out to be an effective model nationwide.

At that point, drug offenses accounted for more than 30 percent of all convictions in state courts, and state prison costs for low-level drug offenders was exceeding $1.2 billion annually.[100]

Two years after Miami's break-the-mold approach began, four additional drug treatment courts had emerged. By 1993, 19 drug treatment courts existed. They grew to 75 by 1995, when the first drug treatment court for juveniles opened its doors in Visalia, California. By 1997, the figure had exploded to 230, and within two years, the number had more than doubled to 472![101]

For the ten years after 1997, the number of drug treatment courts continued to grow by an average of almost 200 a year, reaching 2,147 in 2007! At any given time, across the country, more than 70,000 drug offenders are participating in drug court treatment programs.[102]

In my own state of Tennessee, according to the Tennessee Office of Criminal Justice Programs, 58 out of 95 counties are served with some form of drug treatment court. Most are part-time, with the judge and prosecutors in these courts handling other types of cases as well. Most serve only adults, but eight also serve juveniles. Ten other counties are in the planning stages for drug treatment courts.

The largest area of growth in types of drug treatment courts is with hybrid drug/impaired driving courts. From 2004 through 2007, drug treatment courts that also serve drunk drivers (primarily repeat offenders) increased by

233 percent, representing 24 percent of all drug courts for adults.[103] Of the 2,147 drug treatment courts in existence as of the end of 2007, 110 were set up purely to offer post-conviction treatment to drunk drivers. Treating repeat drunk drivers through drug treatment courts is supported by Mothers Against Drunk Drivers (MADD) so long as it is in addition to a record of conviction and mandatory sanctions required by state laws (such as mandatory jail time and loss of one's drivers license).

The number of drug treatment courts has exploded because, when they are administered properly and in a way that stays true to basic principles such as accountability, consequences for behavior, random drug testing, and intense supervision by a judge, drug treatment courts work! As the Treatment Research Institute at the University of Pennsylvania reported in 2003, To put it bluntly, we know that drug courts out perform virtually all other strategies that have been used with drug-involved offenders.[104]

A study of nine drug treatment courts in California for adults showed that the re-arrest rate for drug treatment court graduates was 17 percent over a four year period compared to 41 percent for similar drug offenders who did not participate in drug court treatment.[105] A study in Suffolk County (Boston), Massachusetts showed that drug treatment court participants were 13 percent less likely to be re-arrested and 24 percent less likely to be re-incarcerated than comparable defendants placed on probation without the benefit of drug court treatment.[106]

In 2005, the U.S. Government Accountability Office concluded that adult drug treatment court programs substantially reduce crime by lowering re-arrest and conviction rates among drug court graduates well after program completion.[107]

In an October 14, 2008 article in *The New York Times*, Erik Eckholm noted that current studies show drug court treatment to be one of the few initiatives that reduces recidivism and saves the taxpayers money. He cited John Roman, a researcher at The Urban Institute, who believes that the recidivism rate of drug treatment court participants depends to some degree on the quality of the judges and treatment programs.

In my hometown of Memphis, a total of 1,141 defendants had graduated from the Shelby County Drug Treatment Court program through the end of 2007. Of those graduates, 354, or 31 percent, had been rearrested.[108] A study conducted by The University of Memphis revealed that 24 percent of drug court treatment graduates were rearrested within three years. However, about 80 percent of comparable defendants who did not complete the drug court treatment program became repeat offenders within three years.[109]

DRUG COURT GRADUATES IN MEMPHIS
PERCENT REARRESTED WITHIN THREE YEARS

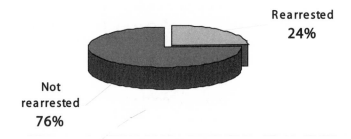

Rearrested
24%

Not
rearrested
76%

COMPARABLE NON-DRUG COURT
DEFENDANTS IN MEMPHIS
PERCENT REARRESTED WITHIN THREE YEARS

Not
rearrested
20%

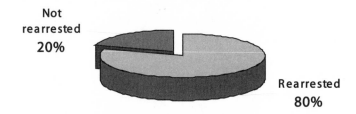

Rearrested
80%

When a Shelby County Drug Treatment Court graduate does return to the justice system in Memphis, it's a blow to Judge Dwyer. It hurts, he admitted.

But for every drug court graduate who makes a return, there are many more who seize the opportunity and change their lives for good. It helped me put my family back together, said graduate James Long. I had a good life, Long continued, explaining how he once lived as a successful business owner. But, counseling people, this is where I was meant to be. I lost everything, but if I had planned it, life could not have turned out this good.

During the early years of the drug court phenomenon, most participants entered treatment before conviction. Today, most drug treatment courts handle participants who plead guilty on the front end. The National Drug Court Institute sees a trend toward drug courts working more with higher risk offenders. It suggests that the drug court model has the greatest effects on high-risk offenders with a severe history of drug abuse and who cannot be handled effectively through typical probation.[110]

The types of drug addictions tackled through drug court treatment vary among urban, suburban, and rural areas. For urban drug courts, crack cocaine is the number one drug of choice among treatment participants. But it's marijuana among suburban drug court participants and meth among rural participants.[111]

While still not the prevalent drug problem in most urban and suburban areas, the increasing use of meth is affecting drug courts in all geographic areas. In a recent report by the National Association of Counties, 50 percent of counties surveyed estimated that one in five of their jail inmates were arrested because of meth-related crimes.[112]

If meth becomes the drug of choice on the streets of our major cities, it will make the crack cocaine epidemic look like a walk in the park! The effects of meth use are devastating to the users, their families, and their communities. It's a difficult addiction to overcome and usually requires long-term inpatient treatment.

But the drug court treatment model works even with meth addicts. The largest controlled study of meth treatment efforts conducted in 2007 evaluated 1,000 meth addicts from eight different treatment sites using eight different models. Compared to the other seven sites, the drug court model produced the best results.[113] Because addiction to meth is so difficult to overcome, an increase in meth-addicted participants will increase the average cost of drug court treatment, but the alternatives are far worse.

In Tennessee, one key recommendation of the Governor's Task Force on Methamphetamine Abuse Final Report in 2004 is for the state to invest in treatment programs with durations of at least 12 months. This includes placement of non-violent meth offenders in a residential drug court setting with a tightly controlled environment, similar to the one operated by Judge Seth Norman in Nashville/Davidson County. Tennessee legislators responded in 2005 by appropriating $1.7 million to launch an inpatient drug court pilot project to tackle addiction to meth. Since then, the Tennessee General Assembly has appropriated more funds for drug court residential, inpatient programs geared primarily to meth users.

It's safe to say that some of the more than 2,000 drug courts in existence today are not properly run and don't produce the kind of results produced in drug courts that are well run and grounded on the fundamental principles of the drug court model. However, the overriding need is to make sure that well run drug courts are in a position to make treatment available to all who are eligible and want the treatment.

With support from the D.A.'s office, Brooklyn has initiated the Comprehensive Screening Project as a way of insuring that all defendants eligible for a court-monitored drug treatment program are given the opportunity to participate. The Comprehensive Screening Project surveys more than 80,000 criminal defendants each year for eligibility in court-monitored drug abuse treatment. The screening is completed within 48 hours of arrest and includes a review of the defendant's case before his or her first court appearance. It includes a detailed assessment as well as a toxicology screen by a treatment professional. Eligible defendants are then given the opportunity to participate.[114]

I've tried to focus on what works, but some words of caution about what won't work are in order. Automatic, mandated programs with no certainty of punishment for failure to adhere to treatment and with no decision-making discretion by judges and prosecutors won't work! Efforts like California's recent misleading Proposition 5 referendum requiring treatment without any sanctions undermine drug treatment courts and other treatment programs that hold offenders accountable.

Proponents of Proposition 5 named their 36 single-spaced page proposal the Non Violent Offender Rehabilitation Act. Truth in advertising would have required a name like the No Accountability Act or the Drug Dealers Bill of Rights! Some of its provisions included:

- Limiting the target population of drug treatment courts to serious repeat offenders, with the eligibility and termination criteria mandated by law rather than based upon the judgment of courts and prosecutors;
- Shortening to six months the period of parole supervision for non-violent drug offenses (including some drug sales) and property crimes such as thefts;
- Expanding the automatic right to pretrial, pre-disposition treatment;
- Re-defining marijuana possession as a fineable infraction only;
- Requiring access-on-demand to substance abuse treatment for addicted offenders; and
- Prohibiting use of any of the proposed funding for drug testing.[115]

Enactment of California's Proposition 5 would have given drug offenders and offenders who commit crimes to support their habits get-out-of-jail free cards and allowed continued drug use during treatment. Its passage would have undermined prosecutor-driven treatment programs that demand results. Simply put, higher treatment success rates come with increased certainty of punishment.

Faced with a concerted effort to pass Proposition 5, voters in California responded in November of 2008 with a resounding no vote. Many of California's prosecutors led the charge in defeating the ill-conceived proposal.

Some go beyond supporting proposals like California's Proposition 5 and advocate legalization of all drugs. They argue that if users can buy drugs at free-market prices, they'll no longer have to steal to support their habits. Therefore, crime will drop.

James Q. Wilson, a professor of public policy at Pepperdine University, summed up the fallacy of this argument in an excellent column in *The Wall Street Journal,* pointing out a serious error in the reasoning of those who make it. He noted that ...the consumption of low-priced drugs would increase dramatically.... The average user would probably commit fewer crimes if those drugs were sold legally. But the total number of users would increase sharply. A large fraction of these new users would be unable to keep a steady job. Unless we are prepared to support them with welfare payments, crime would be one of their main sources of income. That is, the number of drug-related crimes per user might fall even as the total number of drug-related crimes increased. Add to the list of harms more deaths from overdose, more babies born to addicted mothers, more accidents by drug-influenced automobile drivers, and fewer people able to hold jobs or act as competent parents.[116]

Wilson goes on to note that effectively treating people's addictions under a legalized system would prove to be far more difficult because the hammer or threat of prison used by prosecutors and courts would be totally missing! There would simply be less incentive to enter or stay in treatment.[117]

Clearly, the more we currently use a common sense approach to steer drug users into effective, prosecutor-driven, judge-monitored treatment programs, ranging from the standard drug treatment court model to the Brooklyn DTAP model for repeat felony offenders, the more likely we are to break the obvious cycle of drug addiction and crime. **Prosecutor-driven, judge monitored treatment programs can move drug addicts in the right direction rather than allowing them to become or remain parasites on their families and menaces to their communities.**

CHAPTER 14

Prevent Addiction at an Earlier Age

While most drug treatment courts are designed to help adult offenders, many of these specialized courts have been established in jurisdictions across the country to treat juvenile addicts. Many drug addicts get hooked well before they turn 18, and as these young people grow, so do their addictions. The percentage of adolescents who use illicit drugs or alcohol has declined over the past 10 years, from its peak in the 1990s. But, half of all teens who participated in a national study in 2005 admitted they had tried an illicit drug by the time they finished high school.[118]

During the mid 1990s, just as adult drug treatment courts began to emerge across the country, juvenile court judges felt the pressures of increasing caseloads due to an increase in juvenile drug offenses. The number of drug offense cases in juvenile courts increased an alarming 145 percent from 1991 to 1995.[119] The same factors that led to the increase in adult drug offenses created a wave of juvenile drug and alcohol addicts. After witnessing the success rates of adult drug treatment courts, some innovative juvenile court judges thought creating similar treatment programs for younger addicts made perfect sense. Between 1995 and 2001, communities across the country launched more than 140 juvenile drug treatment courts, and some 125 more were in the planning stages.[120]

One of those juvenile drug treatment court programs took off in rural Tennessee. The program was launched in the Upper Cumberland area just northeast of Nashville. It was created in late 2002 to service nine counties, but because of budget cuts, by 2008 the program served just four counties. Through mid 2008, 195 juveniles had entered the program, and 113 of them had successfully graduated.[121] Most of the graduates had either finished high school, earned GEDs, or were still attending high school and doing well. Some had even progressed well enough in their academic studies to earn Tennessee HOPE scholarships to attend college. The program boasted a low eight percent recidivism rate.[122]

One of those graduates is Justin, a teenager from Cumberland County, Tennessee who had a severe drug dependency problem. Justin (whose name has been changed to protect his identity) smoked marijuana daily and had experiments with both cocaine and prescription drugs. At the time he entered the Cumberland County Juvenile Drug Court, Justin had been suspended from school for drug possession and placed in an alternative school where he made very poor grades and constantly disrupted his class. Justin had slip-ups during the first few months of his treatment, but soon he began to see the light and what his life could ultimately become if he remained in the program. His treatment providers said Justin's attitude seemed to change when his mind was clear of drugs. He began to behave in school, started earning As and Bs and even got a part time job. Justin went on to graduate from the program and began working full time to save money for college. His future was brighter than he ever imagined.

Juvenile drug courts don't just help the individual teen. They can also have positive effects on the juvenile's entire family. A good example is a Dekalb County, Tennessee teenager named Allison. She was raised in a family plagued with drug problems. Allison (whose name has been changed to protect her identity) smoked pot and popped prescription pills daily. She was referred to the juvenile drug court after being kicked out of her high school, which enforced a zero-tolerance policy for those caught with drugs on campus. Allison's story took a twist, however. Within a month of entering the program, she became pregnant. Allison was now committed to completing the program and remaining drug-free. Before she entered the juvenile drug court, Allison was a poor student with attendance problems. However, under the court's tight supervision, Allison entered a new school and attended daily. She maintained total abstinence from drugs during her pregnancy and delivered a drug-free baby. Allison went on to earn a GED while in the program and upon graduation started working a full time job. Not only did Allison benefit from the juvenile drug treatment court, but her child would have a greater chance of growing up healthy. Allison's story was a double success.

In 1996, State Attorney Harry Shorstein (Florida's equivalent to district attorney) successfully lobbied for the implementation of a drug court for juveniles in Jacksonville. Launched in 1997, it was one of the first juvenile drug courts in the country. Juveniles accepted into the drug court enroll in a six to twelve month multi-phased treatment program with an inpatient component for those who need it. Just like a standard adult drug treatment court, the Jacksonville Juvenile Drug Court includes frequent drug testing and regular status hearings before a judge. In addition, there are education and family counseling components. Through 2007, more than 350 juveniles had successfully graduated from the Jacksonville Juvenile Drug Court.

In 1998, the National Association of Drug Court Professionals selected the Jacksonville Juvenile Drug Court as a mentor court site. As a national mentor court, it helps train people from other communities who are in the planning stages of creating juvenile drug courts or those seeking ways to improve programs they are already executing.

While juvenile drug treatment courts follow the same basic principles as adult treatment courts, they are not simply carbon copies. Juveniles are definitely not 'little adults' and should not be treated as such, explained Referee Alan Calhoun, who oversees the drug treatment court for the Nashville Metro Juvenile Court. While the adult drug court model can be applied to juveniles, you need to be far more flexible with them, he added, noting that juveniles may not fully understand or realize the consequences of drug abuse the same way an adult may.

Referee Calhoun also stressed the importance of getting the whole family involved. My experience has been that traditional outpatient or residential treatments have their place but that a family counseling model also needs to be implemented. There have been many cases in the Nashville Metro Juvenile Drug Treatment Court in which close scrutiny of the juveniles has led to the discovery of substance abuse or addiction by the parents. In one case that I specifically recall, we discovered that the child's mother would frequent the home in which our client lived and was a cocaine addict. Needless to say, when she would visit, the juvenile would use. The juvenile's custodian was unwilling to bar her from the premises. We changed custody to a different person, and our client never tested positive for drugs again, Calhoun said.

What began as a model approach to addictions among adult offenders has now expanded to drug treatment courts for juveniles in many communities across the country. **The drug treatment court model is an effective community tool to combat juvenile drug abuse and crime.**

\

CHAPTER 15

Save Money Through Effective Treatment

In tough economic times, many state and local governments tighten their budgets. And innovative efforts such as drug treatment courts far too often face the consequences while government's business as usual keeps getting funded. In fact, according to the National Drug Court Institute, a survey of drug court professionals across the country shows the number one reason for a limit on drug court capacity is lack of funding. An overwhelming 72 percent of those who responded to the survey listed budgetary reasons for their drug courts not being fully utilized.[123]

In Memphis, our drug treatment court costs taxpayers a fraction of the price tag to incarcerate an offender for a drug offense. The cost for outpatient drug court treatment is about $9 per day, compared to about $50 a day to incarcerate someone at the Shelby County Correctional Center, about $62 a day to keep someone in state prison, and about $95 per day to house an individual in the Shelby County Jail.

Yet, like so many other drug treatment courts in Tennessee and across the country, the Shelby County Drug Treatment Court has lacked the funding to operate at full capacity. One of the strategies of our local Operation: Safe Community strategic plan is to bring our drug treatment court up to full operational capacity. That means about $2 million in treatment funds per year. It would be a very wise investment.

We know that funding well-run drug treatment courts saves tax dollars. A study in the state of Washington concluded that drug courts cost an average of $4,333 per participant, but save some $4,705 for taxpayers and $4,395 for potential victims of crime. This yields a net cost benefit of $4,767 per participant.[124] Another study in California concluded that drug courts cost about $3,000 per participant but save about $11,000 per participant.[125]

Back in 2001, we took a look at 43 defendants participating in our drug treatment court program and calculated the likely time each would have served had he or she not participated in the program. The savings for these 43 defendants alone was $372,199. In 2004, we ran another calculation based on the likely time 31 drug treatment court participants would have been incarcerated, coming up with a savings of $262,276. In both instances, most defendants were looking at relatively short sentences under our state laws, with very little likelihood of the sentences having any impact on the defendants' patterns of criminal behavior.

In Brooklyn, the D.A.'s Drug Treatment Alternative-to-Prison Program (DTAP) has saved tens of millions of dollars on corrections, health care, public assistance, and recidivism costs, plus the tax revenue generated by DTAP graduates who become employed legitimately instead of selling drugs for a living. By late 2007, 1,066 offenders had graduated from DTAP, and the Brooklyn D.A.'s office estimated the following economic benefits:

Corrections savings	$33,015,953
Health care savings	$1,084,122
Public assistance savings	$4,047,900
Recidivism savings	$3,307,346
Increased tax revenue	$1,010,568
TOTAL BENEFITS	$42,465,899[126]

In his October 14, 2008 article in *The New York Times*, Erik Eckholm cited a 2008 report by The Urban Institute that the country spends about half a billion dollars a year on adult drug treatment courts but benefits from more than a billion dollars in reduced law enforcement, prison, and victim costs.

Memphis is not alone in its struggle to invest wisely in drug treatment court efforts, and, as a result, reduce repeat offenders and save tax dollars. Far too many states and communities are short-sighted and don't invest the necessary funds to operate their courts at full capacity.

Eckholm also noted in his article that, while the King County (Seattle), Washington Drug Court is cited by experts as a national model, state budget restraints were forcing a reduction in the number of participants, from about 500 offenders at a time to about 300 offenders.

Study after study proves that correctly run drug treatment courts are investments that work. We just need the will and vision to more aggressively use this common-sense approach in tackling what is the primary cause of crime in our communities.

Beginning in the 1990s, the federal government made a commitment to support the establishment of effective drug treatment courts through initial grant funding. Federal funding was never intended to be permanent. Nor should it be. The funds were appropriated as seed money rather than as funding for just another long-lasting federal program.

The issue facing many drug treatment courts now is how to sustain them. In fact, these courts need to expand to give treatment to more who are eligible. This is creating a serious issue as the federal money dries up. Many states and communities are responding to the challenge in creative ways.

At the state level, responses to the need for drug court maintenance and expansion have included straight budget appropriations, legislatively approved court assessments and fees, interagency agreements under which treatment funds available to various state agencies are funneled into drug treatment courts rather than less effective programs run by government bureaucracies, and use of Medicaid dollars. In Tennessee, the Governor's Task Force on Methamphetamine Abuse recommended that the state consider covering long-term drug treatment as a public health priority under the TennCare program (Tennessee's version of Medicaid).[127]

Locally, city and county governments have come forward in some cases with budget appropriations. Local fines have been imposed on drug offenders as a way of funding treatment. Drug courts are also finding it more and more advisable to assess fees from treatment participants. Fee scales based on income and ability to pay can be developed. Such fee arrangements can help convince other potential funding sources to lend support. Most importantly, it is a way of insuring accountability and responsibility among participating offenders.[128]

Support from local police and sheriffs can be a critical funding source and add credibility to the drug treatment program as the public safety measure that it is. In Memphis, decisions by the Memphis Police Department and Shelby County Sheriff's office to allocate significant portions of drug forfeiture funds to drug court treatment have been critical to sustaining our drug court.

Community groups such as Rotary clubs and faith-based congregations have stepped forward in many localities to offer important financial support to drug court treatment efforts.[129] Another increasing vehicle for raising local treatment funds is through the creation of private foundations through which tax deductible contributions can be made to support drug courts. In Memphis, we created the Drug Court Foundation to help raise private funds and expand the drug court program. The Nashville Drug Court Support Foundation raises private funds to support the city's one-of-a-kind court-operated, judicially managed, long-term residential drug court program.[130]

We know that drug addiction is the driving force behind most property crimes, crimes in which addicts are desperately seeking ways to come up with the cash to buy more drugs to feed their dependencies. And we know that, absent effective treatment, many drug addicts will graduate to violent crime as a result of their continuing and worsening habits. **Effective treatment with the active oversight of judges and prosecutors not only works to reduce the cause of much of our crime, but saves tax dollars in the long-run by reducing repeat offenders and cutting prison costs.**

CHAPTER 16

Convey the Dangers of Abuse

Done the right way, treatment for addictions is a vital tool in making our communities safer. In addition, citizens are more productive and families stay together. Curtailing the number of people who become addicted in the first place is another important factor in curbing crime.

There have been a lot of effective national public awareness campaigns about the perils of drug abuse. However, it is especially important to understand that states and communities can also do a lot to increase public awareness about the dangers of specific drug trends they face.

Such has been the case in recent years in Tennessee, where we have worked to inform the public about the use of methamphetamine, or meth. Faced with an alarming rise in meth use in parts of our state, D.A.s across Tennessee joined the governor and state legislators in launching a multi-pronged battle plan. It included tougher laws to deal with the manufacture, delivery, and sale of meth. The plan also added laws to make it more difficult to obtain all the ingredients necessary for local meth production. The last prong was an important public awareness campaign about the consequences of meth abuse.

This comprehensive, balanced approach was not new. It was based in large part on best practices already adopted in some other states. And it was the outgrowth of the 2004 final report of the Governor's Task Force on Methamphetamine Abuse.

The 20-member task force included law enforcement officials, state administration officials, medical experts, a mayor, and a couple of legislators. Over a four-month period, the group examined the beginning of a meth epidemic in parts of Tennessee. They met a total of eight times throughout the state and heard testimony from over 30 experts.

The task force's final report painted a grim picture about the effects of meth use. It noted that up to 90 percent of meth addicts will return to the drug. This is a much higher return rate than for most other abused substances and reflects the highly addictive nature of meth. As Dr. John Averitt, Ph.D., a psychologist and drug treatment counselor in Cookeville, Tennessee, told the Task Force, A chronic meth user's brain is never the same again. Normal pleasures, like a trip to the beach or a pleasant meal, no longer feel good. You've got to keep using the drug to feel that pleasure, or take the drug to stop the terrible feelings that result.

The task force's final report noted that the street value of a gram of meth is about the same as cocaine. But while the effects of cocaine typically last a few hours, a meth high can last six hours or longer.

A 2005 Youth Risk Behavior Survey revealed that 5.6 percent of high school students in Tennessee acknowledged using meth. And many younger children were being exposed to the perils of meth. As Tommy Walker, program manager at the Child Advocacy Center in Athens, Tennessee told the task force, I have seen eight-year-olds who can tell you from beginning to end how to cook methamphetamine, what it looks like and how much it costs. They do not know what they are saying. They just know that methamphetamine is scary, and they see their parents in trouble.

What we were seeing in Tennessee was a reflection of what many other states, primarily in the south and west, were seeing as well. A 2003 National Survey on Drug Use and Health showed more than 12.3 million Americans (about 5.2 percent of the population) had tried meth, and 1.5 million were regular users.[131] A 2005 National Association of Counties survey found that 40 percent of child welfare officials reported that meth had led to an increase in the number of children removed from homes.[132]   From 2000 through 2004, more than 15,000 children were found at meth labs.[133] And it is hard to recruit and retain foster parents for children of meth addicts because they have so many behavioral problems.[134]   The National Association of Counties survey also found that meth is, in the view of law enforcement, the number one illegal drug problem in 58 percent of the counties surveyed, with 70 percent responding that meth use is driving up the number of robberies and burglaries.[135]

Meth is a very adaptable drug that can come in the form of white powder; rock-like chunks that are clear, white, yellow or darker; and even pills. Various forms are known by different names, such as glass, ice, speed, or chalk. It can be smoked, snorted, eaten, or injected.

The main ingredient in meth is usually pseudoephedrine, a decongestant commonly found in most cold and sinus medicines. Making meth is very dangerous, often being made in make-shift labs that produce toxic fumes and hazardous waste. When you look at various other ingredients such as drain cleaner, engine starter fluid, battery acid, hydrogen peroxide, and farm fertilizer, it's no wonder that manufacturing meth is a potential disaster.

Every now and then, I'll run into someone who I suspect is a meth addict. Some symptoms are outwardly obvious, such as rotting teeth, discolored skin, loss of weight, and body odor. Other symptoms are sometimes apparent and sometimes not. These symptoms may be anxiety, paranoia, increased aggression, a sensation of bugs crawling under the addict's skin, seizures, and memory loss. Other symptoms are hidden, such as increased risk of heart attack and stroke, loss of appetite, and internal bleeding.

Faced with the debilitating effects on the addicts, as well as the effects on family members and communities, the Governor's Task Force suggested that Tennessee follow what a number of other states had done by launching a broad-based public awareness campaign on the dangers of meth. Upon Governor Phil Bredesen's recommendation, the Tennessee General Assembly appropriated $1.5 million to launch the Meth Destroys public awareness campaign, with the D.A.s being pegged as the organizers of the effort.

Our goal was to get ahead of the curve before meth became an out-of-control epidemic in parts of our state. As the D.A. from our state's largest and most urban jurisdiction, I was especially concerned about meth becoming the drug of choice on our city streets. Crack cocaine is bad enough. Meth is even worse.

Our campaign emphasized the effects of meth on individuals who use it and the effects on their families, neighborhoods, and communities. It was designed to carry an aggressive, proactive message to all Tennesseans about the dangers of meth but especially to middle school and high school students.

The effort included hard-hitting television spots and radio commercials, billboards, graphic posters for schools, media kits, teacher guides for both middle and high schools, informational brochures, DVDs for use in presentations, and a website (www.MethFreeTN.org). We recruited a lot of partners to join us in this public awareness blitz, including, but not limited to, the Tennessee Farm Bureau Federation, Tennessee Sheriffs' Association, Tennessee Association of Chiefs of Police, Tennessee Bankers Association, Tennessee Chamber of Commerce and Industry, Outdoor Advertising Association, Tennessee Association of Broadcasters, Tennessee Department of Health, and Tennessee Department of Education.

The TV spots and DVDs used in the awareness campaign included vivid, candid testimonials from former meth addicts. One of the most compelling testimonials was from David Parnell of Martin, Tennessee, whose disfigured face is a reminder of the perils of meth. I tried to commit suicide while I was high on methamphetamine. I took an SKS assault rifle, stuck it under my chin and pulled the trigger.... The physical wounds can heal, and I can get over it. The thing that I cannot get over is the emotional pain that this drug has caused to my family. That will be with me for the rest of my life, he said in his testimonial.

In one of the DVDs, a teenager from Chattanooga talked about his father's addiction and how his father ended his life by hanging himself. He noted that, the night before he died, his father admitted, I've got hold of something that won't let me go. A woman probably in her thirties said in her testimonial, Before I started meth, I was a PTO mom and a marketing executive. It was killing me, but I couldn't live without it. They took my children from me. I went to jail. I lost my whole life at that point.

In stemming the tide of meth addiction in Tennessee, we weren't reinventing the wheel. Other states had taken similar steps, some on their own and some with the help of the Partnership for a Drug Free America. Our efforts and those in other states show how prosecutors can join with others to get the word out about the dangers of specific kinds of drug abuse. We can't simply sit back and wait for someone to become addicted, and then possibly move into producing and trafficking, or stealing to support his or her habit. We must be willing to aggressively take steps to reduce the number of individuals who ever reach that point. That may mean that some prosecutors will have to step out of their comfort zone and exercise their influence in broader ways than what they are accustomed to doing. It's important that we use what influence we have to reduce drug abuse. The benefit will be a drop in our crime rate.

We need to keep using a common sense approach to addressing at the state and local levels use of illegal, addictive drugs. Our success against meth production is a good model. My prediction is that abuse of prescription drugs will be our next major challenge. It's not just limited to adults but is becoming an increasing drug problem among teenagers as well. And they do not have to buy them from drug dealers. Most teenagers are getting access to prescription drugs, in many cases addictive pain killers, in their own homes or the homes of relatives or friends. It will take law enforcement, physicians, pharmacists, parents, and legislators working together to come up with effective, common sense ways to curtail the abuse of addictive prescription drugs. **By aggressively conveying the dangers of drug abuse, we can curtail demand.**

CHAPTER 17

Turn Lives Around Before It's Too Late

Both the D.A.'s office and the Drug Treatment Court presided over by Judge Tim Dwyer are located at the Criminal Justice Center at 201 Poplar Avenue in Memphis. It's the busiest building in Shelby County, with thousands of defendants, victims, lawyers, and law enforcement officers coming through its doors each day. Most people, including news reporters, just refer to it as 201 Poplar or 201. I've attended student assemblies and asked, Where's the jail? The students routinely shout back, 201!

Judge Dwyer's courtroom is in the basement of the building. It's rather dark. It can be depressing to some and scary to others. (I like to think of our building as having a certain ambience that makes it almost a scene out of a movie.) Each morning it is filled with thousands of people. Prosecutors, defense lawyers, and others who work in the building jokingly refer to the basement level as the pit or The Hall of the People. There's not much uplifting that goes on at 201. It is where we see the ugly, frightening side of our community.

But once a month, there is a break from the darkness. Whatever happens out there, it's not worth getting high, echoed a voice from the front of the courtroom. The statement was made with a strong, commanding voice to an audience of family, friends, and fellow drug court graduates.

For more than a decade, Drug Court graduation has been a day that signifies the new start of the rest of their lives. One recent Thursday afternoon during the sweltering summer, all was quiet in the lower level of 201, except for the roaring sound of applause coming from the Division 8 courtroom. Inside, it was standing room only. The room was filled with people whose hearts were filled with pride. They were the family and friends of the graduating class of Shelby County Drug Treatment Court participants. There was a sense of optimism about the future as they watched their loved ones thank the judge, his staff, and the prosecutors for giving them a second chance. I can't buy that feeling, said graduate James Long. He was one of several former drug addicts and drug court graduates who attended the ceremony to offer enthusiastic support to the new class of people starting their lives drug free.

Judge Dwyer always has a little something personal to say about each graduate. That day was no exception. You've all worked hard. You should be proud, he said shaking the hands of each male graduate and presenting the female graduates with flowers after embracing them with hugs. I left that drug court graduation as I always do, with a feeling of hope, a feeling that people's lives can be turned around before it's too late.

Many drug court graduates are people who had all but given up on their lives. Then they found a way to break the vicious cycle of drug addiction and crime. This was all meant to happen to me, Long explained about his arrests and alternative sentencing. And Judge Dwyer feels the same about his calling to the court. Law is my profession. This is my vocation, he proclaimed.

We must use our laws and law enforcement resources to go after the home cookers, the dealers in our neighborhoods, and the drug traffickers on our highways. But we must also focus on effective ways to reduce demand. Where there is demand, there will always be those who try to supply. Turning lives around by reducing addiction and making citizens aware of the consequences of addiction will reduce demand. And that will have a significant impact on the supply of dangerous drugs in our community. **Ultimately, the best way to reduce the supply of drugs is to reduce the demand.**

PART 4

Tackle Problems at the Neighborhood Level

Back in the mid 1980s, when I was serving a term on the Memphis City Council, the Cooper-Young neighborhood was at a turning point. It could have gone in either of two directions. One direction was high crime, falling property values, and commercial instability. The other direction was a rebirth of a historic neighborhood, with renovation, redevelopment, and rising property values.

Cooper-Young had been a stable, middle income residential area developed in the 1920s. But the 1960s and 1970s brought some decline to the area, with some of the properties deteriorating and much of the family-owned homes changing to rental properties. With that change came a rise in crime. In the 1980s, young professionals and families began to buy some of the homes and renovate them. They, along with many long-time residents, developed a common interest in seeing a safer, revitalized Cooper-Young. This included redevelopment of a vibrant commercial area in the middle of the neighborhood. Everyone agreed that a key element was a reduction in crime.

May Taylor was a leader in the Cooper-Young Neighborhood Association and a long-time resident. With my encouragement, May and other neighborhood leaders decided to organize a neighborhood watch effort that included a car patrol manned by neighborhood volunteers. They weren't interested in being vigilantes. They did not want to take the place of police. They wanted to serve as their eyes and ears. While many patrolmen welcomed such citizen involvement, a large number of the police brass was skeptical.

The Cooper-Young Neighborhood Watch Patrol took off and helped energize neighborhood residents who had become true partners in the battle to make their community safer. Investment in Cooper-Young increased. Home renovation became common place. The commercial area blossomed with restaurants and specialty shops, along with a police mini-precinct. Today, the Cooper-Young neighborhood is clearly on its way up. Each year, the Cooper-Young Festival draws tens of thousands of people. And it began with the neighborhood leaders' determination to come up with a battle plan to tackle crime.

Using Cooper-Young as an example for other neighborhoods, I worked as a member of city council to obtain grant funds for a non-profit whose sole function was to help neighborhoods organize effective neighborhood watch efforts in conjunction with law enforcement. Law enforcement agreed to provide the basic citizen training. They focused on the kinds of suspicious activities about which citizens should be alert and the steps citizens could take to better protect their homes and themselves. Within a short period of time, hundreds of neighborhood watch groups had formed throughout Memphis, creating a strong partnership between law enforcement and concerned citizens at the neighborhood level.

I took my strong belief in partnerships between neighborhoods and law enforcement with me to the D.A.'s office. We use a network of community courts to address code violations and problem properties in a decentralized, neighborhood-based way. We have worked to respond to the specific needs of neighborhoods, ranging from ridding them of drug houses to going after prostitution. A successful battle plan against crime must include a strong partnership with neighborhoods that focuses on addressing their unique needs.

❀ ❀ ❀

Traditionally, the justice system is based on an arrest, prosecution, and then punishment. This has been the standard thinking for hundreds of years. Many prosecutors view themselves in reactive roles. They respond to a crime that has already been committed, holding offenders accountable under the law.

Community prosecution, however, has changed that thinking. The concept of community prosecution can vary greatly from jurisdiction to jurisdiction. But no matter where it is being practiced, community prosecution is a form of proactive problem solving. Community prosecution is prosecutors, law enforcement, other government agencies, and citizens collaborating to make their communities safer. It's a grassroots effort by the local elected prosecutor to get assistant prosecutors, citizens, local government resources, police, and other stakeholders in the community involved in identifying low-level criminal offenses and neighborhood livability issues and engaging in long-term solutions to those offenses, said Mike Kuykendall, previously a prosecutor in Portland, Oregon and the former director of the Community Prosecution Program for American Prosecutors Research Institute. The emphasis is not on arrest and prosecution, but on learning new ways to prevent crime from occurring,[136] added Kuykendall, who went on to become vice president of the Portland Business Alliance.

Community prosecution most often addresses the broken windows in a community. The term broken windows was first introduced in 1982 by George Kelling, a criminal justice professor, and James Q. Wilson, a public policy professor, in an article the pair wrote for *The Atlantic* magazine.[137] Social psychologists and police officers tend to agree that if a window in a building is broken and is not repaired, all the rest of the windows will soon be broken, they wrote.[138] The professors focused on minor crimes and violations, such as public drunkenness, prostitution, overgrown grass and weeds, and, quite literally, broken windows in abandoned houses. They argued that failure to address such problems created an environment more susceptible to serious crime.

After this article was published, many cities across the country initiated community policing. One of the greatest examples of a city that dramatically reduced its crime rate in part because of its commitment to the broken windows theory of crime is New York City. During the 1990s, under Mayor Rudy Giuliani, crime rates in New York City plummeted. They dropped significantly more than the national average. Violent crime declined by more than 56 percent in New York City, compared to about 28 percent nationwide. Property crimes fell by about 65 percent, while decreasing 26 percent nationally. The decreases came as the number of misdemeanor arrests increased by some 70 percent.[139] Mayor Guiliani's policy of aggressively policing lower-level crimes has been credited for being a major factor in this turnaround. Obviously murder and graffiti are two vastly different crimes. But they are part of the same continuum, and a climate that tolerates one is more likely to tolerate the other, Mayor Guiliani told the media in 1998.[140]

The broken windows theory of crime prevention has been challenged over the years. For example, some critics attribute the decline in New York City's crime statistics to other factors, such as the booming economy, low unemployment rates of the 1990s, and the decline of crack cocaine. Yet another study released in late 2008 supported the broken windows theory. In a study published in the journal *Science*, Dutch sociologists tested the spread of disorder and found that when people observe that others violate a certain social norm or legitimate rule, they are more likely to violate other norms or rules, which causes disorder to spread.[141] We reduce crime in our neighborhoods by tackling head on the signs of disorder and neglect.

CHAPTER 18

Partner with the Neighborhoods

The message on the billboard towering over Brooks Road in Memphis could not have been clearer. Hire a hooker – do it on the news. The controversial marketing campaign was one strategic component of a community-based action plan to rid one Memphis neighborhood of prostitution and related crimes. And exactly as we had hoped, the billboards created quite a buzz around the city!

The concept for the marketing component was simple: we would try to stop would-be johns from picking up prostitutes on a major Memphis thoroughfare with a reputation for street walkers by using the threat of humiliation. The billboards and other communication efforts would support the initiative to help reduce the number of drug charges and related crimes in the area. The idea was conceived though an open dialogue and partnership between the Shelby County District Attorney's office, the Memphis Police Department and the Brooks Road Corridor committee. This committee was composed of business owners and community leaders who were tired of the traffic and crime prostitutes and their promoters were bringing to the area. The business owners in the neighborhood agreed that prostitution and related crimes could be reduced if a targeted, coordinated effort was made. Most importantly, they knew it would take a partnership to make it work.

Before the efforts could take shape, the group met to put together an action plan. First, the D.A.'s office would focus a number of prosecution tools on the Brooks Road area. Working with the police, we would use a state law that prostitutes and those patronizing prostitution receive a mandatory minimum sentence of seven days in jail if prosecutors can prove through police testimony that the crime occurred within 1.5 miles of a school. We would work with the police to make sure they documented properly the location of each arrest. The D.A.'s office would also concentrate efforts to use the Tennessee nuisance law to close down any business that condoned or allowed prostitution to occur on its property. With the assistance of the Memphis police, arrests made in the Brooks Road Corridor area would be tracked regarding disposition and imposed sentences. And, the D.A.'s office would concentrate efforts on enforcing its Drug Dealer Eviction Program to rid rental properties in the area of those charged with drug-related crimes.

Second, the Memphis Police Department would step up its enforcement efforts through the area precinct and its Vice and Narcotics Unit. The department would immediately initiate community policing efforts through meetings with businesses and community groups. And the Memphis police would open a substation in a nearby apartment complex and another in the area on the other side of the Brooks Road Corridor.

Finally, the businesses in the Brooks Road Corridor agreed to privately fund an intensive marketing effort that would include billboards, bus shelter signs, and in-store posters to warn the community about the consequences of prostitution and patronizing prostitution. The Memphis-based Conaway Brown marketing firm agreed to do the creative work on an at-cost basis. The marketing effort would also include funds for creating and mailing brochures into the area communicating information about our Drug Dealer Eviction Program.

The stakeholders met with a local television station that provided a key element to the marketing efforts of this action plan. WMC-TV, the NBC affiliate in Memphis, agreed to produce a news story weekly naming and showing the mug shots of those convicted of patronizing prostitution. This attention-getting move had been done in other cities across the country and was the focus of the marketing message. It was a pro-active, preventive approach to stopping prostitution in the area and was truly a partnership between the community, businesses, and law enforcement. Some criticized publicizing the names and faces of convicted johns on television, but a poll conducted by WMC-TV showed that more than 72 percent of those who responded thought the billboard and poster campaign was a good idea.[142]

This coordinated effort worked. In 2002, the year the innovative partnership was implemented, the D.A.'s office reported a total of 973 convictions for prostitution and 288 convictions for patronizing prostitution. The previous year, there were 769 convictions for prostitution and 405 for patronizing prostitution.[143] The efforts of police and the community resulted in the arrests of more individuals for prostitution and fewer johns out soliciting them.

Prostitution remains a problem in many communities across the country. In Indianapolis, a partnership was formed between community prosecutors, the police, and the public to produce a plan to tackle the problem. With significant community involvement, the Red Zone Program targeted prostitution in the city's East District. Community and business leaders had constantly complained about prostitution in their neighborhood, in front of both their homes and businesses. Some business owners claimed their employees and customers were propositioned on a regular basis. Health problems also created a concern among community organizers. Knowing that most prostitutes act to support addictions, the partners thought they would have a better chance of reducing the prostitution problem by focusing on the supply side of the crime: the customers.

The Indianapolis partners brainstormed and developed a diversion program for first-time offenders. If offenders admitted to patronizing a prostitute, they had to be tested for syphilis, then attend a program in which they learn about the health risks of sexually transmitted diseases. The offenders also had to participate in a neighborhood impact panel discussion during which residents spoke about prostitution and how it plagued their community. The panel is basically volunteers from the neighborhood who get to say things like, 'Hey, I live here. My kids have to deal with it. You're using our park where our kids play,' explained Reverend Jay Height, who helped plan the Red Zone Program. The neighborhood volunteers felt empowered when they had the chance to confront the offenders who patronized the prostitutes. The neighbors got the opportunity to describe to the offenders the problems generated by prostitution. It's not a victimless crime, County Prosecuting Attorney Carl Brizzi, who has sometimes participated in the panel, told a group of offenders. The women are victims, and the community is a victim, he stressed.[144] Anywhere from six to 30 offenders participate in the panel on a given day. The session often begins with a participant grumbling, but by the end of the panel discussion, many express regret. One offender responded to a survey about the program by writing, I'm glad I got caught. It kept me from a deviant lifestyle. The guilt and shame has been excruciating, yet beneficial. Thank you.[145]

The partners who created the Red Zone Program also felt it was important that offenders pay back the community. As part of the diversion, offenders, wearing orange vests to identify them as program participants, pick up litter and trash in the neighborhood where the crime occurred. Additionally, offenders must agree to stay outside a one-mile radius from where they were arrested, with waivers available for those who live, work, or otherwise have valid reasons to be there. Offenders must avoid committing any additional criminal offense over the next two years or face the possibility of being re-charged in the prostitution case.

The Indianapolis police carry out the final component of the Red Zone Program by conducting regular sting operations to arrest offenders. The program hasn't eliminated prostitution; it does force hot spots to move, and the police stings to move with them.

Just west of Indianapolis, another partnership was forged between the community and law enforcement. This program addressed the common low-level crime of car break-ins in a unique way.

The 3rd District is one of the oldest neighborhoods in St. Louis. It is home to Anheuser-Busch and has been experiencing an urban revitalization. In mid-2007, the 3rd District was also experiencing a rash of thefts from vehicles parked outside newly refurbished condominiums, trendy restaurants, and chic shops.

The St. Louis Police Department for years had warned people not to leave valuables in their vehicles and tried to teach residents and visitors how to avoid being victims of crime. Their pleas seemed to fall on deaf ears. People don't like to be told what to do, said Bill Shelton, of Left Field Creative. Shelton is also a member of the 3rd District Business Partnership, a grass-roots organization established by area business leaders to improve communications between the businesses, police, and neighborhoods in the community. Shelton's agency worked with the St. Louis police officers in the 3rd District to create a unique marketing campaign to reduce the number of break-ins. The messages illustrated what a thief sees when he notices four quarters sitting in the cup-holder or a cell phone lying on the seat. It was not the items the thief wanted. It was the beer, food, cigarettes, or drugs he was going to buy with them.

The anti-theft campaign was funded by local businesses and donations from the community. It included bus shelter signs, posters, and table tents inside stores and restaurants with the simple message of Free Beer or Free Food in big, bold letters as a way of conveying to citizens the consequences of leaving money and personal items in their vehicles in clear view. The campaign kicked off in the fourth quarter of 2007 and received a lot of additional promotion through media coverage. The local businesses really loved the idea. They plastered the message all over the district. Some restaurant managers even posted the signs in their bathrooms! The signs really catch their attention and make them do a double take, Shelton said. He also made the important point that in order to change behavior, his agency had to stop and make people think about the bigger picture. That loose change in your car is just another 'tall boy' to a thief, he noted. And the campaign did change behavior. Thefts from vehicles decreased 35 percent from the fourth quarter of 2007 to the first quarter of 2008. Car break-ins were down 40 percent in the first quarter of 2008 compared to the first quarter of 2007.

The anti-crime campaign was working so well in St. Louis, Left Field Creative decided to franchise it to law enforcement agencies in other jurisdictions. The police department in Shreveport, Louisiana joined in. After implementing its marketing efforts, the city experienced a 75 percent reduction in vehicle break-ins.

While the efforts in Memphis, Indianapolis and St. Louis are each uniquely different, they do have one common element: none would have worked without a partnership between the community and law enforcement. Neither the community nor law enforcement could have taken on these initiatives without the other's participation.

Denver is another city that has focused on successful partnerships between law enforcement and the broader community. The goal is to support community capacity-building efforts so that neighbors can identify problems and come up with effective strategies for dealing with crime and quality-of-life problems, said Susan Motika, former director of the Community Prosecution Division in the Office of the Denver District Attorney. She described the relationship with the community as an essential foundation on which to build any community prosecution plans. We involve the community as a partner to develop solutions, she said.[146]

But how do these community-based initiatives come about? How do you get the community, the neighborhoods, and the citizens engaged and part of the solution? You have to be proactive. You have to give citizens an opportunity to form relationships with law enforcement. You cannot take your community's support for granted. To achieve a strong community justice initiative, engaging the community should become a top priority.

In Memphis, the Brooks Road Corridor initiative to reduce prostitution and patronizing prostitution was the direct outgrowth of a series of meetings I attended with others in law enforcement, business leaders from the Brooks Road area, and other Brooks Road area leaders. Dexter Muller of the Memphis Regional Chamber of Commerce took the lead in bringing us all together. We brainstormed how to tackle the problem. Out of that brainstorming came the plan that included the marketing effort and the recruitment of a television station to participate with us as a partner.

The Center for Court Innovation suggests three principle reasons for engaging citizens before initiating a community-based criminal justice program. *First, the relationship needs to be developed early.* People who live and work in the area should be involved in identifying issues, setting priorities, and crafting solutions. The organizers must earn the trust of skeptics in the community by listening to them and demonstrating that law enforcement will follow through. We are the community. If we show that, it helps us build a foundation to move forward together, said Richard A. Devine, the state's attorney in Cook County (Chicago), Illinois.[147] For a relationship to endure there must be common interests among the parties. Those interests must be addressed in a way that benefits all parties. By connecting with the community as soon as possible, prosecutors and others in law enforcement can build trust to sustain a long-lasting relationship.

Second, whether the community-based justice initiative begins with the courts, police, prosecutors or any other local agency, they should be designed to address the unique needs and concerns of that particular community. There is no one-size-fits-all model for these types of programs. Each community is diverse. They have different problems. Each one deserves a distinctive approach.[148]

Finally, when planning a community-based justice initiative, financial, political and material resources must be organized in order for the effort to come together. This means building support among fundraisers, social service providers, elected officials, community leaders, and the media. The only way to develop these types of partnerships is to have an active and visible presence in the neighborhood. That is accomplished by attending public meetings, interviewing local stakeholders, and convening discussion groups.[149] It is labor-intensive, but the effort pays off with positive results.

Brad Holland serves as a deputy county attorney in Pima County (Tucson), Arizona. Speaking of himself, he said, I was a loud mouth activist for twenty years then had a mid-life crisis and went to law school. During his years of community activism, Holland worked as a jazz pianist, and out of his own home he bank-rolled a free legal aid clinic.

Tucson's chief prosecutor, County Attorney Barbara LaWall, had followed Holland's activities over the years. As Holland put it, One day she called and said, 'I've heard about the work you're doing. Would it be easier to do it with a badge?'

Holland spent his first year in the county attorney's office handling a variety of cases and getting adjusted to the system. Then, in 1997, LaWall thought he was ready and made him deputy county attorney for neighborhood prosecution.

LaWall is a believer in the broken windows theory of crime. When she was elected county attorney in 1996, she was determined to focus on the broken windows, such as abandoned houses and graffiti in the neighborhoods, in order to create an atmosphere less conducive to criminal activity. She started in three target areas in 1997, but the office started getting calls from all areas of Tucson very quickly because of the public's interest.

When Holland assumed his leadership role in neighborhood prosecution, it was with the understanding that he would address problems identified by neighborhood groups throughout Tucson. These problems ranged from getting slumlords to clean up properties to working with the police to go after drug trafficking.

Holland hands actual cases off to others in the office. His job is to troubleshoot and put out the bonfires. He works closely with community activists and, while he's careful not to give them legal advice, he tries to point them in the right direction. I'm kind of a community ombudsman, he noted.

Holland spends considerable time dealing with problem properties. Many of these are drug houses. The first step is to figure out who actually owns the property. Once he's done that and gets the owner's attention, he can get a lot of the properties cleaned up pretty quickly. In a lot of situations, I attempt to figure out whether the landlord is clueless or evil. Many landlords attempt to convince me that they are, in fact, clueless, not evil.

One tool Holland uses is Good Neighbor Agreements under which owners agree to take certain steps to remedy criminal activities on their properties, or conditions that tend to encourage criminal activities. In some cases, the agreements include formation of a neighborhood board to monitor activities and compliance with the agreement.

Through the efforts of LaWall and Holland, the Tucson prosecutor's office has become a strong advocate for safer neighborhoods, working hand-in-hand with community activists. It is a partnership that is benefiting Tucson.

In California's capital city, the top prosecutor realized the crucial need for partnerships. I thought it was important that the D.A.'s office that represented citizens in the courtroom develop stronger relationships within the community, stressed Sacramento County District Attorney Jan Scully. We also recognized that addressing quality-of-life issues requires forming partnerships with community organizations. To me, community prosecution is another side of the face of a prosecutor—meaning that it's a positive, proactive face. Typically, when citizens deal with a prosecutor's office it's because they've been involved in a crime of some fashion and are being forced to participate in the system, whether as a victim, witness, or defendant. When prosecutors actually go out into the community to help identify issues, it's a more positive relationship, Scully said.[150]

Sacramento is a city with several strong ethnic communities. Scully has used community forums to forge relationships with the individual groups, including the Muslim community, the Asian Pacific Islander community, and the Slavic community. These ethnic groups traditionally distrust the criminal justice system and don't necessarily bring us their issues, she said.[151] To help develop those relationships with a segment of the population that is very diverse and comes from various ethnic and immigrant backgrounds, Scully formed a multicultural community council.

Another way to partner with the community is to create volunteer opportunities for citizens. People often want to help. They just don't know how. Volunteers can strengthen the bond between law enforcement and the community by reporting back to their neighbors. Citizen volunteers can perform office duties, conduct surveys, sit on advisory boards, and serve as mentors to young people. Once citizens feel that they are part of the team, they are more likely to buy into a community-based justice initiative. This relationship-building is vital to any program's success.

There is no substitute for 'face time,' said Greg Berman, director of The Center for Court Innovation. Berman was one of the founding forces behind the Red Hook Community Justice Center in Brooklyn, New York. While planning for the court, Berman spent a lot of time getting to know the Red Hook community. He attended events; convened focus groups of residents to identify community needs and resources; and held discussions with community leaders, social service providers, young people, older neighbors, single moms, and different groups of residents that made up the neighborhood. The conversations were extremely lively. Once people started talking, it was difficult to get them to stop, he noted.[152]

As the months passed, I found my connections with community leaders deepening. I met their children, attended their church services, and shared meals with them. I saw them in good times and bad, at public gatherings and in more intimate settings. These ties would serve the community court well when it was necessary to mobilize neighborhood support, Berman added.[153] Today, the Red Hook Community Justice Center is an anchor in the diverse Brooklyn neighborhood in which it sits. And, it is the partnership with the neighborhood that made it that way. **Forming strong partnerships with neighborhoods is critical to responding effectively to their unique needs in the battle against crime.**

CHAPTER 19

Take the Prosecutors to the Neighborhoods

The ideological shift among prosecutors in fighting crime naturally led to the community prosecution strategy we see in many jurisdictions today. In the early 1990s, only a handful of prosecutors' offices practiced community prosecution. But in 2003, American Prosecutors Research Institute (APRI) estimated that nearly half of all prosecutors' offices practiced some sort of community-based prosecution.[154] In 1993, the U.S. Department of Justice's Bureau of Justice Assistance and APRI formed an advisory group to define community prosecution. The group agreed that …community prosecution focuses on targeted areas and involves a long-term, proactive partnership among the prosecutor's office, law enforcement, the community, and public and private organizations, whereby the authority of the prosecutor's office is used to solve problems, improve public safety, and enhance the quality of life in the community.[155]

In 2003, the National Center for Community Prosecution at the National District Attorneys Association took this definition a step further and developed a set of four key principles that outline the community prosecution approach. In late 2008, the Center, in conjunction with the Center for Court Innovation, updated the four principles which provide a framework for prosecutors to construct their own community based prosecution strategies.

The first principle is recognizing the community's role in public safety. For so many years, prosecutors and police dictated to the public how to handle crime and safety issues, often without taking into consideration the public's specific concerns or needs. By inviting the stakeholders to express their points of view and by coming together to brain-storm solutions, citizens will take pride in making their neighborhoods safer. Problem-solving prosecutors must work with and through their constituents in the community while, at the same time, seeking to achieve their primary objective of reducing crime and the perception of crime, Portland's Mike Kuykendall said. In the words of Abraham Lincoln,

'With public sentiment, nothing can fail; without it, nothing can succeed,' he added.[156] This principle can be achieved in several different ways. Prosecutors can be assigned to neighborhoods to focus on local crime and safety issues. Volunteer opportunities can be created for citizens in the justice system. Regular channels of communication can be made available with citizens.

Engaging in problem solving is the second principle. This is where non-traditional thinking comes into play for the prosecutor whose customary practice is to focus on individual crimes once committed. Community prosecutors are more than just reactive case processors. We use proactive problem solving to attack crime at its source with a goal of preventing cases from happening in the first place, said Seattle City Attorney Thomas A. Carr.[157] Community prosecutors must think creatively and view individual acts as having a history, potentially a future, and as part of a problem or set of problems within a community. The ultimate goal is to prevent the next crime by relying on a wide range of tools. They must be both traditional and non-traditional, and, when appropriate, should enlist the assistance of agencies outside of the justice system. We use every tool available, and if we don't have one, we fashion a new one, Carr added.[158]

Prosecutors' offices can achieve the third principle by *establishing and maintaining partnerships.* Prosecutors know that traditionally they must work with other law enforcement agencies and offices to get their jobs done. After all, there would be no case without an investigation and, ultimately, an arrest. But, community prosecutors must take that relationship a step further. They should build on natural connections, encourage greater communication, improve coordination, and strengthen partnerships. Community prosecutors don't rely solely on others in the criminal justice system. They understand that private citizens and private agencies are often necessary partners in problem-solving efforts. Prosecutors across the country are redefining their role in helping solve the complex issues that result in over-reliance on the criminal justice system, said Milwaukee County District Attorney John Chisholm.[159] Comprehensive crime prevention and reduction efforts crafted by prosecutors, or in which prosecutors participate with other partners, can generally have a greater impact in the community. That's why D.A. Chisholm believes partnerships are so critical. Prosecutors must acknowledge and embrace the leadership role they have in problem-solving and work with others in the community to develop long term, community based solutions to public safety issues, he said.[160]

The final key principle to effective community prosecution is *evaluating the outcomes of activities.* Data is the key element to determining the effectiveness of any initiative. But community prosecutors cannot simply rely on conviction rates and other figures to make certain their efforts are successful.

Quantitative results are important to evaluate a specific program. Qualitative results are also necessary to truly find out if the goals of the program have been met. Community prosecutors must evaluate their activities and the impact on neighborhoods, continuously adapting to the community's needs. Community prosecutors should continue to evaluate crime reduction. They should monitor calls for service in a particular area, the perception of safety in the neighborhood, and the increase in community participation through neighborhood meetings, school presentations, or community events. Are we involving the community in our work? Are we taking into account the community's priorities? Are we addressing the problems that fuel crime? Are we capitalizing on partnerships? asked Greg Berman, director of the Center for Court Innovation. By quantifying our answers to these important questions, we're not only holding ourselves accountable but we're strengthening our ability to pursue justice.[161]

The Milwaukee D.A.'s Community Prosecution Unit was originally created in 2001 ...to provide a more direct linkage between the community and law enforcement and to deal with drug houses and nuisance properties within Milwaukee, said prosecutor Jeff Altenburg.[162] We're proactive, not reactive, said Altenburg, the office's Community Prosecution Team captain. While the program may be prosecutor-driven, it is definitely a collaborative effort. The Community Prosecution Program is made up of Target Teams. There is one team housed at six of the seven Milwaukee Police Department district stations. Each Target Team consists of an assistant D.A., two police officers assigned to the community prosecutor in that district, and agents from the Department of Corrections as well as the Department of Probation and Parole.

Like many community-based prosecution programs, the efforts of the Milwaukee D.A.'s Community Prosecution Unit have evolved over the years. We continue to do a fair amount of work in the nuisance abatement area, but we've expanded our efforts to include law enforcement intelligence sharing through our Target Teams and targeted investigations through our Major Violators Program (MVP), and district level case review. This includes all of the non-victim misdemeanor cases and some of the felony gun and drug cases, Altenburg said.[163] The MVP effort focuses on a list of approximately 20 individuals in each district determined by prosecutors, police, and partner agencies to be the most violent individuals within each of those districts. Those individuals are then specifically targeted by the district Target Teams. By working together through the Community Prosecution Unit, information on these individuals is shared among the agencies. Such efforts are ways for the assistant D.A.s assigned to the Community Prosecution Unit to ensure that various levels within law enforcement start talking to each other.

In Indianapolis, community prosecution is nothing new. Initiated in the early 1990s, it has been a component of the Marion County Prosecuting Attorney's office under three administrations. Former Marion County Prosecuting Attorney Jeff Modisett first established the program by placing deputy prosecutors in each of two police district headquarters on a part-time basis. These soon developed into full-time positions. His successor, Scott C. Newman, expanded the program to four of the city's five police districts. County Prosecuting Attorney Carl Brizzi, elected in 2002, increased the community prosecution efforts, assigning a prosecutor to work on problem-solving in the county's suburbs.

Community prosecution is highly effective because it broadens the mission of prosecution from simply prosecuting to preventing and reducing crime, Brizzi said.[164] He believes that one of the most important goals of community prosecution is to give the members of our community a greater voice in solving the problems in their neighborhoods. The problems in their neighborhoods are unique, and law enforcement can't solve them by itself.[165]

Indianapolis residents appreciate the prosecutor's efforts and say the community prosecution program gives them better access to the prosecutor's office. The prosecutor is so distant in normal cases where they're in the downtown office. You might see them when you go to court and that's it. But I know here if I have something that needs to be addressed by a prosecutor, I can call over there and I'm on a first name basis, said Pam Cole, vice president of Northwest Neighborhood Association Cooperative, Inc., a coalition of seven neighborhood associations.[166] Brizzi thinks community prosecutors in effect serve as emissaries for the entire office. Most of the prosecutors in his office venture out of the main office only to go to the courthouse, to crime scenes, or on investigations with law enforcement. That's not the case for the community prosecutors who Brizzi calls ambassadors. They're interacting with the public and I think generating a very positive image for the office, which translates into better cooperation with law enforcement, he said.[167]

It's what Brizzi has labeled a global approach to problem-solving prosecution that has led to many effective solutions to long-standing problems in Indianapolis, including prostitution, nuisance properties, gun crime, and juvenile delinquency.

Communities across the country are taking that same global approach when it comes to community prosecution and policing. **Instead of simply being reactive to community issues, prosecutors must be proactive and use a problem-solving approach when addressing local neighborhood concerns.**

CHAPTER 20

Bring the Courts to the Neighborhoods

As long as you obey my court order, we're… The judge was cut off mid-sentence by the thunderous roar of a FedEx airbus as its screeching tires touched down at Memphis International Airport. The runway is just across the street from a former church transformed into a courthouse in the Memphis neighborhood known as Whitehaven. The routine interruptions created by aircrafts that take off and land never seem to bother Judge Larry Potter, who holds environmental community court here once a month. As I was saying, as long as you obey my court order, we're not going to have any problems, Judge Potter continued after the brief pause, without missing a beat. The judge had ordered a young man to pay a fine and court costs, and, most importantly, pay closer attention to the volume on his car stereo. Memphis police had issued the defendant a citation for excessively loud music blasting from his car while driving down a nearby street. It seems almost appropriate that a loud jetliner briefly halted the case of loud music being handled in the Whitehaven Environmental Community Court that day.

The Whitehaven Environmental Community Court is one of six community courts held throughout Shelby County, Tennessee. Judge Potter splits his time sitting on his permanent bench inside his courtroom in downtown Memphis and the six satellite benches across the community.

Most community courts across the country handle various misdemeanor criminal cases. Our community courts are a little different. They are problem-solving courts that handle the literal broken windows cases. We refer to them as environmental cases. They include problems such as building, health, and fire code violations generated from deteriorated buildings, vacant lots, and unkempt yards. At our community court locations, these are the kinds of cases we most often handle. An assistant D.A. and an entire staff travel with the judge each week. The staff assigned to the judge's courtroom includes clerks needed to keep records and sheriff's deputies required to secure the courtroom.

It's as if someone picked up the courtroom and placed it right in the middle of a neighborhood. The proximity helps these cases move swiftly through the system. Because the courtroom is just a few blocks away, instead of miles away, community police and code enforcement officers can work quickly. They inspect the properties in question to see if owners are in compliance, then immediately report back to the court. Also of importance, the community courts enable the citizens to have greater access to the judicial system.

Most prosecutors don't have jurisdiction over the literal broken windows cases involving problem properties. But under a law passed by our state legislature back in the 1980s, the D.A. has the authority to prosecute such cases, even though they involve violations of local ordinances rather than state criminal laws.

Soon after taking office, I saw an opportunity to address problem properties at the neighborhood level through community courts. I approached Judge Potter about the possibility of trying it out in the Frayser community of Memphis, an area that was once a thriving, primarily blue-collar residential area composed mostly of families dependent on jobs at the then-flourishing International Harvester and Firestone manufacturing plants. But as those plants closed, Frayser lost its stable economic base and began a downward spiral, with deteriorating properties and rising crime. But there remained in Frayser a strong core of citizens committed to its future. And establishing a community court in the heart of Frayser represented an opportunity to partner with those citizens.

When I approached him, Judge Potter committed without hesitation. I reached out to a leading real estate development company, Belz Enterprises, regarding some space for a community court at a shopping center it owned in Frayser. It was a shopping center that had seen better days, had vacant space, and might benefit from the presence of a community court. Belz Enterprises agreed to provide the space if we would renovate it. We completed a renovation with the help of funds from the county and the non-profit Assisi Foundation.

In the newly renovated space, we kicked off our first community court in 1999. Feeling that their community had been long neglected, the Frayser leadership was thrilled by the court's presence. The community court also motivated the police to be more aggressive in citing people for code violations.

The results in Frayser did not go unnoticed. Judge Potter was ready and willing to expand the concept to other areas. The Memphis-Shelby County Airport Authority owned property in the community of Whitehaven, including a former church. It provided the former church for creation of the Whitehaven Community Court. That was followed by opening four more community courts in the Orange Mound and Hickory Hill communities of

Memphis, and the towns of Millington and Arlington.

The Center for Court Innovation in New York City, a non-profit think tank that assists courts and criminal justice agencies, describes community courts as neighborhood-focused courts that attempt to harness the power of the justice system to address local problems.[168] They can take many forms, but all of these courts focus on creative partnerships and problem-solving. Community courts are yet another important component to the concept of community prosecution. And this is a concept which usually has the added benefit of creating unity between the citizens and the justice system.

The Center for Court Innovation helped launch the Midtown Community Court in Manhattan in 1993. It has served as the model community court for dozens of communities across the country. The Center for Court Innovation suggests six principles that are significant to establishing a community court that handles low level criminal cases, primarily misdemeanors. These principles were derived from the community court established in Midtown Manhattan.

The first principle of a community court is *restoring the community.*[169] Quality of life crimes can damage a community, sometimes more so than individual crimes. A community court realizes that unaddressed, low-level crimes can erode a community. These crimes lead to economic hardship and neighborhood decay. They create an environment conducive to serious crime. To create a better quality of life in the neighborhood, a community court uses punishment to pay back the community, combines punishment with help for the offender, gives the community a voice in shaping the types of restorative punishments, and makes social services at the court available to residents.

Bridging the gap between communities and courts is the second principle.[170] By making justice visible, accessible, and proactive, the court becomes more of a partner with the community instead of an adversary. A community court puts offenders to work in places where neighbors can see it. It welcomes observers and visitors. It becomes a central location for neighborhood events and meetings. A community court's staff can keep close tabs on crime conditions in the community and look for ways to address problems as they develop instead of reacting to them after the fact. A community court also reaches out to victims by providing faster services and less intimidation than a traditional court.

The third principle of a community court is *knitting together a fractured criminal justice system.*[171] Sometimes, criminal justice agencies just don't communicate with each other. Because separate agencies have different missions, they often work in isolation. By providing a central location, a community court can act as a hub in the justice system. It serves as a place where all concerned agencies can come together to focus on a case. A community court can also help criminal justice professionals and social service providers form more productive relationships. This provides better supervision and results in each individual case.

One very different principle of a community court is *helping offenders deal with problems that lead to crime.*[172] By putting an offender's problems first, a community court can be used as a gateway to treatment. Drug treatment, medical services, educational programs, and counseling can all be incorporated into sentences. Because of the accessibility to the community, the court can remain involved beyond the disposition of the immediate case. Police, staff, and even neighbors can update the court on how the individual is doing.

Providing better information is another key principle of a community court.[173] Making as much information as possible available at the defendant's first court appearance allows for a significantly more rapid response and disposition of the case. Instant updates on a defendant's progress enable the court to better monitor the defendant's compliance.

The final principle is *designing the courthouse.*[174] The courthouse should be a physical expression of the court's goals and values. After hours, the community court can become a resource for community groups to convene and hold public meetings. Putting community meetings, events, and people under one roof serves the needs of the court by making it easier for a judge to craft sentences that combine punishment and help.

These principles were used as the foundation to form another very successful community court in a Brooklyn, New York neighborhood. It's a great example of how these six principles work together to make a community safer.

On one recent hot and steamy August afternoon, the smell of hot dogs roasting on a nearby grill wafted through the air. The sound of someone banging on a bongo drum competed with the chatter and laughter of families speaking to police officers and prosecutors. Balloons and streamers decorated tables from one end of Red Hook Park to the other. It was National Night Out in Brooklyn's Red Hook community, and it was clearly a celebration.

The scene that day was a far cry from what Red Hook looked like in the late 1980s and early 1990s. Back then, not many residents ventured into Red Hook Park. Mostly gang members walked the streets, and guns and drugs were prevalent. My son's baseball team would sometimes have games right here, and security guards were always nearby, says one Brooklyn prosecutor remembering the fear that most people felt walking the streets of this community back then. But, times have changed. Many attribute that to a tragic event in 1992, when the problems Red Hook faced came to a head. The principal of a nearby elementary school was gunned down while walking through the Red Hook Housing Development. Principal Patrick Daly was searching for a student who had run out of the nearby school when Daly was caught in the crossfire of rival gang members. It was a senseless crime that prompted Brooklyn District Attorney Charles Joe Hynes to take action. Following the conviction of Mr. Daly's killers, D.A. Hynes helped create and implement The Red Hook Community Justice Center. The center opened its doors to hear its first case in 2000.

One step inside the refurbished former Catholic school located in the heart of this low-income neighborhood causes one to immediately sense the difference between The Red Hook Community Justice Center and a traditional court building. Maybe it's the neighborhood children's drawings posted on the walls. Or perhaps it's the bulletin board covered in flyers announcing various community events. Most noticeably, it's the friendly greetings of community volunteers who welcome area residents into the center.

Inside the center, Judge Alex Calabrese hears every single case. Most of the matters brought to the court are misdemeanor crimes. Low-level drug cases, domestic violence cases, simple assaults, theft cases involving small amounts, and driving without a license cases are common on the court's docket. In 2007, the court heard approximately 4,000 criminal misdemeanor cases in which the defendants were arrested and about 8,000 other cases in which the defendants were summoned to the court. Each of these cases originates in Red Hook or neighboring communities. The court also has jurisdiction to hear selected family court and civil court cases stemming from the Red Hook community.

I think a lot of what we do is common-sense justice, said Brooklyn Assistant D.A. Gerianne Abriano, who serves as the chief prosecutor at The Red Hook Community Justice Center. Abriano tries to achieve three goals with every case that comes before her: a defendant must give back to the community; a defendant must make the victim whole again; and the defendant must try to make himself a better person.

Returning to that August day when the neighborhood would celebrate National Night Out, an 18-year-old young woman stood before Judge Calabrese. She was six months pregnant and had been charged with a felony theft for stealing her friend's debit card and using it to make purchases. Taking into consideration the nature of the crime and the fact that, if convicted, this woman would give birth while in prison, the judge allowed the defendant to plead guilty to a misdemeanor theft charge and ordered her to undergo court-supervised counseling. The judge also ordered her to pay back her friend the full amount she spent using the card and ordered five days of service in the community. If her punishment was successfully completed, she would benefit the community as well as her unborn child.

The judge at The Red Hook Community Justice Center has an array of sanctions and services at his disposal, including community restitution projects, on-site educational workshops and GED classes, drug treatment, and mental health counseling. All of these are rigorously monitored to ensure accountability and drive home notions of individual responsibility.[175]

Back in my own community of Shelby County, Tennessee, as the judge looked around the community courtroom, he took notice of something you don't see very often at the courthouse downtown. The defendant before the court who had been cited for playing loud music stopped to shake the hand of the officer who cited him for the violation. You see that? Judge Potter asked. If we had more people who acted like that, there would be a lot fewer problems in this city, he added, to the chuckle of the crowd gathered. Most left the community court that day with a better understanding of the criminal justice system and a greater appreciation of what is being done to help their community thrive. **Bringing the courts to the neighborhoods increases the success level of any battle plan for safer communities.**

CHAPTER 21

Go After the Literal Broken Windows

Neighborhood blight is an issue that concerns nearly all of us. The main reason is because its impact is not limited to one particular piece of property. It affects all property throughout the entire community. It takes only one house, one building, one property to bring down the quality of life and the sense of security on a block. Of course citizens are concerned with violent crimes, gangs, and other more serious offenses that occur throughout their community. But neighborhood blight is something that most homeowners can relate to or have had to deal with at one time or another. Whenever I attend a town-hall style meeting or a neighborhood watch meeting, it's the one topic that consistently comes up for discussion. Whether I'm eating dinner at a restaurant with my wife or at the grocery store picking up some things for dinner at home, citizens tend to approach me most often about this one problem.

Neighborhood blight goes right to the heart of the broken windows theory of fighting crime. No one in the neighborhood wants an unkempt yard with tall grass and weeds. No one wants to see an old, rusty, broken-down car sitting idle on his neighbor's lawn for months. No one wants a dilapidated building sitting on the corner. No one wants a big rig parked on a residential block. No one wants to live next to a home with a yard full of debris. While these minor offenses don't warrant calling 911, citizens have a right to be concerned.

As professors George Kelling and James Q. Wilson first wrote in 1982, these situations send signals that people living in the neighborhood do not care. However, most neighbors do care. The professors explained how any one of these conditions can create an environment conducive to crime. They perpetuate the broken windows theory. Repairing the literal broken windows can lead to community pride, a sense of safety, and less crime.

In Memphis, there is an overwhelming number of properties facing one code violation or another. There are several agencies involved in enforcing the codes and looking for violations. Some are city divisions, others represent the county. While the Shelby County D.A.'s office mainly prosecutes violations of state law, it does have the authority to prosecute violations of city and county building, health, and fire codes in a special court division established by the Tennessee General Assembly. In the Shelby County Environmental Court, any number of agencies can bring cases. But, after the D.A.'s office began prosecuting city and county code violations, we soon realized that not every agency involved in code enforcement was communicating with other agencies. We learned that in some cases there was duplication, and in others no action taken because one agency thought another was handling the issue.

Finding permanent solutions to the number of problem properties in Memphis was becoming increasingly difficult. Something needed to be done to focus on specific properties for the following reasons:

- Code violations on certain properties cannot be resolved through the normal work processes of individual agencies;
- Violations often fall under the purview of more than one agency (with many violations occurring on one property);
- Problem properties pose an eminent danger to human health and safety; and
- Owners of problem properties often cannot be located.

Several years ago I approached our city and county mayors to address these issues. I asked if they would help me implement a team approach to fighting these eyesores and public nuisances. With their assistance, we created the Environmental Team (E-Team). The D.A.'s office and various city and county agencies that handle environmental, building, and health codes signed a memorandum of understanding. These divisions, offices, and agencies agreed to use their combined resources to investigate and create solutions for problem properties. Each agency has designated a representative to be a member of the E-Team. This individual must be a key staff member who is authorized to make decisions in his or her office.

Presently, the E-Team meets every month in order to work together in a collaborative and comprehensive way to find solutions to solve the problem properties in our community. I try to attend the meetings myself to the extent possible. The team devises a list of problem properties to tackle. That is the easy part. Some are eyesores, others are health hazards. The list is always changing. As one property comes off, another is added. Decision makers from each agency establish specific, coordinated game-plans for each property. The E-Team assigns detailed responsibilities to different agencies and sets detailed timetables for completion. The team gives some priority to properties located within the Memphis Police Department's targeted hot spots as established by its data-based policing initiative called Blue Crush™. The team also focuses on properties that are closed or secured by the D.A.'s office and police through public nuisance actions.

One such location was the Lucky 7 Food Mart. The D.A.'s office filed a public nuisance petition against the owners of the Lucky 7. It was the central hub of an identified drug hot-spot controlled by gang members. Citizens living in the surrounding neighborhood routinely called police for help regarding crimes of violence, drug trafficking, and drug related-burglaries and thefts. Many of these crimes were generated at the Lucky 7, which anchored a block of run-down homes tagged with gang graffiti and littered with evidence of drug sales and drug use. We filed six nuisance actions against home owners on that street as well as the Lucky 7.

The Lucky 7 was not just the central meeting place for drug dealers and gang members. It was in serious disrepair and posed a substantial risk to the health and safety of the community. Rev. Dwight Montgomery, head of the local chapter of the Southern Christian Leadership Conference (SCLC), pledged his organization's support and assistance in removing the graffiti from the market and other properties on the block. Their efforts helped salvage some of the homes on that street. But a fresh coat of paint would have never been enough to remedy the multiple code violations the Lucky 7 faced.

Police boarded up the market and it never reopened. The E-Team stepped in and coordinated a joint effort between the D.A.'s office, the health department, the county code enforcement office, and the Memphis Police Department to demolish the property. Ultimately, the environmental court judge ordered the owner to tear it down. Today, an empty lot sits where the Lucky 7 Food Mart once operated.

Many government agencies responsible for addressing blighted properties have very tight budgets, and funds are hard to come by. Many times there are not enough physical or financial resources available to address every property that needs attention. And for every problem property that is corrected there are that many more that fall into violation. Many citizens realize this. Understanding this led to an idea generated by one of our local community groups. PACA (Police and Citizens Alliance) is a group of concerned citizens that addresses quality of life issues in the Hickory Hill area of Memphis. The group works out of a Memphis police precinct in Hickory Hill. A gentleman by the name of Bob Morgan has worked in the PACA office and been a community leader for some time. He had heard of a program in Plano, Texas that educates rather than disciplines property owners who are first time code violators. He believes that many people don't even realize they may be in violation of a city or county code ordinance. He came up with the idea of volunteers walking door-to-door through their neighborhoods, distributing educational materials about code violations. A few weeks later, the volunteers would survey the streets for possible violations. The idea was to reduce the number of calls made to city or county agencies, freeing those agencies up to focus on more serious violations.

We initiated the Community Improvement Project on a pilot basis after listening to Mr. Morgan and other PACA members. Crucial to the success of the program was the involvement of PACA and other community groups including SEMBA (Southeast Memphis Business Association), SEMI (Southeast Memphis Initiative), and the Center for Community Building and Neighborhood Action at the University of Memphis.

The collaborative group implemented the Community Improvement Project in three phases. In phase one, working with the Memphis Mayor's Citizen Service Center, we created a flyer outlining the top ten most common code violations. We described each violation in detail and included a photo to illustrate the problem. These violations included accumulation of junk, trash, and debris; open storage of materials and furnishings; parking and storing inoperable or junk motor vehicles; excessive weeds, grass, trees and vegetation; off street parking; substandard structures and fences; parking special use and recreational vehicles and equipment; abandoned and derelict structures; and general service and repair shops in residentially zoned areas.

In phase two, after the flyers were produced, a group of community volunteers educated through a volunteer training session led by code enforcement officials distributed the flyers door-to-door. Volunteers distributed flyers to approximately 1,500 homes in two specific Hickory Hill neighborhoods during the pilot project. In addition to delivering the flyers, the volunteers also reviewed the neighborhoods for possible code violations. This step provided dozens of additional sets of eyes to scope out the neighborhood and helped overburdened code enforcement officers.

Two weeks after the flyers hit the streets the volunteers went back to survey the neighborhood as part of the second phase of the Community Improvement Project. Several homeowners had come into compliance since the flyers were passed out two weeks prior. Some people just don't realize what they're doing is in violation, Morgan said at the time. That's why educating them and pointing out the violations is such a helpful first step. We can correct it before code enforcement is even called, he added.

In phase three, the D.A.'s office sent warning letters to the property owners who appeared to remain in violation. The letters stated that the property owners would be prosecuted in environmental court if the violations were not rectified. Two weeks after we sent the letters, volunteers conducted a third and final follow-up survey. The addresses of houses that continued to be in violation of city or county codes were forwarded to the proper code enforcement office for appropriate action.

We partnered concerned citizens with public agencies responsible for addressing problem properties. As a result, we were able to make a significant dent in the broken windows of specific neighborhoods.

Working together to tackle the broken windows in our communities sends the message that someone does care and that crime will not be tolerated. **The fight against crime must include an attack on problem properties that create an atmosphere conducive to crime.**

PART 5

Develop a Sense of Urgency About Juvenile Crime

I have seen thousands of defendants in criminal cases in Shelby County courtrooms. Many of the ones who concern me the most are juveniles transferred from juvenile court to criminal court at our request. This means they will be tried under the same laws that apply to adults.

The juveniles who end up being transferred are usually violent offenders with a history of criminal acts and gang involvement. They represent a small percentage of the cases in juvenile court. Some are charged with murder, others with serious violent crimes such as armed robberies and carjackings.

As I observe these juveniles in court, what disturbs me most is their lack of emotion. I sense they have no remorse for their actions. Their eyes only show blank, cold stares. Most of them will harm others again if given the chance. They have little value for the lives of others or their own lives. I know that we must do our job to protect citizens from juveniles who have become predators. It is not an enjoyable part of my job, but it is my duty to do what I can to protect the public under our state laws.

The middle school students, sixth, seventh, and eighth graders, must be reached before it is too late. I've talked to student assemblies at every single public middle school in my community, around 40 in all, about the consequences of making bad choices and engaging in serious violence. I've visited many of the schools numerous times.

Arguably, my job description does not include alerting juveniles that they are looking at prison time if they commit serious acts of violence. I could sit back and let them screw up, then try to slam the prison doors on them. But I'd rather young people make good choices. If my presentations at schools have salvaged just a handful of young people who were headed down the path of gang involvement and a life of violence, then every minute of my time has been worth it.

* * *

Demarrius Banks was a seventh grader at Airways Middle School in Memphis. Demarrius saw the consequences of violence up close when he arrived home from school one day to find his mother's lifeless body. She was a homicide victim. The perpetrator was convicted and is serving a life sentence. Though the killer is in prison where he belongs, the emotional scars as a result of his mother's murder will remain with Demarrius the rest of his life.

Back in 2005, I decided the D.A.'s office needed to do what it could to make young people part of the solution rather than the problem. One small step was to sponsor the Do The Write Thing essay contest. The idea is simple. Get middle school students to write about violence in the community, how it affects their lives, and what they think should be done about it. Nationally, the contest has been funded with donations from the nation of Kuwait as a way of thanking our nation for securing the sovereignty of Kuwait in the Gulf War.

We have set up a program in which English teachers in our middle schools are encouraged to have their students participate. Graduate students at the University of Memphis' Department of Criminology score the essays and pick a female and male winner from each participating school. Next, a committee of community leaders reviews the winning essays from each school and picks a community-wide male and female winner. A local church, Hope Presbyterian, hosts a banquet for all the winners each spring. It's an uplifting experience, with students, proud parents, and teachers in attendance. The overall community-wide winners get an expense paid trip to Washington, D.C. to attend the national Do the Write Thing banquet, visit with their senators and congressman, and see some of the sites of our nation's capital. Memphis main daily newspaper, *The Commercial Appeal*, publishes the winning essays on its editorial page, and our local NBA franchise, the Memphis Grizzlies, gives special recognition to the winners at one of the team's home games.

The Do the Write Thing essay contest significantly changed the life of young Demarrius. As an Airways Middle School student, he decided to participate in the essay contest. Demarrius lived in a neighborhood where poverty and violence are common ways of life. He could have gone down the path of violence pretty easily. But Demarrius saw the violence against his mother as a reason to stand up and speak out. His essay caught the attention of the essay contest judges. He ended up being the community-wide male winner.

Much can be learned from the following words of Demarrius in his essay:

How has violence affected me? What are the causes of violence? What can I do about violence?

Violence has affected my life in many ways. The effects of gang activities, drive-by shootings, and peer pressure are some of the causes of violence. Certain environments, one parent homes, and a low self-esteem in a person can contribute to violence. A person doesn't have to give in to anyone who chooses to not do the right thing. If everyone does what is right we can overcome violence....

I am raised by my grandmother. My grandmother told me to do what is right. If I do see my uncles and brother involved in gangs and doing drugs, I should not start their bad habits. I should continue to be a leader and not a follower. It does get hard for me at times. My mother was killed in an act of violence. It is painful for me to talk about it at times. However, when I am feeling down, I talk to my grandmother, and she encourages me to stay on task.

I have an uncle who is in a gang. He is one of my favorite uncles who I looked up to.... I was hurt when I discovered that he was involved in gang activities. I know gangs are dangerous, and they are people you do not want to associate with. I have a brother who is in a gang. My brother joined a gang because of my uncle. My uncle helped influence by brother to join.

I am a seventh grade young man who is on the honor roll at my school. I am very respectful to my classmates, friends, teachers and everyone I come in contact with. My grandmother taught me to treat others the way I want to be treated. I do treat my friends right, but sometimes they do not show any respect toward me. For example, when we have class work or homework, I will complete my assignments on time. Most of my classmates do not do their assignments. If I do not let my friends see my class work they get angry with me and start calling me names. It hurts me when they say mean things to me, but I have learned how to ignore them. My teacher told me if I ignore students when they are disrespectful to me, they will eventually leave me alone. It works most of the time.

One reason for violence is gang activity.... gang members do all kinds of things. For example, they steal cars, break in people's houses and smoke and drink. I told my friends that I do not want to get involved. They said, 'When you are in a gang no one will want to fight you, and you will have someone to protect you at all times.' I told my friends that gangs are for cowards and they should be arrested for the things they do. I do not like violence because it brings back memories of my mother.

> *In order to prevent violence, I can join a community center and create a fight-free club. In this club, we will focus on ways to read better and write more. I would like to start this club because I have some family members who are in gangs. I believe this program will help them want to improve their lives. I have decided that Demarrius Banks is going to think for himself. I am an honor roll student and I am going to continue studying and reading daily so I can become a successful person. If I become successful, I can help others turn their lives around so they would not want to participate in negative activities such as violence.*

Through the simple act of writing an essay, Demarrius decided to stand up and be part of the solution. He traveled to Washington, D.C. with his father and English teacher. He met his senators and congressman. He was recognized at center court at a Grizzles game. His essay appeared in *The Commercial Appeal.* His whole life changed.

✳ ✳ ✳

I can't say I had a happy childhood. My father abandoned us when I was four years of age. We fell into poverty, and I felt it. I knew there had been better times, just from looking at family photograph albums, the remnants of our farm, and our household belongings that were being sold piece by piece to put food on the table. I remember well the winter I had no coat to wear, the days my mother had nothing to put on the dinner table but rice and water, and the hurtful comments from other kids when our farm sold at foreclosure.

Looking back on it, I was embarrassed by our poverty. I had the feeling of being trapped with no way out. I started skipping school on a pretty regular basis. I was headed down the wrong path. But I was lucky. Some adults helped steer me on the right course. My mother deserves much credit. We didn't have a car, a telephone, or a television, during most of my younger years. But my mother had an appreciation for education. While selling other items to make ends meet, she held on to hundreds of books. While other kids were watching television, I was reading! She had given me one of the most valuable gifts of my life. My fourth grade teacher, Mrs. White, had a tremendous impact on me with just a few words. Because I had missed so many days of school, Mrs. White told me I was supposed to repeat the fourth grade. However, because of all of my mother's books, I was the best reader in the class. Mrs. White explained to me that she was going to let me pass to the fifth grade even though it was technically against school policy. I remember her words, You can be anything you want to be, but in order to do it, you must come to school. Those few words were powerful in turning a sense of hopelessness into ambition and a darn good work ethic. I didn't skip school after that conversation with Mrs. White. As Mrs. White was helping me connect the dots and see a way out of poverty, my older brother Gordon was showing me that determination and focus really did pay off. He was a senior in high school at that time and had chosen football as his ticket out. One of my early memories was of LSU Assistant Coach Charlie McClendon sitting in our home talking to my brother and mother. (McClendon would later become the head coach.) Gordon ended up getting a scholarship to play football at LSU. His drive and focus helped motivate me to strive for a better life.

Then Frank Humphreys entered my childhood. He bought our farm after foreclosure. My mother and I moved across the highway to a small house. Frank Humphreys hired me to work on the farm after school and on weekends. He helped me with school projects and introduced me to the world of political campaigns. His acts changed the course of my future.

At a critical point when I was headed in the wrong direction, a handful of adults instilled in me the importance of achieving, doing my best, and setting goals. I often wonder what direction my life would have taken had it not been for their influences. My own community of Memphis has thousands of juveniles skipping school on a regular basis, and it's a big problem in many other communities. We must insure positive role models in the lives of young people and give them encouragement before it is too late to make a difference.

CHAPTER 22

Take a Tough Stance
Against Serious Juvenile Offenders

On October 5, 2002, 15-year-old William BJ Hall was shot and killed at 4400 American Way in my hometown of Memphis. This was a location frequented by young teenagers who referred to it as The Fro because of the appearance of the trees which, to them, resembled an Afro style hairdo.

BJ was murdered by his 14-year-old friend and fellow Five Deuce Hoova Street Crips gang member, Deandre Kendall. Deandre shot BJ at close range with a shotgun in the back of the head. According to witnesses and fellow gang members, the murder took place because BJ had dishonored the gang by losing a fight to a weaker individual. Several teenagers stood by and watched in horror that day. Worst of all, they did nothing. Some knew of Deandre's intention to execute BJ. Only one person had tried to talk Deandre out of murdering his friend. Most of these teens probably stood by and did nothing out of fear that they might be Deandre's next target. One 14-year-old witness stated that Deandre had told him beforehand that he was going to get BJ because there was something about him he didn't like. The witness said when BJ looked away, Kendall saw his chance and took the shot. According to all the witnesses, none of the youngsters checked on BJ or even approached his body after Deandre shot him. They just ran away. They told no one. The body was discovered in The Fro a couple of days later.

At our request, juvenile court transferred Deandre Kendall to stand trial as an adult. He was and remains one of the youngest juveniles tried as an adult in Memphis. His prior juvenile history was for disorderly conduct in 2001. There were no other indicators in his court file that he had any propensity for this level of violence. Spectators attended each of the court hearings dressed in orange, the Hoova Street Crips' signature color. Some of the victim's family members wore orange as well, even though it was the gang life that had led to BJ's death.

After prosecutors interviewed potential witnesses, it was obvious to us that the gang members weren't going to be very reliable on the stand. Given that problem, we made an exception to our no plea bargaining policy on violent crimes. Even though the grand jury indicted Deandre Kendall for first degree murder, we allowed him to plead guilty to second degree murder. Deandre Kendall is serving a 30 year sentence.

Jean Williams was a 76-year-old retired school teacher who lived alone in her home in the Raleigh area of Memphis. On January 28, 2004, she answered a knock on her door. A young male teenager introduced himself as Terry. He asked if he could use her telephone to call someone to pick him up and give him a ride home. She agreed to dial a number for him. She called the number and spoke to someone she suspected was also a teenager. She cracked open her door to hand Terry the phone. He immediately pulled a gun on her and forced his way inside her home. Terry demanded money and started searching her home for cash and other valuables. He took a small amount of cash and some heirloom jewelry. He started to take an antique necklace but left it behind when Jean Williams pleaded with him not to take the necklace because it had been given to her by her grandmother. Terry told the victim he was going to take her car. He took her car keys and removed the phone from her home so that she could not call the police. He left in her car but inexplicably returned and abandoned the running car in her driveway. Jean Williams will never forget how Terry looked right at her while pointing the gun at her and asked her if she was going to call the police. She watched in horror as the young boy inserted a clip in the gun and racked the slide. Police officers later collected as evidence a round of 9mm ammunition that had ejected from his gun. Jean Williams felt certain Terry was thinking of killing her. She told him she was going to call her son, but not the police. She recalled asking Terry what his mother would think of what he was doing. During the robbery, Jean Williams was pushed down at least twice to the floor, causing her to hurt her back.

On January 29, 2004, Karla Baker was shot and killed in her home. She lived near Jean Williams, who had been victimized one day earlier. Karla Baker was a cancer patient and was returning home after receiving her chemotherapy treatment. When she entered her home, she found a young male inside. She started screaming. The intruder shot Karla Baker in the leg, the torso, and finally the head, killing her. Police found three unspent and three spent 9mm rounds inside the Baker home. Karla Baker's mini van was missing, along with her purse and property from her home, including a large television set. Officers located 15-year-old Terry Caraway driving her van shortly after the murder occurred. They found Karla's purse and contents, including personal identification papers with Karla Baker's name on them, in a dumpster near Caraway's home. Other items taken from the Baker residence were recovered in the suspect's home. Terry's sister, Ebonie, told police her brother acknowledged getting the items from a robbery. Ebonie Caraway gave a statement to police investigators that her brother admitted killing Karla Baker.

Terry Caraway gave a written confession to the murder of Karla Baker. Jean Williams identified him as the same juvenile who had forced his way into her home at gunpoint. He was charged with aggravated robbery of Jean Williams and first degree murder in the perpetration of the aggravated burglary of Karla Baker. At our request, Terry Caraway was transferred by juvenile court to stand trial as an adult for these crimes. He entered a guilty plea to the charges. He is serving a life sentence with no possibility of parole until he has served a minimum of 51 years.

Prior to the 2004 crimes, Terry Caraway had a juvenile delinquency record for two assaults, three incidents of disorderly conduct, being a runaway, and ungovernable behavior. Caraway was one of a group of youths who carjacked Burton Callicott in October 2002. The late Memphis artist, then 94 years old, was knocked to the ground, and his car was taken near the Memphis College of Art. Caraway was 13 at the time and spent nearly one year at a youth detention facility for that offense. The victim himself had asked the court for leniency for the boys due to their young age. In fact, a parent of one of the other juveniles paid court ordered restitution to Mr. Callicott. He sent the payment back to the court, asking that it be donated to a worthy cause.

An interesting footnote to this case regards the 3 unspent 9 mm rounds found in Karla Baker's home. Police investigators concluded that the suspect, being only 15 and unpracticed in the use of a 9 mm weapon, had racked the slide between the 3 shots he fired into Mrs. Baker's body. He apparently did not understand that this action was not necessary on a weapon that automatically chambered the next round. This was the action he took in Jean Williams' home when he pointed the 9 mm at her. The rounds found at both crime scenes matched. The police believed that Terry Caraway was trying to get up his nerve to shoot and kill someone the previous day. They were pretty sure he had considered killing Jean Williams, since the unspent rounds were found at both crime scenes. The police always suspected that Terry Caraway did not act alone during the robbery and murder of Karla Baker. An extensive amount of property was taken from the Baker residence, including a large television. Police investigators did not feel Caraway could have loaded it into the Baker minivan without the assistance of at least one other individual. According to the Baker family members, Karla Baker always opened the automatic garage door when she pulled into the driveway, stopped at the mailbox, and let out the family pet before going into her home. If she did not deviate from her routine on the day of her murder, Terry Caraway had ample opportunity to exit the residence undetected through the back side of the home. Instead, he chose to remain inside the home when the victim entered. He then confronted and killed Karla Baker.

Harry Shorstein served as state attorney (Florida's equivalent to district attorney) from 1991 through 2008 for Florida's fourth judicial circuit, which includes the city of Jacksonville. Soon after taking office, he made the conscious decision to place more of his office's resources on combating the escalating juvenile crime problem facing the Jacksonville area. He doubled the number of prosecutors assigned to his juvenile division. Many of these were his top prosecutors. He did so out of a commitment to more aggressively prosecute juvenile cases. His efforts sent a powerful message to the community that he was making the reduction of juvenile crime a top priority.

From the start, Shorstein made it clear that his battle plan to tackle juvenile crime involved a two-pronged approach. First, he was committed to going beyond the traditional role of the prosecutor by using a preemptive strike. He implemented aggressive preventive steps to curtail the number of would-be juvenile criminals and intervention steps to influence juveniles going down the wrong path before it was too late. Shorstein's second mode of attack was to incarcerate repeat and violent juvenile offenders.

When prevention and intervention steps were unsuccessful, Shorstein believed that he should hold habitual and violent juvenile criminals just as accountable as adults. Under Florida law, he aggressively dealt with habitual and violent juvenile offenders as adults, with the intention of placing them in jail or prison. In an ideal system, Shorstein did not actually believe incarcerating juveniles as adults was the best approach. But his hands were tied by the juvenile system's inability to handle dangerous criminals.

This is the only way to effectively protect the public and is certainly more effective than leaving them in the juvenile justice system where they often bounce from rehabilitative program to program without any positive results, said Shorstein.

Shorstein felt that aggressively prosecuting chronic juvenile offenders as adults would serve the dual purpose of holding those juveniles accountable *and* providing an incentive to at-risk youth to avoid the same consequences. Prevention efforts cannot succeed if those not abiding by the law do not believe there is a consequence to criminal behavior. I believe that incarceration of juveniles as adults is a critical deterrent to juveniles not to break the law, noted Shorstein. As a part of his deterrence message, Shorstein sent a personal letter to the principal of the last school where each incarcerated juvenile was enrolled. He hoped that communicating the consequences of engaging in serious crime would persuade other students to make better choices.

According to Shorstein, when he took office, Jacksonville faced a 27 percent increase in the number of juveniles arrested from 1990 to 1991. While he was state attorney, his office prosecuted more than 2,700 juvenile cases in adult court. From 1993 through 2007, around 1200 juveniles prosecuted by his office were incarcerated locally in the Duval County (Jacksonville) Jail. Approximately 370 juveniles were sentenced to time in the Florida state prison system, with 26 violent juveniles being sentenced to life in prison. Our goal, of course, was to succeed in our preventive efforts and to never be forced to prosecute a juvenile as an adult. Our statistics in this regard were very promising. In 1993, we referred 483 cases to adult court. In 2006, even with tougher laws mandating adult prosecution in certain cases, we only transferred 79 juveniles cases to adult court, said Shorstein.

Shorstein's goal of holding serious juvenile offenders accountable and deterring others from such acts was achieved. In recent years, the juvenile crime trend in Jacksonville has been encouraging. From 1997 through 2006, overall juvenile arrests in Jacksonville were down 40 percent. Shorstein noted that the reduction in juvenile arrests corresponded with an increase of more than 20,000 in the preteen and teenage population in Jacksonville.

DUVAL COUNTY (JACKSONVILLE) Number of Juveniles Arrested[176]			
CRIME	**1993**	**2006**	**% OF CHANGE**
Murder	18	8	-56%
Rape/Sex Offenses	178	74	-58%
Robbery	294	152	-48%
Aggravated Assault	576	224	-61%
Weapons	251	203	-19%
Residential Burglary	694	228	-67%
Vehicle Theft	782	185	-76%

Shorstein noted that an evaluation of his approach concluded that over 7,200 robberies, burglaries, and motor vehicle thefts were prevented by incarcerating habitual juvenile offenders as adults during the study period of 1992-1995. He said the evaluation's conservative estimate of the economic benefit of the reduced level of property crime alone was $6 million a year.

Many of the juveniles held accountable as adults and incarcerated spent their time at the local jail in Jacksonville. Shorstein knew that simply warehousing them wasn't the answer. He wanted to insure the juvenile inmates in the jail had access to education. He also knew they needed good role models. He organized the Jailed Juvenile Mentor Program. Volunteer mentors were recruited throughout the community including the military, local organizations, the Chamber of Commerce, and faith institutions. The mentors visited the inmates a minimum of one hour per week at the jail.

In 1997, Shorstein implemented a new group mentoring program called Inside/Outside. Shorstein's idea was to get a group of volunteers associated with local churches and synagogues to meet with juveniles in the jail once a week. Then the group would continue to meet monthly with the juveniles after they completed their jail sentences. That was the outside portion of the program. The volunteers worked to create a sense of community and provide positive influences to counteract the negative influences the juveniles inevitably faced when they returned to their communities.

Shorstein believed the most significant proof that his approach worked was the reduction in the number of juveniles meeting his criteria for prosecution as adults and the resulting tremendous decrease in the number of juveniles imprisoned. Shorstein noted that the number of juveniles incarcerated increased nearly 90 percent nationwide between 1993 and 1998. Even though the number dropped after peaking in the late 1990s, there was still a 65 percent increase nationwide between 1993 and 2004. In our program, despite expansion in the criteria qualifying a juvenile for prosecution as an adult, the number of juveniles in our jail decreased from a high of 200 in 1994 to an average of 50 in 2007. Since my philosophy remained the same, the only explanation is a decrease in the number of juveniles committing offenses which would qualify them for prosecution in adult court, he said. He emphasized that the purpose of his approach was to reduce crime not to increase the number of juveniles spending time behind bars.

From Jacksonville to Memphis to St. Louis, many of our communities face the threat of a hard-core group of juveniles intent on being violent. Many are armed with guns and determined to use them. Most of them are driven by gang involvement. And most prosecutors are determined to take a tough stance against them.

The scope of the problem is driven home in a study issued in December of 2008. This study compared gun use by both adult and juvenile arrestees in St. Louis, Missouri.[177] It was based on interviews of more than 950 arrestees detained in St. Louis, 629 adults and 338 juveniles. The interviews were conducted with inmates held in the adult jail and the juvenile detention facility at six points in time from 2003 through 2007. All arrestees were eligible to participate in the interview study, and about 90 percent agreed to interviews.[178]

Consistently, St. Louis has had one of the highest violent crime rates among America's major cities. In recent years, its homicide rate has been four times the national average. Law enforcement routinely seizes over 2,000 guns per year either used or possessed illegally. Over a quarter of the city's population is under 18 years of age. [179] Disturbingly, the study found that the possession and use of guns was more prevalent among the juvenile arrestees than among the adult arrestees!

The study revealed that gun toting outside the home on a daily basis was four times more likely among the juvenile arrestees than among the adults. Nearly half (46 percent) of the juveniles reported carrying guns outside the home most or all of the time. In contrast, only 12 percent of the adult arrestees said they carried a gun on a regular basis outside the home. Another 19 percent of adult arrestees said they sometimes carried a gun but not regularly. [180]

An even more upsetting result from the study was the finding that the juvenile arrestees were more than twice as likely as adults to have used a gun in the year prior to the interview. Over half of the juveniles (55 percent) who acknowledged possessing a gun also acknowledged using it. Only 24 percent of the adult arrestees fell into this category.[181]

These conclusions are consistent with earlier studies noted by the researchers. A 1994 study based on a sample of 1,900 male felons from 11 adult prisons in 10 states revealed that 75 percent had possessed guns. [182] A 1995 study of 835 serious male juvenile offenders detained in six juvenile detention facilities in four states revealed that 84 percent had carried a gun outside the home during a two-year period before confinement and that an amazing 76 percent had shot at someone.[183] And a 2001 study looked at patterns of gun use by 14,285 juvenile and adult offenders (male and female) serving time in 275 state prisons. Offenders 20 years of age or younger were more than twice as likely to have been armed during their most recent offense (36 percent) than were offenders 21 years of age or older (17 percent).[184]

The 2008 study concludes that illegal gun possession and use by adult offenders are influenced by a combination of access, fear of the streets, and the risks of arrest.[185] On the other hand, fear and perceived risks are not major factors in juvenile offenders acquiring, carrying, and using guns.[186] As noted by the researchers, the greater willingness of juvenile arrestees to carry and use guns seems to indicate that juveniles view the purpose of gun possession very different from adults.[187]

The overriding factor in this different reasoning for gun toting and use by juveniles is gang membership. Simply put, the study showed that gang membership was the central indicator of gun use by juvenile offenders.[188]

Gang members are more likely to be involved in criminal activity than their non-gang counterparts, especially gun-related violent crime.[189] In the 2008 study, juvenile arrestees who reported gang membership were five times more likely to report having a gun. Likewise, adult arrestees reporting gang affiliation were six times more likely to have a gun.[190] What put the juveniles so far ahead of the adults in gun use was that juvenile arrestees were much more likely to report current gang membership (56 percent) than were adult arrestees (31 percent).[191]

Juveniles participating in the study who reported gang membership were four times more likely to have actually fired a gun in the year prior to arrest than juvenile non-gang members. The effect of gang membership on adult use of guns was also strong but only about half what it was on juveniles.[192]

The gang culture has already created a group of juveniles who are ready and willing to use violence. We must recognize it for what it is and deal with it. We cannot let violent juvenile predators threaten the peace and safety of our neighborhoods.

Despite the obvious presence of violent juvenile predators on our streets, we have seen attacks in recent years on even the limited application of adult sanctions on serious juvenile offenders. In 2007, the National District Attorneys Association (NDAA) felt compelled to speak out against consideration by the American Bar Association (ABA) of a resolution encouraging state legislators to change state laws to make it more difficult to prosecute serious juvenile offenders as adults and to punish such offenders less severely solely because of their perceived immaturity.

The NDAA argued that the proposed ABA resolution failed to recognize the importance of public safety and ignored other important factors, such as the circumstances surrounding the offense, the impact on the victim, the juvenile offender's criminal history, and the need for certainty of punishment. The NDAA specifically rejected the notion that juvenile offenders are categorically less culpable than the average criminal, which appeared to be the main rationale behind the ABA resolution.

The NDAA advocated a balanced approach to the challenge of juvenile crime that took into consideration all relevant factors in determining how to handle a juvenile offender. After the NDAA had voiced its opposition to the original resolution, a revised resolution was adopted that stated sentences for youthful offenders should generally be less punitive than sentences for adults and urged states to adopt sentencing laws that recognized mitigating considerations of age and maturity of youthful offenders. As a result of the NDAA's stand, the resolution also noted the need to protect public safety and to consider the seriousness of the offense and the delinquent and criminal history of the offender. It's an example of prosecutors taking a stand in the public's interest and for the protection of citizens against a limited number of serious juvenile offenders in our midst.

Senseless, horrific crimes by juveniles are a source of fear in communities across America. Charged with protecting the public's interest, most prosecutors are hesitant to leave brutal juvenile perpetrators in juvenile justice systems with no meaningful accountability.

As part of its effort to combat the original ABA resolution, the NDAA accumulated examples from America's prosecutors of juveniles who faced adult sanctions as a result of the seriousness of their crimes. Numerous examples were supplied as part of a document submitted to the ABA. The following are just a few of the examples set forth in that document.

In Hartford County, Maryland, a 17-year-old was told he had to commit a robbery as initiation into a gang. He called a cab, waited in the dark for it to arrive, shot the cab driver in the head and then robbed him. The cab driver was the father of nine children. He had recently moved his family out of the city to get them away from crime. He had decided to start driving a cab as a second job to help pay for their new home. The 17-year-old was handled as an adult and sentenced to life in prison.

In Birmingham, Alabama, a 14-year-old girl mixed together rubbing alcohol, fingernail polish remover, and charcoal lighter fluid. She stole a gun as well and gave it to her 16-year-old boyfriend. Together, they shot, stabbed, and used the mixture to set fire to the 14-year-old's grandfather. Then they shot and stabbed her aunt, stabbed and set her grandmother on fire, and stabbed her ten-year-old sister approximately 12 times. Both were sentenced as adults to life in prison without the possibility of parole.

In Pima County (Tucson), Arizona, a 17-year-old held up a Quick Mart at gunpoint. When the clerk hesitated to hand over the money, the juvenile fired the gun just over the clerk's arm. He left merely to rob another store. A previous felony conviction had been handled in juvenile court. This time, he faced charges as an adult and was sentenced to seven years and eight months in prison.

Two 17-year-olds in Minnesota plotted with an 18-year-old (an adult under Minnesota law) to kill one of the juvenile's parents. The initial plan was to stage a nighttime robbery at the family home and use a shotgun to kill the parents. This original plan went awry when an alarm was activated. Undeterred, the two 17-year-olds drove to the family business the next afternoon. One of the juveniles murdered his own father by shooting him five times with a .22 caliber handgun. While the mother was attempting to help her husband after he had been shot, the other juvenile murdered the mother with a shotgun blast to the back of her head. The juvenile defendants received life sentences under the adult system, with eligibility for parole after serving 30 years.

In Polk County (Des Moines), Iowa, a 17-year-old juvenile had been at a party and gotten into a fight with a rival gang member. The next day he retaliated by shooting and killing his rival. He received a life sentence. In the same community, another 17-year-old entered a restaurant, put a gun to the head of a waitress and fired. She died instantly. As a manager attempted to come to her aid, the 17-year-old shot and killed him too. He is facing a life sentence as well.

A 16-year-old St. Louis juvenile was sentenced to prison as a result of murdering another student in a high school bathroom. Several years later, after he was no longer a juvenile, he was sentenced to death for killing his prison cellmate.

In my home state of Tennessee, a 16-year-old Nashvillian robbed a gas station and fled the scene by stealing a car. He drove the stolen vehicle to a shopping mall, where he shot and killed a shoe store security guard who was trying to stop him from stealing a pair of tennis shoes. The juvenile attempted to flee the shopping mall by carjacking a family. He fired several shots at the family, hitting a ten-year-old boy in the face. He was transferred to be tried as an adult and is serving a life sentence.

In another Nashville incident, during an attempted robbery, a 15-year-old fired 13 shots at an undercover police officer posing as a pizza delivery man after a string of pizza delivery robberies. Transferred to be tried as an adult, he was sentenced to 17 years in prison.

A 15-year-old Montgomery County (Dayton), Ohio juvenile had been committed to a juvenile detention facility on a receiving stolen property charge for supposedly a six-month minimum period. But he was judicially released under Ohio law after serving 45 days. Within less than two months of his release, he robbed a woman at gunpoint while trying to push her into her apartment. She managed to resist. Then he proceeded to rape another woman in her car after she had pulled into the parking lot of her apartment complex. The juvenile pleaded guilty and was sentenced as an adult to a mandatory 10 years. And in another Montgomery County case, a 15-year-old upset at his mother for taking his cell phone privileges away murdered her by stabbing her 14 times. He left the knife in her back as he fled the scene with her credit cards. He was indicted for murder, which carries a life sentence, making him eligible for parole after serving 20 years.

Then there's the brutal murder of a man in Snohomish County, Washington. He was viciously killed by five juveniles recruited by one of the juvenile's mother, who had been hired by the victim to care for his elderly mother.

The participants included a 13-year-old daughter, a 14-year-old friend, the daughter's 17-year-old boyfriend, and two of his friends, 13 and 14 years of age. The mother had access to the victim's bank account, and the plan was to murder him and take about $40,000 in the account. An earlier plan had failed when some juveniles recruited for the task had second thoughts. All juveniles were promised something of value for their participation.

When the victim walked into his home, the three male teenagers proceeded to beat him with a baseball bat. Once he was down for good, the two female teenagers stabbed him with knives. The victim's mother watched the horrific scene from her wheelchair, helpless to do anything about it. The mother of one of the participants who had planned the murder recruited her two younger children, seven and ten years of age, to help clean up the murder scene. That night, the victim's remains were dumped down a hillside on a nearby reservation. The mother rewarded the juvenile participants and began spending money out of the victim's account. They abandoned the victim's elderly mother, who was unable to look after herself. All but one of the juvenile participants received adult prison sentences, ranging from 18 to 50 years.

A very small percentage of juvenile offenders face adult sanctions. In most states it is no more than one to two percent of all juvenile offenders.

A lot of citizens feel that the percentage is too small. A national poll conducted in 1993 showed that 73 percent of those surveyed felt that violent juveniles should be treated as adults rather than as defendants in lenient juvenile courts.[193]

It is imperative that prosecutors and courts have the ability to hold those juveniles who are serious, violent offenders accountable in the same manner as adults. First, and foremost, as a matter of public safety, a limited number of juveniles who are serious threats to communities must be taken off our streets. Second, if the consequences are communicated effectively, such action will hopefully deter juveniles from making the bad choice of engaging in serious, violent crime.

In Tennessee, our choices are limited when it comes to handling juveniles charged with serious offenses. Many of these are committed by gun-toting gang members hell-bent on proving their worth to the gangs to which they belong.

As D.A., I can decide to leave a 16-year-old juvenile charged with first degree murder in our juvenile justice system. If convicted, he'll get a sentence which can last through age 19, but that's it. His longest period of confinement for murdering someone will be three years. [194] And the chances are high under our state law that the sentence will not be for any fixed, determinate time. So he can get out earlier if deemed rehabilitated.[195]

My other option is to ask the juvenile court judge to transfer him to criminal court to be tried in the same manner as an adult.[196] If the judge agrees and transfers him he's looking at a life sentence if convicted. (Juveniles aren't eligible for the death penalty.)

I have no other options. It's either three years or less or a life sentence. Given those two options, after looking at all the circumstances, I have to make the call, keeping the public's interest uppermost in my mind.

A juvenile facing a first degree murder charge is the most extreme example in Tennessee of the difference between leaving the offender in the juvenile system and transferring the offender to the adult system. Other cases are not quite as extreme but still involve difficult decisions.

One such decision I faced recently involved a 14-year-old charged with second degree murder, not first degree murder. He was charged as well with attempted second degree murder of a second person. Luckily, the gun had misfired. The choice was either leaving him in the juvenile system where he would face a maximum sentence of five years, and quite possibly less than that, or seeking a transfer to the adult system where he would likely get the minimum sentence of 15 years without parole. After receiving his evaluation, it was obvious to us he could tell right from wrong. The shooting in which he was involved was an act of retaliation, and I was concerned about an escalation of violence. I felt it was critical to send a strong message to all involved that we would not tolerate more violence and that anyone who engaged in prolonging the feud through violence would be held fully accountable under our state laws. We decided to seek a transfer of the 14-year-old to criminal court to be tried as an adult. The juvenile court granted our request.

We have up to 15,000 juvenile crime cases per year in my community. In recent years, we've been averaging about 150 transfers per year to criminal court, or about one percent of the total. I take no pleasure in these transfers but believe there are a certain number of juvenile predators whose actions and records reflect an alarming choice of violence as a way of life. They must be taken off our streets in the interest of public safety.

I prefer juveniles to make good choices and reject the choice of violence. That's why I address as many middle school assemblies as I can to warn students of the consequences of engaging in serious acts of violence. Our presentation includes the names and photographs of juveniles who were given long sentences in prison, sometimes life. The presentation seems to get most of the students' attention.

Our state law contains a somewhat shocking, but apparently not unusual, provision stating, in part, that the purpose of our juvenile code is to …remove from children committing delinquent acts the taint of criminality and the consequences of criminal behavior.[197] It's a philosophy that goes back at least to the 1960s and pre-dates the kind of juvenile gang violence and callous disregard for the lives and property of others we see today. We need to seek rehabilitation whenever possible, but it is equally important to understand the necessity of holding juveniles accountable for their actions. In the late 1990s, I served on a state Juvenile Justice Reform Commission appointed by then Governor Don Sundquist and chaired by my colleague, District Attorney Jerry Woodall, from Jackson, Tennessee. The commission recommended a more balanced approach of rehabilitation and accountability, but that change in our law has not occurred. Specifically, the commission came up with language declaring the purpose of the juvenile code to be:

- Holding a youth accountable for his or her unacceptable behavior;
- Holding parents or legal guardians accountable where appropriate, including payment of detention costs and restitution to victims and attendance at programs to develop parenting skills;
- Protecting the public from the consequences of unacceptable behavior of youth; and
- Providing services to youth and their families to prevent further unacceptable conduct, with emphasis on early intervention, effective rehabilitation programs, and post-release services upon return to the community.

States vary widely in their laws relating to the transfer of juveniles to the adult system. Basically they fall into the following categories:

- Judicial discretion, under which the ultimate decision is up to the juvenile court judge (the system we have in Tennessee);
- Automatic transfer as mandated under the law enacted by a state's legislature;
- Prosecutorial discretion, under which the prosecutor makes the decision; and
- Some combination of the above, depending upon the age of the juvenile and the type of crime.

In August of 2008, the U.S. Department of Justice's Office of Juvenile Justice and Delinquency Prevention issued an overview of juvenile transfer laws. According to the overview, 40 states have some form of a judicial system under which the juvenile court judge has the discretion to transfer a juvenile to the adult system.[198] It's usually done at the request of the prosecutor, and most states have some limit on the conditions under which a transfer can occur. For example, in Tennessee, the judge can transfer any case involving a juvenile 16 years of age or older but only cases involving certain stipulated violent crimes if the juvenile is younger than 16 years of age.[199]

The overview notes that 29 states have automatic transfer provisions under which a juvenile is automatically transferred if certain criteria are met, such as age or specific types of crimes.[200]

Fourteen states have laws giving prosecutors the authority to decide whether to prosecute a juvenile in the adult system. Usually there are some restrictions related to age or type of crime.[201]

How to handle a juvenile facing criminal charges can be a two-way street. About half of the states have reverse waiver laws allowing a judge in the adult system to transfer a juvenile back to the juvenile system under certain circumstances.[202]

The Juvenile Justice Reform Commission on which I served in the late 1990s recommended a change in our state law to provide for the automatic treatment of juveniles 15 years of age or older as adults if charged with murder, rape, robbery, or kidnapping with use of a deadly weapon. Another important recommendation was the creation of a blended sentencing option that would allow both juvenile and criminal court judges to sentence juveniles not charged with serious violent crimes to fixed sentences. The fixed sentences would be similar in length to those given adults, but the juveniles would be placed in separate facilities with intensive educational, vocational, and treatment programs. Our state legislators did not act on the blended sentence recommendation, probably because of the projected expense.

Many states have adopted some form of blended sentencing. While blended sentencing laws vary widely from state to state, the basic idea is to expose juveniles to adult criminal sanctions, or at least to the possibility of such sanctions.

As of 2003, 15 states had what are referred to as *juvenile blended sentencing provisions* that allow juvenile courts to impose adult sanctions on certain types of juvenile offenders. The usual approach is a combination or blend of a juvenile sentence combined with a suspended criminal sentence. If the juvenile maintains good behavior, he or she remains in the juvenile system. If not, the juvenile faces a sentence to an adult facility. It's a way of encouraging good conduct.[203]

Massachusetts is an example of a state with a juvenile blended sentencing system. A juvenile 14 years of age or older found guilty of one of the crimes covered by blended sentencing is designated as a Youthful Offender. The juvenile court may take one of the following steps:

- An extended commitment in a juvenile facility until 21 years of age;
- A straight criminal sentence in the adult system; or
- A combination or blending of the two, with the adult sentence suspended pending successful completion of the juvenile sentence.[204]

In most states with some form of blended sentencing, juveniles are eligible for such a sentence based on a variety of factors, including age, prior record, and the nature of the offense. In some states, these factors are the same as those considered in determining transfers to criminal court. For example, in Minnesota, a juvenile 14 years of age or older facing a felony charge may, at the juvenile court judge's discretion, be transferred for prosecution as an adult or be placed under an extended juvenile commitment.[205]

Some states such as Alaska and Illinois have blended sentencing criteria that are actually more narrowly defined than transfer criteria.[206] However, most states with juvenile blending sentencing have broader eligibility criteria than those for transfer eligibility.[207] It serves as a tool to hold juvenile offenders more accountable than does the standard juvenile justice system approach. But it does so in a way that avoids committing them to the adult system.

As of 2003, 17 states had what are known as *criminal blended sentencing laws.* These are laws under which adult criminal courts having jurisdiction over transferred juveniles can impose sanctions ordinarily available just to juvenile courts, conditioned upon those juveniles maintaining good behavior.[208]

In the criminal blending sentencing states, criminal courts which try and convict juveniles as adults can, under certain circumstances, impose juvenile sanctions. Some states allow the judge to make a choice between adult sanctions and juvenile sanctions. Others allow a true blended sentence in which both are imposed in some combination. It usually takes the form of a juvenile system disposition coupled with a suspended criminal sentence pending successful completion of the juvenile system portion.

Missouri is an example of a criminal blended sentencing state. If a criminal court judge does not wish to impose a straight adult sentence on a transferred juvenile, an option is a combination juvenile system/adult system sentence. The adult portion is suspended pending completion of the juvenile portion. If the sentenced juvenile violates the conditions of the juvenile sanctions or picks up a new offense, the court can revoke the juvenile portion and impose the adult sentence.[209]

Whether it is imposed by a juvenile court judge or an adult criminal court judge, the option of some form of blended sentence is an important tool in combating serious crime. Under the right circumstances, it gives prosecutors and courts a viable alternative to, on the one hand, juvenile justice systems simply not founded on the notion of meaningful accountability, and on the other hand, straight adult prison sentences. It's a needed tool which I hope my own state will adopt.

Whether it is transfers to adult court, or a system of blended sentencing, or a combination of both, the prospect of fixed sentences for serious juvenile offenders is the bedrock to any true accountability. Only those who still believe juveniles should not be held accountable for their criminal conduct would reject such an approach. Accountability for actions must be a cornerstone of today's juvenile justice system as well as part of any battle plan to make our communities safer.

Will holding serious juvenile offenders accountable through fixed sentences deter other juveniles from going down that path? Opinions are mixed on that. The keys to deterrence are two fold:

- Clearly communicating the consequences of engaging in such behavior and
- Doing so before juveniles become involved in gang activity and gun violence.

One multi-state study which covered a 15-year period (1978-1983) suggested that tougher adult sanctions can have some deterrent effect on juvenile crime. Controlling for demographics and economic variables, researchers found some decreases in juvenile crime as juveniles reached the age that puts them in the adult system with more accountability and tougher sanctions.[210] This decrease occurred only in states where the sanctions under the adult system were significantly greater than under the juvenile system. This finding suggested recognition on the part of juveniles that the risk to them was greater once they became eligible for punishment in the adult system.[211] Similar results came from a study in New York back in the 1980s. A relatively small number of juvenile offenders were interviewed and indicated they had decided to stop their criminal behavior once they became eligible for adult sentencing.[212]

However, a number of studies have indicated little effect on criminal behavior upon facing adult sanctions. A Florida study examining data from 1989 through 2002 showed no significant impact on criminal behavior as a result of a juvenile reaching 18 years of age and becoming an adult for sentencing purposes.[213] Another study looked at 14 states that had enacted laws giving prosecutors the authority to transfer juveniles to the adult system. Researchers looked at juvenile arrest rates five years before and after enactment of each state's prosecutorial discretion transfer law and, with the exception of Michigan, found no significant deterrent effect.[214]

A key to whether the prospect of tougher sanctions has a deterrent effect in juveniles appears to be awareness of that prospect! A study issued in 2004 of Georgia's juveniles automatically tried as adults for murder and armed robbery showed an unawareness of the law, with less than 30 percent knowing they could be tried as adults. Even among those who knew about the law, none thought the law would be enforced against them. They thought they would end up getting light sanctions under the juvenile system.[215] On the other hand, 75 percent of the transferred juveniles interviewed in the study said that they may not have committed the crimes for which they were convicted had they known they faced adult sanctions. They also felt their experiences in the adult system had taught them the consequences of engaging in criminal behavior.[216]

The Georgia study concluded that there is a significant need to implement successful, targeted awareness campaigns in states where adult sanctions are possible and even probable. These campaigns can help make juveniles actually aware of the consequences of engaging in serious crime.[217]

Awareness of tough sanctions and the likelihood of facing them can sometimes have a deterrent effect on would-be offenders.[218] As noted in the August 2008 overview by the U.S. Department of Justice's Office of Juvenile Justice and Delinquency Prevention, It is useful to consider… each of the necessary preconditions for successful deterrence… A law can act as a deterrent only if the targeted population is aware that the law exists and believes that it will be enforced.[219]

If tough sanctions are going to be imposed against serious juvenile offenders, we must convey that message successfully if it is to serve as a deterrent. This is another reason I spend as much time as I can talking to middle school assemblies about the consequences of engaging in violent crime and giving them real-life examples of juveniles sentenced to lengthy prison terms. I am the first to admit that the visits I make to schools are not enough. It's a message that needs to be repeated over and over. Our office continues to work with schools, churches, and other community institutions to develop more ways to get the word out.

The study issued in 2008 on gun use among juvenile and adult arrestees in St. Louis revealed that the perceived threat of punishment has the least impact on hard-core juveniles already heavily involved in the mix of gangs and guns. Almost 40 percent of juvenile arrestees in St. Louis interviewed in the study reported that they would consider the penalties before possessing or using a gun. But once a juvenile becomes involved with a gang, a significant drop occurs in that deterrent effect. The study concludes that …the youth most heavily involved in gun use may be the least to be influenced by deterrence messages.[220]

The same study showed that the perceived threat of punishment did affect the likelihood of gun use by adults. Adult arrestees who perceived that the chances of getting caught had increased were less likely to use a gun. It suggested that adults were more receptive than juveniles to a deterrence message on the consequences of using a gun.[221]

The study noted that, This finding supports recent work which suggests that [adult] offenders, in general, are amenable to a deterrence message because they are more acquainted with criminal sanctions.[222]

Focusing on the distinction between juvenile and adult arrestees, the study concludes, Adults were more amenable to measures of perceptual deterrence than juveniles. The key finding for policy is that juveniles seemed impervious to deterrence messages, particularly with regard to gun carrying and gun use. (This was the case even though the mean age of the juvenile sample was 15).[223]

The study noted several clear implications for combating juvenile gun violence:

- Start with early prevention efforts among juveniles *before* they become involved in gangs and guns, possibly targeting juveniles as young as 8 - 10 years of age;
- Consider reaching the more hard-core group with deterrence messages delivered directly in small groups with peers and criminal justice officials using innovative ways; and
- Alternatively, find ways to increase the impact of deterrence policies on this hard-core group.[224]

These conclusions go to the heart of holding serious juvenile offenders accountable for their actions. For there to be deterrence, we must first have tough sanctions. Second, we must communicate the consequences effectively so that would-be offenders understand them and believe those consequences will apply directly to them. And third, communicating the message early is much more effective than waiting until a juvenile is already heavily involved in violence.

The sanctions must be real! Otherwise, they will not serve to hold violent juveniles accountable and will have no chance of deterring others. The 2008 study concludes with the disturbing but correct observation that a ...group of deep-end juvenile offenders is not being reached effectively by current efforts... These findings suggest the challenges of dealing with gangs and guns remain a key topic in the crime control agenda.[225]

Clearly, one reason to deal firmly with serious juvenile offenders is to try to deter other juveniles from going down that road. But what should be done regarding the juveniles who do commit serious crimes and face sentencing in adult systems? Some of the worst predators, in particular, those convicted of first degree murder, will never get out of prison. If they do, it will be at an advanced age. By transferring them to the adult system, we are taking them off the streets permanently for the good of society. But the juvenile sentenced in the adult system for a crime such as armed robbery will probably return to his community at a fairly early age. The chances are fairly certain he will become a repeat offender. Arguably, we are giving up on a 17-year-old juvenile transferred to the adult system to be tried for armed robbery. But, unfortunately, the only alternative in many states, including my state of Tennessee, is to leave him in a juvenile justice system legally based on the notion that he should not be held accountable and under which he cannot be detained beyond 19 years of age.

I've taken a clear stand that, while every case should be based on its own unique circumstances, we should not hesitate to seek justice in the adult system when it is in the public's interest to do so. We need a third choice. That choice is the blended sentencing approach adopted by a number of states under which courts can impose a mix, or blend, of juvenile and adult sanctions with the adult sanctions hinging on the successful completion of the juvenile sanctions. It's a tool every prosecutor needs to deal effectively with serious juvenile crime. We must not let a small group of serious juvenile offenders create a climate of fear in our neighborhoods and schools. **Serious juvenile offenders must be held accountable and removed as threats to the peace and safety of our communities.**

CHAPTER 23

Deal Effectively With Other Juvenile Offenders Through a Preemptive Strike

Getting the limited number of juveniles who have chosen a life of violence off our streets is essential to a successful battle plan to curb crime. We cannot look the other way and allow communities to be terrorized by a limited group of dangerous juvenile predators. But what about the vast majority of juveniles who end up in the system for everything from property crimes to simple drug possession? We must be smart enough to use our resources and systems in ways that have a positive impact rather than a negative one. A juvenile's contact with the criminal justice system does not have to be something that escalates into increasingly more serious offenses. We should gear our efforts toward turning lives around before it's too late.

When Jim Backstrom took office in 1987 as the county attorney for Dakota County, Minnesota (Minnesota's equivalent to district attorney), the office had in place a system under which first offender juveniles could be diverted from standard prosecution and avoid getting a record. The problem was that the program …amounted to getting a letter in the mail saying, 'don't break the law again,' said Backstrom.

Backstrom believed in giving most first time juvenile offenders a second chance. He also knew that there had to be some accountability in order to produce any positive results. In 1992, he launched his Youth Accountability Program (YAP). The program was available to:

- First time juvenile offenders facing alcohol and marijuana possession or consumption cases not involving the use of a vehicle;
- Juveniles referred by school officials because of alcohol or drug use; and
- Juveniles voluntarily enrolling.

Backstrom knew that the vast majority of crimes committed are in some way related to drug or alcohol use. He wanted a program of accountability that would prevent further alcohol or marijuana use by juveniles. He came up with a straight-forward approach that required the following:

- ❦ Attendance by the participating juvenile and at least one parent at an educational class concerning alcohol and drug use;
- ❦ Payment of a fee at the start of the class (with adjustments being made for families who demonstrated an inability to pay); and
- ❦ Completion of a chemical use questionnaire prior to attending class.

Backstrom's approach is still being followed today. If a juvenile successfully completes the program, the case is dismissed. Failure to participate in, or complete, the program results in the case going to court. In court, the juvenile will probably face a fine, driver's license suspension, and a record for the offense.

In 1994, Backstrom expanded YAP to cover first time juvenile offenders charged with misdemeanor property crimes such as shoplifting and vandalism. He used a similar common-sense approach for these low-level misdemeanor property offenses, requiring the following of the participants:

- ❦ Attendance with at least one parent or guardian at an educational class focusing on community values, morals, and respect for others and their property;
- ❦ Payment of a fee, with consideration given to ability to pay; and
- ❦ Importantly, if the victim incurred a loss, payment by the juvenile of restitution in an amount determined by the county attorney.

While completion of the program results in dismissal of the case, failure to be a participant in or complete the program results in the case proceeding to court. This will most likely result in payment of restitution, community service of some sort, placement on probation, and a record from having committed the offense.

In 1994, Minnesota's legislators enacted legislation requiring all county attorneys by July 1, 1995 to establish pre-trial diversion programs for juvenile first offenders charged with property crimes that would result in dismissal of the charges upon successful completion of the program. By the time the new law was enacted, Dakota County already had YAP up and running. Expanding the concept to meet the requirements of the new law was fairly easy.

The following year, Dakota County followed the new law by taking the leap of expanding the YAP concept to more serious misdemeanors and low-level felony property offenses. There was some risk involved, but Backstrom was encouraged by the success of the YAP model for alcohol/drug *and* low-level misdemeanor cases. Now the program covers cases in which the value of property stolen or damaged is $2,500 or less. The components are very similar to YAP for low-level misdemeanors, but with the addition of required community service.

Under Dakota County's YAP initiative, juveniles don't get a second bite at the apple. It's a one-time opportunity for a juvenile to avoid getting a record while at the same time being held accountable.

What are the results of YAP? Under the program for low-level misdemeanors, from 1998 through 2007, 80 percent of participants completed the program successfully. The repeat offender rate was calculated by tracking juveniles for a period of two years from the date of completing the program. The result showed a low repeat offender rate of 12 percent. For the YAP covering more serious misdemeanor and low-level felony property crimes, the completion rate from 1996 - 2007 is 70 percent, with a low repeat offender rate of just 10 percent.

The key to the success of YAP seems to be a hands-on approach with clear elements of accountability. The old system of diverting juveniles from prosecution but with no oversight or follow-up was not working. It sent the wrong message that no one took the violations seriously. That has changed in Dakota County, Minnesota.

In 1997, soon after becoming county attorney in Pima County (Tucson), Arizona, Barbara LaWall heard a disturbing report on the radio about a stabbing at Marona High School in the northwest suburbs of Tucson. The rumors had already started that it was gang-related. LaWall met with the school principal to talk about the incident. As it turned out, the stabbing was a continuation of a long-standing feud between two families in that part of Tucson. She learned that law enforcement knew about the feud, which had involved assaults and threats by members of both families. But that hadn't been communicated to school officials, who were unaware of any need to take special precautions to keep the two students apart.

LaWall saw a need for prosecutors, the police, school officials, and juvenile court probation officers to share information about juveniles who had cases in juvenile court or were at risk of being court-involved. She decided the way to get it done was through a school-based team approach.

In 1997, LaWall created the School Multi-Agency Response Team (S.M.A.R.T.). The idea was to develop a team at each school that would meet regularly to discuss students attending that school who had pending cases, were on juvenile court probation, or were known to be involved in questionable activities.

Initially, in 1997, the S.M.A.R.T. approach started in six schools. Government bureaucracies are hard to change, and LaWall and her staff faced the challenge of getting various government entities to actually share information. It took a lot of energy, commitment, and persistence to get it done, but it did not take long for all those involved to see the benefits. As one middle school principal observed, The S.M.A.R.T. meetings are lively and informative. If you attend one, it would be evident that the team members are all professionals who have developed a relationship based on mutual support.... S.M.A.R.T began to change the dynamics of addressing juvenile crime in Tucson.

By the 2007-2008 school year, the S.M.A.R.T. approach had grown to more than 50 high schools. This figure represents about 75 percent of all the public high schools and middle schools in Pima County. Seven prosecutors in the juvenile division of the county attorney's office participate in S.M.A.R.T., with each taking schools in certain geographic areas. Just as important is the willingness of the Pima County Juvenile Court to assign safe school probation officers to specific schools.

Each school team discusses the best way to handle each matter and the underlying reasons for a particular occurrence, such as whether a fight at school was a random act or part of a gang rivalry. They place emphasis on school attendance, compliance with counseling plans, and adherence to probation requirements. They use the meetings as well to gather information about gang activity, drugs, and guns at the schools.

S.M.A.R.T. is a results oriented effort. Goals are straight-forward:

- Reduce juvenile crime;
- Eliminate gang activity, drugs, guns, and violence on school property, at school activities, and on school buses; and
- Intervene in a positive way in the lives of at-risk juveniles.

As Dale Cardy, the Pima County Attorney's Juvenile Division supervisor, put it, S.M.A.R.T. just makes sense. Schools have become much more comfortable with our office as a result of going to the schools and rolling up our sleeves. The trust level has increased. Subpoenas for information, for example, are more readily honored promptly. And he noted that he goes to basketball and football games at the schools to which he's assigned. He's become part of the school community.

Through the S.M.A.R.T. approach, there's a better chance of finding out what's really going on and handling situations the right way. It is not another expensive new program. It relies primarily on resources that were already in place and are now being more effectively channeled. Along with other steps taken in Arizona, such as tough laws to deal with juvenile violence, S.M.A.R.T. seems to be working to make Tucson a safer community. Juvenile arrests for major violent crimes had dropped almost 55 percent in 2007 compared to 1995! That includes an 83 percent drop in juvenile arrests for homicides and a 70 percent drop in juvenile arrests for robberies! Juveniles arrested for property crimes, such as burglaries, larcenies, and auto thefts, had dropped 46 percent in 2007 compared to 1995.[226]

Not all the news is good in Tucson. The number of juveniles arrested for drug offenses actually went up about six percent during the 1995-2007 time period. But, the rate of juvenile crime continues to decrease, making Tucson a safer place to live.

In Memphis, our juvenile court handles about 15,000 delinquency cases per year. Up to about 5,000 of these will be officially placed on the court docket. This is where the D.A.'s office gets involved. Serious repeat offenders, violent offenders, and those facing gun possession charges are examples of cases that usually get docketed automatically. But another 10,000 or so involve primarily first time offenders who have committed relatively minor offenses. Under our state law, juvenile court officials have the authority to administratively handle the cases without placing them on the court docket. Court counselors do what they can to make sure those juveniles are not repeat offenders, but they are limited in what they can do. They can't devote the hands-on time needed with each juvenile and the juvenile's family members in order to dramatically decrease the odds of a return to juvenile court.

Based on national research, and supported by our own local experience, about 80 out of every 100 juveniles age 10 to 16 coming into contact with the court system will have at least one other contact with the system.[227] Of those 80, eight will likely become serious and chronic juvenile offenders.[228]

In November of 2006, community leaders convened the Memphis Crime Summit in direct response to the increase in crime we were facing, including an alarming increase in juvenile crime. The Crime Summit resulted in our plan of attack known as Operation: Safe Community. A lot of communities develop strategic plans for many different things. Far too often, they sit on shelves and collect dust. We were determined to make our plan a real roadmap, an actual battle plan. One of the key strategies pushed by our juvenile court judge, Curtis Person, was the launching of the JustCare 180° approach. Its purpose is to turnaround juveniles charged with unruly and low-level delinquent acts.

We weren't re-inventing the wheel in deciding to start JustCare 180°. We looked at Boston's widely acclaimed systematic approach to youth violence in the mid to late 1990s. We observed Cincinnati's Teen Violence Prevention Program that was a local, community-based endeavor to provide an expanded range of individual and group services. And we looked at Wrap-Around Milwaukee as a model of how individualized service plans can be developed and executed for juveniles and their families.

The JustCare 180° concept is common sense driven and based on early intervention with juveniles who are making their initial contacts with the juvenile court system. We saw a need to link those juveniles and their families with appropriate pre-existing resources in their own communities. The idea was to build community-based networks to strengthen families and help them navigate through the maze of services readily available to a large degree but not being utilized adequately. This idea of wraparound services for the juvenile and other family members is critical to the JustCare 180° approach. The idea is to pull together key stakeholder groups at the community level. This includes faith-based groups, health facilities, schools, community centers, job training facilities, and others that need to be made accessible. While the concept is practical, in our world of multiple systems, agencies, and bureaucracies, such a practical approach requires a lot of work. Therefore, under JustCare 180°, neighborhood-based lead agencies are being identified for each geographical area. Through the lead agencies, case coordinators are responsible for identifying and linking individual juveniles and their families to local services using an approach that stresses family decision-making and self direction.

JustCare 180° is premised on the notion that we can do a better job of utilizing existing community-based resources rather than creating a whole new agency with its own turf to protect. The additional funding needed to implement JustCare 180° focuses on putting into place sufficient staff members to coordinate efforts at the neighborhood level. Driven by some newly-elected members committed to fighting crime and pushing implementation of our Operation: Safe Community plan, the Memphis City Council appropriated $800,000 to get the JustCare 180° effort underway.

While it's too early to measure the results, based on the research results of similar efforts, we expect JustCare 180° to reduce juvenile repeat offenders by 50 percent in the designated geographic areas. It's an ambitious undertaking. Correctly, conservatives emphasize parental responsibility and the importance of the family. Liberals argue that it takes a village to raise a child. One point of view is not exclusive of the other. JustCare 180° combines both viewpoints. It focuses on parental involvement and decision-making as well as the need to more effectively mobilize the help available at the community level.

During his tenure as state attorney for the fourth judicial circuit of Florida (the Jacksonville area), Harry Shorstein developed a well-deserved reputation for using his state's laws to get serious violent juvenile offenders off the streets and behind bars. He was a tough, no-nonsense prosecutor. But Shorstein also knew the importance of intervening effectively to re-direct juveniles down the right path before it was too late. He wanted to engage in what he termed a preemptive strike by aggressively intervening to influence the direction of juveniles before it became necessary to incarcerate them.

During Shorstein's tenure from 1991 through 2008, he developed a national reputation for being on the cutting edge in effective approaches to curtailing juvenile crime. He worked tirelessly with school officials and youth service institutions and agencies on cooperative, team efforts.

His approach included regular presentations at schools designed to alert students about the potential penalties they faced if they chose a life of violence. It's an approach I've admittedly copied. Additionally, he sent letters to schools letting students know that juveniles who are serious repeat offenders and commit violent crimes should expect to be treated just like adults.

Shorstein's efforts to turn juveniles' lives around before it was too late were extensive, and I won't attempt to cover all of those efforts. I would be remiss, though, if I didn't mention some of the efforts initiated by this cutting edge prosecutor during his time in office.

Shorstein knew that no comprehensive juvenile program could be complete without focusing on juveniles and guns. In 1994, he joined forces with the National Rifle Association to educate elementary school students about the dangers of gun use and to teach them that guns are not toys.

In 1996, Shorstein started a program with a local hospital where juveniles charged with violent misdemeanors or weapons offenses were ordered to tour the hospital's emergency room. He expanded the idea and created the Turning Point: Rethinking Violence program. Turning Point was a six week court-ordered program. The program's goal was to teach the participating juveniles and their parents ways to avoid incidents that trigger violence. Juveniles and parents met with medical professionals and were given a first hand look at the emergency room and the hospital morgue as a way of understanding the results of violence. These visits were followed by five weeks of group sessions for the teens focusing on anger and impulse control and conflict resolution. The group sessions included hearing first-hand from victims of violence about the impact it has had on their lives.

While Shorstein advocated tough measures to get serious juvenile offenders off the streets, he believed as well that an effective battle plan against juvenile crime must include a strong component under which appropriate non-violent juvenile offenders are diverted out of overcrowded courts.

For those juveniles, Shorstein set up several juvenile diversion programs collectively called the Youth Offender Program (YOP). YOP included two arbitration programs and the Multi-Agency Assessment Program.

The primary juvenile arbitration program used volunteers from the community and was designed for juveniles arrested for misdemeanor offenses and without any prior record. Juveniles with minor records were eligible for a second arbitration program. Juveniles accepted into the programs paid restitution and were assigned sanctions such as work hours, essays, letters of apology, and jail tours. They were referred to community programs for counseling as the need arose. To communicate the consequences of criminal behavior to these early offenders, Shorstein decided to use juveniles incarcerated as adults who discussed the increased sanctions they would face if they continued to commit crimes.

Shorstein hired eight case managers to oversee participating juveniles. In 2006, his office placed more than 2,100 juveniles into the program. These juveniles performed nearly 22,000 hours of community service and paid nearly $60,000 in restitution.

Shorstein reported that approximately 70 percent of juveniles referred to diversion programs did not re-offend. The diversion programs …provide consequences for criminal behavior while at the same time offer an opportunity for change. I believe we can make a difference with young offenders diverted from the criminal system before they become chronic offenders, said Shorstein.

Shorstein acknowledged that his community had suffered greatly from disjointed efforts to serve juveniles who faced criminal charges but weren't yet serious offenders. In response, he set up the Multi-Agency Assessment Program (MAAP), a diversionary program based on inter-agency cooperation. The state attorney's office organized regular meetings between law enforcement, the schools, the Department of Children and Families, and the Department of Juvenile Justice. Professionals from these agencies met with the state attorney's staff and closely examined the backgrounds of first offenders.

The MAAP partners attempted to identify juveniles who were at-risk of becoming chronic offenders. Potential participants underwent diagnostic evaluation. Juveniles accepted into MAAP were assigned a case manager from the state attorney's office. Each MAAP case manager kept a case load of no more than twenty juveniles and provided intensive supervision, including visits to homes and schools. The case managers met with each juvenile three times a week and with parents once a week. They kept in close contact with the school of each child. In 2006, case managers conducted over 14,000 visits with juveniles in the program, parents of participants, and professionals familiar with the juveniles. A variety of services were available to MAAP participants through contracts with local agencies. Case managers also had the option of referring parents to a parenting skills course and juveniles to Camp Consequences, a two-day wilderness experience designed to teach responsibility and effective communication skills.

Shorstein believed MAAP was a successful way to intervene with juveniles before they became serious offenders. School suspensions and arrests decreased among participants, and school attendance and performance improved. He noted that the Florida Department of Juvenile Justice adopted the MAAP concept state-wide through the Intensive Delinquency Diversion Services Program.

Communities must have effective preemptive strikes in place to move juveniles in the right direction and stop the influence of gang culture and drugs before it's too late.

CHAPTER 24

Empower Juveniles to
Make the Right Choices

Each year, Memphis has anywhere from 12,000 to 15,000 juveniles coming through its juvenile court as a result of being arrested and charged with a crime. A limited number have become violent thugs who must be taken off the streets and out of our neighborhoods. Most can still move in the right direction if given the right kind of help and guidance as highlighted in the previous chapter. But how do we reduce the number of juveniles who go to juvenile court in the first place for committing a crime?

Most of the answers to that question reside outside the realm of law enforcement and prosecutors, in particular. They reside in our homes, churches, and schools. But there's one area over which most prosecutors across the country do have some authority to act. That area of authority deals with truancy, kids skipping school without an excuse. While laws vary from state to state, most states have laws under which parents or guardians can be criminally prosecuted for failure to get their kids to school, although it's usually a low-level misdemeanor. Most states have laws under which truancy is a status offense by the juvenile instead of a criminal offense. But status offenses give juvenile courts jurisdiction and prosecutors a case to pursue.

There is a connection between skipping school and juvenile crime. On a school day in Memphis, roughly 25 percent of all of the juveniles brought to juvenile court are charged with committing crimes during school hours and off school property. Almost by definition, these crimes are being committed by juveniles who are either truant from school or who have been suspended.

That problem in Memphis is consistent with findings in other communities as well. Law enforcement officials have linked high truancy rates with daytime burglaries and acts of vandalism.[229] As noted by the U.S. Department of Justice's Office of Juvenile Justice and Delinquency Prevention in a 2001 report, Tacoma, Washington law enforcement officials reported that juveniles committed a third of all burglaries and a fifth of aggravated assaults occurring between 8 a.m. and 1 p.m. on weekdays. In Contra Costa County, California, police reported that 60 percent of all juvenile crime on weekdays occurred between 8 a.m. and 3 p.m.[230] A study by the Office of Juvenile Justice and Delinquency Prevention indicates that truancy may be a key predicator of criminal offenses, and the connection is especially strong among males.[231]

Truancy has been linked to gang activity and substance abuse, as well as other particular types of crimes, such as auto theft, burglary and vandalism.[232] And truant behavior that goes unchecked is often a gateway to escalating criminal behavior in adulthood, including an increased chance of violent behavior.[233] Judge Kenneth Turner served as our juvenile court judge for over 40 years, retiring in 2006. On many occasions, in our discussions, he noted, Not every truant is a delinquent, but every habitual delinquent is also a habitual truant. In a column in the September 22, 2008 edition of *The Tennessean* newspaper, Metro Nashville Juvenile Court Judge Betty Adams Green sounded a similar note stating, Children who are truant do not all grow up to be delinquents who prey on our community, but virtually all of our delinquents have extremely poor school performance and truancy in their background.

Students with high rates of truancy are likely to have low academic achievement and ultimately become dropouts.[234] And dropouts are more likely to experience unstable marriages, engage in criminal conduct, and end up in prison.[235] Add those to all the other financial drains, ranging from higher welfare costs to less funding for school systems operating on funding formulas based on average daily attendance to understand even more of the burden dropouts place on a community.

From my own experience, I know that truancy figures are not always accurate and often understate the scope of the problem. For example, in Memphis, we've had a software system which automatically counts each student present unless the teacher takes the time to record an absence, which sometimes doesn't happen. One high profile incident that reflected the problem involved a robbery spree during school hours by a number of high school students who were miles from their school. They were recorded present for the day! (They actually did go by school to eat lunch.) What's more, they were recorded present the next day even though they were being detained at juvenile court! Even with these shortcomings, the data shows thousands of habitual truants in our schools each year.

The scope of truancy has been extensive in many communities across America. In Detroit, officials investigated over 66,000 complaints of chronic absenteeism in one school year. And a study of Chicago revealed that the average tenth grader missed six weeks during the school year.[236]

In a national review of discipline issues, public school principals identified student absenteeism, class cutting, and tardiness as their major discipline problems.[237]

In January of 2006, I attended a meeting on juvenile crime sponsored by American Prosecutors Research Institute. It was a fairly intensive, hands-on meeting, with attendees being divided into smaller working groups. At our last session together, the prosecutors in attendance were asked, What is the single most pressing challenge that, if addressed, could have a significant impact on juvenile crime? The overwhelming response was the challenge of truancy.

Ignoring the issue of truancy leads to increased juvenile crime and the likelihood of even more serious criminal behavior in adulthood. Rampant truancy can drag entire communities down. But led by prosecutors who have the force of the law to back them up, many communities are coming up with effective strategies to combat this problem and turn around juveniles who are skipping school before it's too late.

The two public school systems in my community (Memphis City Schools and Shelby County Schools) reported approximately 29,000 habitual truants (defined as absent five days or more without excuse) in the school year 2003 -2004.

Under Tennessee law, schools are required to take action when a child has been absent without excuse for five days. As D.A., I have been designated as the person in my community the superintendents are to notify if a student has reached this benchmark.

We have tried a number of different approaches in an effort to figure out the best way to tackle truancy successfully. As a child who felt trapped in poverty, I skipped school myself. It was adults like my fourth grade teacher, Mrs. White, who steered me in the right direction just by being there and saying the right thing at the right time. She helped me connect the dots between working hard in school and having a brighter future. We are all products of our backgrounds and experiences. In part, my personal experience helped me realize that, if we could put more good role models in the lives of kids skipping school, then they would be more likely to make the good choice of going to school and be less apt to go down the path of crime.

A landmark study by Public/Private Ventures found that at-risk youth with mentors were 46 percent less likely to begin using illegal drugs, 53 percent less likely to skip school, and 33 percent less likely to engage in physical fights. The study also found that young people with mentors were more likely to report positive attitudes about themselves, their families, and their prospects for the future.

Our office launched a program to offer mentors as an alternative to court proceedings for habitual truants (those absent for five or more days without excuse). Participating youth and a parent or guardian enter into an agreement in the form of a court order in which the youth agrees to be matched and cooperate with a designated mentor.

We began operating the effort to reduce habitual truancy in five Memphis public middle schools. Truants participating in the program are given the opportunity to be diverted from traditional prosecution into a mentoring arrangement. We employ a small number of graduate students as case advocates to work with administrators in the middle schools to promptly identify students who are habitually absent from school. Once a truant middle school student is identified, the court issues a summons to appear at a special hearing. At the hearing, if the student and parent or guardian agree, a court order is entered to place a volunteer mentor with the truant child. Prosecution for truancy will be deferred as long as the child and his or her family comply with the court order. Mentors are drawn primarily from churches and other faith-based groups but from area businesses as well.

The program coordinator, the mentor, a case advocate/liaison, and an assistant district attorney assigned to juvenile court assess each youth's successful participation in the program. The following factors signify success:

- School attendance;
- School performance;
- Conduct at home, at school, and with the mentor;
- Participation in any community and/or faith based programs recommended by the mentor; and
- The absence of illegal infractions of any nature.

The case advocates report directly to the program coordinator. The advocates serve as liaisons with the following program partners:

- Each participating school;
- The mentors of students from that school;
- Social service agencies; and
- The D.A.'s office.

Specifically, the advocates track and monitor mentor/student relationships and school attendance. The advocates meet weekly with the program coordinator to go over specific cases and develop action plans to address any problems. Case advocates are responsible for notifying the assistant D.A. in charge of truancy prosecution when students are failing to adhere to the court order.

The process of recruiting mentors involves the active assistance of faith-based groups, specific faith-based congregations, and other community groups.

The program coordinator, Harold Collins, and I make a lot of appearances at churches in the community to personally recruit mentors. The biggest challenge is getting enough mentors for truant kids who want them. I know I have to be personally involved in meeting that challenge.

National Mentoring Network provided initial training to the program coordinator and an assistant D.A., who serve as the lead trainers of mentors. Criminal background checks are conducted by the D.A.'s office on each mentor candidate, including, but not limited to, sex offender registry checks. Upon completion of the training, mentors are certified. Each September, National Mentoring Network comes to Memphis to conduct a refresher course for the mentors.

Mentoring arrangements are expected to last for at least one year. There are criteria such as the number of personal contacts with the mentored youth per month (8 hours). Mentors are expected to identify family problems and needs. With the help of the case advocates, they reach out to social services available, especially those in each student's neighborhood and near his or her school. Mentors also encourage students to participate in after school group activities offered though such groups as Memphis Athletic Ministries (MAM) as well as at community centers. These activities include tutoring and sports activities in a safe, supervised environment. MAM involves participating youth in various after-school team sport activities, providing group mentoring through teamwork.

The University of Memphis' Department of Criminology and Criminal Justice has partnered with the D.A.'s office to conduct the evaluation of the pilot mentoring program.

The quality of the mentor/student activities is an important factor affecting the success of the project. These interactions are affected by how well the program recruits, trains, and retains quality mentor volunteers. The university collects descriptive information for each mentor prior to the first interaction with a child using a Mentor Intake Form, self-administered during the initial mentor orientation and training session. To understand the nature and extent of the mentor/student interactions, mentors are contacted monthly by phone and asked to participate in a brief interview regarding the frequency, duration, and content of interactions with students.

The advocates collect and report information monthly to the evaluation team regarding school attendance, academic performance, mentor participation, and delinquent and/or unsatisfactory behavior at school, home, or in the community. This information is used to measure program compliance.

It's not surprising that our efforts in the five middle schools are encouraging. Attendance is up. Grades are higher.

Alicia was a seventh grader at Cypress Middle School. In the fall of 2006, the then 13-year-old hit the five day mark for unexcused absences. Alicia's mother received notice from the D.A.'s office to attend a meeting with an assistant D.A.

Alicia and her mother accepted our offer to place Alicia in the mentoring program in lieu of prosecution. After talking with Alicia and her mother, we discovered that Alicia had self-esteem issues and that she skipped school because she felt that she was not attractive and other kids made fun of her. Although Alicia skipped school, her grades were better than most, and she enjoyed writing.

It took a while to find the right mentor for Alicia, but soon she was matched with Karen. Karen and Alicia hit it off extremely well. Karen had gone through training and a background check. Both were interviewed to identify common interests. After several months of meeting and engaging, Alicia had a unique opportunity to demonstrate just how much she enjoyed writing. Karen is the publisher of a teen magazine. Alicia became one of Karen's major contributors to the magazine. Alicia would write not only about her trials as a teen with esteem issues but also other issues that most young girls her age encountered. Needless to say, Alicia and Karen's relationship grew into a very special, positive one.

Alicia had perfect attendance in school for the next two years. She was on the honor roll at her school. Karen and Alicia continued to share time with one another even though the required one year commitment ended in 2007.

It was in the fall of 2006 when a 13-year-old sixth grader from Chickasaw Middle School, Timothy, reached the threshold of five unexcused absences.

After receiving notice to attend a meeting with an assistant D.A., Timothy and his mother agreed to our offer to place him in the mentoring program. We learned that Timothy missed his father. He was having a difficult time getting along with other kids at school and wanted to play on the school basketball team. He is a very good player. Timothy would not receive a mentor for another year. The need for male mentors is great, and finding the right one for each kid is important. Although Timothy did not receive a mentor immediately, he stayed in contact with our case advocate assigned to his school. We kept up with his attendance and his behavior.

We ended up matching Timothy with Jonathan. Jonathan was a youth minister in one of our local churches and also working on a master's degree. After Jonathan was trained and interviewed, we found that Jonathan and Timothy had similar likes and feelings about certain things. Our program coordinator, Harold Collins, took Jonathan to meet Timothy. They went to Timothy's home in southwest Memphis. It was an apartment complex.

When they arrived, a resident asked if they were the police, and didn't believe assurances given that they were not. It was only when Timothy came out and told the group who they were that things settled down. He informed them that Harold was there to introduce Jonathan and that Jonathan would be his mentor. In fifteen minutes, all the kids wanted a mentor!

As the mentor arrangement progressed, Timothy's mother called to inform Harold Collins that Timothy was doing extremely well in school. In fact, he was on the honor roll. He was attending Mitchell High School and a major player on the basketball team. Timothy was one of our mentored kids invited by then-basketball Coach John Calipari of the University of Memphis Tigers to attend one of the Tigers' practices. At the practice, Coach Cal implored the young men to never give up on their dreams and to never use tough times as an excuse for not succeeding in life. He invited several of the University of Memphis players to talk to Timothy and the other mentored students and pose for pictures. It was an occasion Timothy and the others will remember the rest of their lives.

I chair the Operation: Safe Community strategic plan initiative, an ambitious effort undertaken by community leaders to tackle crime in my community. One of the strategies is to make our mentoring effort available to all truant middle school students who want it. That's a major undertaking, involving the recruitment of thousands of mentors. If we can pull it off, it will certainly place Memphis on the map. We would be a model for tapping into the energy and commitment of concerned citizens willing to help young people who are headed down the wrong path get on the right path. The main beneficiaries are the students being mentored, although most of the mentors see themselves as being beneficiaries as a result of the experience. The secondary beneficiary, though, is our community. As a result of the mentoring effort, there will be fewer juveniles making the bad choice of skipping school.

Brooklyn D.A. Charles J. Joe Hynes knows that truancy is the first indication that a juvenile is giving up and moving in the wrong direction. He sees skipping school as not only a gateway to juvenile crime but as increasing the likelihood of youth victimization. In 1998, Hynes launched Truancy Reduction Alliance to Contact Kids (TRACK).

The focal point of TRACK is seven truancy centers located throughout Brooklyn which are open during school hours and staffed by personnel from the New York Police Department, the D.A.'s office, and the school system. During school hours, if a police officer sees a student on the street and, upon questioning, determines the student is truant, the officer takes the student to a TRACK truancy center. A truancy counselor on the D.A.'s staff assesses any particular needs of the student that may be cause for skipping school and makes appropriate referrals. School personnel at the TRACK truancy centers are responsible for contacting students' schools. The students' parents/ guardians usually get a call from the N.Y.P.D. to come pick up their children. If a parent or guardian can't be reached, school personnel return the student to his or her school.

A key to the success of TRACK is using the N.Y.P.D. to catch the truants *and* to call the parents/guardians. Usually, it gets their attention. The New York City school system has maintained a truancy program of its own, with its own centers. But the police aren't the ones calling the parents/guardians. Rather, its school personnel. It's not quite the same. Calls from school personnel do not get the same reaction as calls from the police. With a call from the N.Y.P.D., most parents/guardians understand the seriousness of the situation and respond. Many are surprised their kids are skipping school.

The recidivism rate among students picked up under TRACK is extremely low at six percent. In 2000, then Mayor Rudy Giuliani praised the success of TRACK in Brooklyn and called for implementation of the approach throughout all of New York City.

Randy Nichols is the D.A. in Knox County, Tennessee, which includes the city of Knoxville. He's a good friend. One thing I admire about him is that he always speaks his mind. You know where Nichols stands. When it comes to truancy, he is clear in his determination to attack it and equally clear in his opinion that typical bureaucratic approaches don't work. As D.A., he knows he has a stick and is willing to use it.

Fed up with students skipping school, in the late 1990s, Nichols took the lead in organizing the Knox County Truancy Initiative, a partnership composed of the D.A.'s office, the Knox County Juvenile Court, Knox County Schools, the Knoxville Police Department, and the Knox County Sheriff's office. It's a simple but effective approach that depends upon each partnering agency doing its part.

When a student hits five unexcused absences, school officials send the parent/guardian a letter giving notice. A Knox County Schools attendance social worker will follow up with the student, as well as make phone calls to the home. The attendance social worker works with the student through home visits, parent conferences, and referrals for social services.

As part of the effort, the Knoxville Police Department set up a truancy center. The city police and sheriff's office began transporting juveniles found off campus during school hours to the truancy center. But due to budget cuts, the police department was no longer able to keep the truancy center running. Then, in 2006, the Boys & Girls Club assumed responsibility for the center. When a student is brought to the center, the staff notifies the student's school, a parent/guardian, and the D.A.'s office.

Once a student has accumulated 10 unexcused days, both student and parent/guardian are invited to a meeting held by the District Attorney's office. This letter of invitation informs the parent/guardian that the student's name has been turned over to juvenile court by the Knox County Schools and sets out the consequences of continued unexcused absences. At this meeting the D.A., juvenile court judge, and Knox County Schools officials warn of the consequences of further truant behavior. Randy Nichols means exactly what he says. He doesn't hold back in those meetings.

If a student continues missing school after the meeting with the D.A., charges are filed in juvenile court, or the parent/guardian is invited to a Truancy Review Board hearing held at the court. The Truancy Review Board is composed of representatives from the Knox County District Attorney's office, Knox County Schools, and various social service agencies. Knox County Schools provides a registered nurse for the board, and the Knox County Juvenile Court provides a licensed psychologist. The parent/guardian is reminded of the seriousness of the situation, including the criminal charges that may be filed. The board tries to identify the circumstances that are hindering the student from coming to school and will construct a plan of action to alleviate the truant behavior. If the parent or guardian does not comply, or refuses to comply, then charges are filed in juvenile court.

When the effort began back in the 1998-1999 school year, the meeting with the D.A. and other officials was triggered at 15 unexcused absences. That year, 360 letters went out to students and parents inviting them to a meeting with the D.A. In response, 251 parents or guardians attended. For that school year, 41 warrants were filed against the parents or guardians and one petition was filed against a juvenile.

The number continued to grow as the partnership began running on all cylinders. In the 2001-2002 school year, 1171 letters were sent and 524 parents or guardians attended the meeting with the D.A. The police filed 46 warrants against adults, and 73 petitions against students.

Changes were made for the 2002-2003 school year. Instead of 15 unexcused absences serving as the trigger, 10 unexcused absences became the trigger point. With this new threshold, the letters sent out peaked at 2,386 and 1,100 attended the meeting with the D.A. The number of warrants against adults increased to 108, and the number of petitions against juveniles increased to 220. The Truancy Review Board heard 41 cases. The number of referrals was still more than 2,000 in the 2004-2005 school year. This time, 2,253 letters were sent out, and 1,174 attended the meeting. Police filed 42 warrants against adults along with 161 petitions against juveniles. The Truancy review board heard 207 cases.

But after the peak in the 2002-2003 school year, truancy referrals continued to drop, with 2,107 in the 2005-2006 school year and 2,023 in the 2006-2007 school year. At the same time, a higher percentage of parents faced warrants, and a higher portion of the truant students faced petitions in juvenile court. Those numbers reflect a more aggressive stance against those who did not respond.

In 2007-2008, 1,636 letters were sent, with 762 attending the D.A.'s meeting. Police filed 60 warrants against adults and 265 petitions against juveniles. The Truancy Review Board heard 166 cases.

Pima County (Tucson), Arizona chief prosecutor, Barbara LaWall, has been in the forefront of effective practices to deal with juvenile delinquents before they become serious repeat offenders as reflected in the S.M.A.R.T. initiative highlighted in the previous chapter. She recognizes as well the need to address truancy as often being a gateway to delinquency. She knows that combating truancy is the first line of defense in the battle against juvenile crime.

In 1993, the Arizona Criminal Justice Commission had formed a Youth and Crime Task Force to give the governor and state legislature recommendations on the issue of juvenile crime. The task force determined that one major risk factor and early warning sign of a potential delinquent youth was poor school attendance. Its study revealed that about 90 percent of all prison inmates were chronic truants at one time. And it concluded there were many different causes for truancy, including reading deficiencies, abuse, health issues, and family issues. Pima County's truancy rates were among the highest in Arizona, accounting for more than 50 percent of the total reported truants in the state.

Faced with over 1,200 students truant daily and 5,000 dropouts annually, LaWall decided to tackle truancy while she was still the deputy county attorney back in 1994. That's when Arizona enacted a new law to hold parents more accountable for truant kids. The new law exposed parents to a Class 3 misdemeanor charge, with a fine of up to $2500 and a maximum of six months in jail. LeWall saw the new law as an opportunity to put some teeth into efforts to combat truancy, and she hired a retired veteran police officer, Gene Bertie, to help her do it.

There are 16 separate school districts in Pima County. With the new law as a tool, LaWall and Bertie went to three of the school districts to begin the Abolish Chronic Truancy (ACT) Now truancy program to do the following:

- Enforce the new law and hold parents accountable;
- Through a diversion program, provide services to address the root causes of truancy; and
- Sanction parents and students for continued truancy.

The traditional approach had been to process truants through juvenile court and normally place them on a form of diversion, but with no real consequences. Now, there would be a form of diversion with consequences for failure. Also, they brought in the non-profit Center for Juvenile Alternatives (CJA) to help serve the needs of truants and their families.

ACT Now is a step-by-step approach to dealing with truancy:

- After the first unexcused absence, the participating school sends a letter to the parent or guardian, with a warning of possible prosecution;
- When a student has been absent for three days without excuse, the matter is referred to CJA, with all supporting documentation;
- Parents are notified that they are subject to prosecution and that their truant children are subject to juvenile court action, but as an alternative they can contact CJA, and upon signing a written agreement they can participate in the diversion program; and
- Failure to respond results in prosecution under the law enacted in 1994.

Upon entering a written agreement to participate in the diversion program, CJA uses a case management approach, with referrals to groups and agencies that provide counseling, mentoring, parenting skills classes, alcohol and drug programs, and support groups. There is regular follow-up with (1) the schools to check on attendance, (2) the family through home visits and phone contacts, and (3) groups and agencies to which individuals have been referred.

Mike Burns heads up the community justice unit of the Pima County Attorney's office. He sees truancy as an indication of more serious problems in the home. It's pretty predictable that something going on in the home is creating the truancy. It can be drug abuse, drug trafficking, domestic violence, or any number of other things. Dealing with the truancy problem is like opening a door. We usually find a kid with whom we can work and we can change. Rather than just looking at the symptoms, we're looking at the underlying problems, noted Burns.

ACT Now has spread to eight of Pima County's school districts. From fiscal year 1995-1996 through fiscal year 2005-2006, ACT Now handled a total of 5,180 truancy cases, with only 1,061 resulting in citations for prosecution. The compliance rate with the CJA-run diversion program was between 75 and 80 percent. The biggest challenge for ACT Now and its possible expansion to more school districts is the issue of funding. In fact, in the 2007-2008 school year, ACT Now had to reduce the number of referrals to the program due to the drop in Juvenile Accountability Incentive Block Grant (JAIBG) funds available to pay for case managers.

But Pima County remains committed to ACT Now as a significant part of the battle plan to curb juvenile crime. As noted by Mike Burns, We must be committed to working with kids coming in the front door and not wait until it's too late.

According to the National Center for Health Statistics, part of the Centers for Disease Control and Prevention, more babies were born in 2007 in the United States than in any year in our nation's history. This topped the previous record year of 1957. A disturbing trend, though, was the fact that the teen birth rate was up for a second year in a row. In my home state of Tennessee, more than 13 percent of 2007 births were to teen mothers.

District attorneys across Tennessee weighed in on the issue in 2008. Armed with brochures, posters, and an effective video, Tennessee D.A.s spoke to student assemblies across Tennessee, conveying a straight forward message about the far too often following consequences of teen parenting:

- The sons of teen mothers are 13 percent more likely to end up in prison;
- Fewer than half of mothers who have a child before they reach 18 years of age graduate from high school;
- Children of teen mothers are 50 percent more likely to have to repeat a grade in school and are less likely to finish high school;
- The children of teen mothers are two times more likely to suffer abuse and neglect; and
- Teen fathers have less education and earn much less money than teenage boys without children.

By weighing in on this issue, many D.A.s were stepping out of their comfort zones. But it reflected a realization that teen parenting often creates conditions which create an unstable atmosphere that can lead to many bad choices. By speaking out about teen parenting, D.A.s were using their influence to curb conditions which simply add to the number of people going through our criminal justice system. It's an example of an issue that a community's leadership can impact by speaking out and setting the right tone rather than being silent and surrendering to the status quo. Addressing such issues as teen parenting is certainly no quick fix to crime. But it is a great example of how communities and states can look ahead and take action now to have a positive impact down the road. It's another way to encourage juveniles to make good choices with long-term positive impact.

Prosecutors and other community leaders must speak out on the need to tackle patterns of behavior and engrained cultural influences that have a direct, and indirect, impact on crime, both short-term and long-term.

Increasing the odds that juveniles make good choices can have a positive impact on our crime rate.

CONCLUSION

I've not attempted to highlight every useful tool, policy, and practice available to prosecutors and communities in the fight to make our neighborhoods, streets, and schools safer. There are so many great examples of steps prosecutors and other law enforcement officials; business leaders; governors, mayors, and legislators; and neighborhood leaders have implemented all over America. It's simply impossible for me to highlight all of the efforts that have come to my attention. I have attempted to highlight enough examples that, taken together, reflect the kind of multi-front battle plan any community needs to be successful. Some examples have been based on the tools, policies, and practices I've used personally. Some are based on the experiences of other communities.

There is no cookie-cutter approach to developing a battle plan. A lot depends on the tools and resources available, which vary from community to community and state to state and depend upon state laws, funding levels, and other factors. The key is for every community to identify what resources are available then develop a plan to use those resources effectively, while at the same time seeking needed changes in state laws and funding priorities.

All the tools, policies, and practices I've mentioned fall within one or more of three broad approaches to combating crime:

- Holding offenders accountable (commonly called suppression in law enforcement circles);
- Intervening to change behavior (reducing the number of repeat criminals); and
- Preventing criminal behavior (reducing the number of would-be criminals).

The accountability part must come first. For years, the U. S. Department of Justice has funded a weed and seed program in an attempt to turn crime-ridden areas around. The name itself sums up the approach. The weeding means going after those causing the problems. It must come before the seeding. The seeding refers to the intervention and prevention parts.

Violent and other serious offenders, both adult and juvenile, must be held accountable so they are no longer threats to our communities. This means using tough laws as an effective tool, and urging our state legislators to enact such laws where they don't exist. It means having in place policies and practices to take full advantage of the laws on the books. That includes effective use of prosecutor resources to go after serious repeat offenders through such practices as hands-on vertical prosecution, use of a team approach to develop the strongest cases, and holding the line on strong cases rather than engaging in unnecessary plea bargaining.

It means opening up a second front against the violent criminals and drug traffickers by going after their places of business and operation in our neighborhoods while at the same time prosecuting them. And it involves working with specific neighborhoods to effectively suppress particular kinds of activity that, left unchecked, result in even worse conditions. Taken together, such weeding out of the bad actors must take precedence in any successful battle plan.

However, we must be smart enough to know that we can never simply prosecute our way out of the crime challenge. Prosecutors must support, and be in the forefront of, efforts to reduce the number of repeat offenders by breaking the cycle of drug abuse and crime and by giving both adult and juvenile offenders the guidance they need to make better choices in the future.

And we must be visionary enough to reduce the number of individuals who would even be inclined to commit crimes. The bulk of this responsibility lies with families, institutions of faith, and schools and represents a long-range commitment to changing behavior. But there are also short-range steps we can take as part of an immediate battle plan to reduce crime. By working to reduce truancy and taking steps such as reducing teen parenting, we can create a climate that fosters better choices by juveniles.

Many communities face significant challenges to insure the peace and safety of their citizens. Such peace and safety is a fundamental right of all citizens. The preamble to the U. S. Constitution states in part that the reason for creating our national government is to …establish justice, insure domestic tranquility… and secure the blessings of liberty to ourselves and our posterity… Most of our state constitutions have similar provisions regarding the basic reasons for their creation. We are a nation of laws founded on the notion that all citizens have a right to basic safety. **We must never surrender in our fight to preserve the right to feel safe in our homes, neighborhoods, and schools and on our streets.**

A Battle Plan
For Creating Safe Communities

Any realistic battle plan must include tough laws that get the thugs off our streets.

Vertical prosecution is essential to build the strongest cases possible against serious offenders who threaten the very lives of citizens in our communities.

It takes a team approach to fight crime and make our communities safer.

Violent offenders aren't automatically entitled to plea bargains and must be held accountable.

Long-term changes in behavior require a long-term commitment to influencing behavior by communicating the consequences of engaging in crime.

By turning around the lives of those who ultimately return to our communities, we can reduce the number of repeat offenders.

By identifying and shutting down the drug houses, law enforcement and law-abiding citizens can salvage entire neighborhoods and give residents hope for the future.

Prosecutors must have the necessary tools under the law to root out illegal activity occurring in rental properties.

Communities can curtail low-level drug dealers by building good cases, then relying upon the influence of neighborhood leaders and family members to help change behavior.

Our laws must give prosecutors the means to fight back and prevent gangs from controlling any part of any neighborhood.

The battle to take back our neighborhoods, we must include concerted, effective efforts to go after the local production of drugs such as meth and intercept the flow of drugs from the outside.

An essential part of any battle plan must be an effort to break the cycle of drug addiction and crime rather than just overseeing a revolving door of drug addicts cycling through the system.

Prosecutor-driven, judge monitored treatment programs can move drug addicts in the right direction rather than allowing them to become or remain parasites on their families and menaces to their communities.

The drug treatment court model is an effective community tool to combat juvenile drug abuse and crime.

Effective treatment with the active oversight of judges and prosecutors not only works to reduce the cause of so much of our crime, but saves tax dollars in the long-run by reducing repeat offenders and cutting prison costs.

By aggressively conveying the dangers of drug abuse, we can curtail demand.

Ultimately, the best way to reduce the supply of drugs is to reduce the demand.

Forming strong partnerships with neighborhoods is critical to responding effectively to their unique needs in the battle against crime.

Instead of simply being reactive to community issues, prosecutors must be proactive and use a problem-solving approach when addressing local neighborhood concerns.

Bringing the courts to the neighborhoods increases the success level of any battle plan for safer communities.

The fight against crime must include an attack on problem properties that create an atmosphere less conducive to crime.

Serious juvenile offenders must be held accountable and removed as threats to the peace and safety of our communities.

Communities must have effective preemptive strikes in place to move juveniles in the right direction and stop the influence of gang culture and drugs before it's too late.

Increasing the odds that juveniles make good choices can have a positive impact on our crime rate.

ENDNOTES

1   Virginia Criminal Sentencing Commission. (2005). *A Decade of Truth-In-Sentencing in Virginia.* Richmond, VA. Retrieved from http://www.vcsc.state.va.us/Mar_05/TIS_Brochure.pdf

2   Virginia Criminal Sentencing Commission. (2005). *A Decade of Truth-In-Sentencing in Virginia.* Richmond, VA. Retrieved from http://www.vcsc.state.va.us/Mar_05/TIS_Brochure.pdf

3   Virginia Criminal Sentencing Commission. (2005). *A Decade of Truth-In-Sentencing in Virginia.* Richmond, VA. Retrieved from http://www.vcsc.state.va.us/Mar_05/TIS_Brochure.pdf

4   Federal Bureau of Investigation. (1996). Unified Crime Report. *Crime in the US.* Washington, DC: Retrieved from http://www.fbi.gov/ucr/ucr.htm

5   Silver, S. (Speaker of the Assembly), Lentol, J. (Chair, Assembly Codes Committee). (2000) *The Toughest Crime Laws in a Generation: A Summary of Recent Significant Criminal Justice Laws Passed by the New York State Assembly.*

6   New York Division of Criminal Justice Services. (2006) *State Criminal Justice Crimestat Report.*

7   New York Division of Criminal Justice Services. (2006) *State Criminal Justice Crimestat Report*

8   New York Division of Criminal Justice Services. (2006) *State Criminal Justice Crimestat Report*

9   New York Division of Criminal Justice Services. (2006) *State Criminal Justice Crimestat Report*

10 New York Division of Criminal Justice Services. (2006) *State Criminal Justice Crimestat Report*

11 New York Division of Criminal Justice Services. (2006) *State Criminal Justice Crimestat Report*

12 New York Division of Criminal Justice Services. (2006) *State Criminal Justice Crimestat Report*

13 Federal Bureau of Investigation. (1996). Unified Crime Report. *Crime in the US.* Washington, DC: Retrieved from http://www.fbi.gov/ucr/ucr.htm

14 Florida Department of Corrections, Office of Department Initiatives.

15 Florida Department of Corrections. (2007). 1*0-20-LIFE Criminals Sentenced to Florida's Prisons.*

16 Florida Department of Corrections, Office of Department Initiatives.

17 Memphis, TN-MS-AR M.S.A. includes Crittenden County, AR; DeSoto, Marshall, Tate, and Tunica Counties, MS; and Fayette, Shelby, and Tipton Counties, TN

18 Federal Bureau of Investigation. (2006). Unified Crime Report. *Crime in the US.* Washington, DC: Retrieved from http://www.fbi.gov/ucr/ucr.htm

19 Federal Bureau of Investigation. (2006). Unified Crime Report. *Crime in the US.* Washington, DC: Retrieved from http://www.fbi.gov/ucr/ucr.htm

20 Federal Bureau of Investigation. (2007). Unified Crime Report. *Crime in the US.* Washington, DC: Retrieved from http://www.fbi.gov/ucr/ucr.htm

21 Monahan, B., & Burke, T. (2001). Project Exile: Combating Gun Violence in America. *FBI Law Enforcement Bulletin.*

22 Monahan, B., & Burke, T. (2001). Project Exile: Combating Gun Violence in America. *FBI Law Enforcement Bulletin.*

23 United States Attorney's Office. Western District of Tennessee.

24 The National Children's Advocacy Center.

25 Tennessee Code Annotated § 37-1-607

26   Tennessee Code Annotated § 37-1-406(c) and 37-1-609 (b)

27   U.S. Department of Justice. Office of Justice Programs. Bureau of Justice Statistics. (2008) *Criminal Case Processing Statistics*. Retrieved from http://www.ojp.usdoj.gov/bjs/cases.htm#felony

28   U.S. Department of Justice. Office of Justice Programs. Bureau of Justice Statistics. (2008) *Criminal Case Processing Statistics*. Retrieved from http://www.ojp.usdoj.gov/bjs/cases.htm#felony

29   Shelby County, Tennessee District Attorney's Office. (2008). *Annual Report.*

30   New York Criminal Procedure Law sec. 180

31   Federal Bureau of Investigation. (2006-07). Unified Crime Report. *Crime in the US.* Washington, DC: Retrieved from http://www.fbi.gov/ucr/ucr.htm

32   Reed, L., Henderson, E., & Janikowski, R. (2005). *PSN Media Campaign Impact Summary.* Center for Community Criminology and Research. The University of Memphis.

33   Reed, L., Henderson, E., & Janikowski, R. (2005). *PSN Media Campaign Impact Summary.* Center for Community Criminology and Research. The University of Memphis.

34   Cracking Down on Weapons. (2007, November 18). *The Commercial Appeal.*

35   U.S. Attorney's Office. Middle District of Tennessee. (2007) *Project Safe Neighborhoods Continues to Make a Difference in Our Community.*

36   U.S. Department of Justice. Bureau of Justice Statistics. (2002). *Recidivism of Prisoners Released in 1994.* Washington, DC. Langan, P., & Levin, D. Retrieved from http://www.ojp.usdoj.gov/bjs/pub/pdf/rpr94.pdf

37   U.S. Department of Justice. Bureau of Justice Statistics. (2002). *Recidivism of Prisoners Released in 1994.* Washington, DC. Langan, P., & Levin, D. Retrieved from http://www.ojp.usdoj.gov/bjs/pub/pdf/rpr94.pdf

38   Hynes, C. (2008). ComALERT: A Prosecutor's Collaborative Model for Ensuring a Successful Transition from Prison to the Community. *Journal of Court Innovation.*

39   Jacobs, E., & Western, B. (2007). *Report on the Evaluation of the ComALERT Prisoner Reentry Program.* Retrieved from King's County, New York District Attorney's Office Web site: http://www.wjh.harvard.edu/soc/faculty/western/pdfs/report_1009071.pdf

40   Kings County, New York District Attorney's Office.

41   Kings County, New York District Attorney's Office.

42   Kings County, New York District Attorney's Office.

43   Tennessee Code Annotated § 29-3-102

44   Tennessee Code Annotated § 29-3-101

45   Wisconsin State Statute Chapter 823

46   New York Consolidated Laws, Real Property Actions and Proceedings § 715

47   New York Consolidated Laws, Real Property Actions and Proceedings § 715

48   New York Consolidated Laws, Real Property Actions and Proceedings § 715

49   New York Consolidated Laws, Real Property Actions and Proceedings § 715

50   City of New York v. Wright, 162 Misc. 2d 572 (App. Term, 1st Dept. 1994)

51   Tennessee Code Annotated § 66-7-101

52   High Point, North Carolina Police Department.

53   High Point, North Carolina Police Department.

54   Frabutt, J., Gathings, M.J., Hunt, E. & Loggins, T. (2004). *High Point West End Initiative.* The Center for Youth, Family, and Community Partnerships. The University of North Carolina at Greensboro.

55   High Point Police Department.

56   Frabutt, J., Gathings, M.J., Hunt, E. & Loggins, T. (2004). *High Point West End Initiative.* The Center for Youth, Family, and Community Partnerships. The University of North Carolina at Greensboro.

57   Frabutt, J., Gathings, M.J., Hunt, E. & Loggins, T. (2004). *High Point West End Initiative.* The Center for Youth, Family, and Community Partnerships. The University of North Carolina at Greensboro.

58   Frabutt, J., Gathings, M.J., Hunt, E. & Loggins, T. (2004). *High Point West End Initiative.* The Center for Youth, Family, and Community Partnerships. The University of North Carolina at Greensboro.

59   Shiner, M. (2007). Gang Injunctions: Going to Court to Take Back the Streets. *Building Bridges,* Volume 5, Numbers 3 & 4. National District Attorney's Association.

60   California Civil Code §§ 3479, 3480; California Penal Code § 370

61   People ex rel. Gallo v. Acuna (1997) 14 Cal. 4th 1090, 1102

62   Shiner, M. (2007). Gang Injunctions: Going to Court to Take Back the Streets. *Building Bridges,* Volume 5, Numbers 3 & 4. National District Attorney's Association.

63   California Senate Bill 271 (2007)

64   Editorial. (2005, July 15). *The Boston Globe.*

65   Tennessee Governor's Task Force on Methamphetamine Abuse. (2004). *Final Report.*

66   Tennessee Governor's Task Force on Methamphetamine Abuse. (2004). *Final Report.*

67   U.S. Drug Enforcement Administration. (2004).

68   Tennessee Governor's Task Force on Methamphetamine Abuse. (2004). *Final Report.*

69   Tennessee Governor's Task Force on Methamphetamine Abuse. (2004). *Final Report.*

70   Tennessee Governor's Task Force on Methamphetamine Abuse. (2004). *Final Report.*

71   Tennessee Governor's Task Force on Methamphetamine Abuse. (2004). *Final Report.*

72   Tennessee Code Annotated 39-17-417(a) and (c)

73   Tennessee Code Annotated 39-17-433 and 435

74   Tennessee Code Annotated 39-17-431(a)

75   Tennessee Code Annotated 39-17-43(c)

76   Tennessee Code Annotated 39-17-431(d)

77   Tennessee Code Annotated 39-17-431(e)

78   Tennessee Code Annotated 39-17-431(f)

79   Tennessee Code Annotated 39-17-436

80   South/East Tennessee Methamphetamine Task Force. (2006).

81   Tennessee Bureau of Investigation.

82   U.S. Department of Justice. Bureau of Justice Statistics. (1997).

83   King's County, NY District Attorney's Office. (2008). *Drug Treatment Alternative-to-Prison Annual Report.* (Citing data from New York State Division of Criminal Justice Services).

84 King's County, NY District Attorney's Office. (2008). *Drug Treatment Alternative-to-Prison Annual Report.*

85 King's County, NY District Attorney's Office. (2008). *Drug Treatment Alternative-to-Prison Annual Report.* (Citing data from New York State Division of Criminal Justice Services).

86 King's County, NY District Attorney's Office. (2008). *Drug Treatment Alternative-to-Prison Annual Report.* (Citing the Drug Treatment Outcome Studies initiated by the National Institute on Drug Abuse in 1990).

87 King's County, NY District Attorney's Office. (2008). *Drug Treatment Alternative-to-Prison Annual Report.* (Citing the Drug Treatment Outcome Studies initiated by the National Institute on Drug Abuse in 1990).

88 King's County, NY District Attorney's Office. (2008). *Drug Treatment Alternative-to-Prison Annual Report.* (Citing the Drug Treatment Outcome Studies initiated by the National Institute on Drug Abuse in 1990).

89 King's County, NY District Attorney's Office. (2008). *Drug Treatment Alternative-to-Prison Annual Report.* (Citing the Drug Treatment Outcome Studies initiated by the National Institute on Drug Abuse in 1990).

90 King's County, NY District Attorney's Office. (2008). *Drug Treatment Alternative-to-Prison Annual Report.* (Citing the Drug Treatment Outcome Studies initiated by the National Institute on Drug Abuse in 1990).

91 King's County, NY District Attorney's Office. (2008). *Drug Treatment Alternative-to-Prison Annual Report.* (Citing the Drug Treatment Outcome Studies initiated by the National Institute on Drug Abuse in 1990).

92 King's County, NY District Attorney's Office. (2008). *Drug Treatment Alternative-to-Prison Annual Report.* (Citing the Drug Treatment Outcome Studies initiated by the National Institute on Drug Abuse in 1990).

93 *Crossing the Bridge: An Evaluation of the Drug Treatment Alternative-to-Prison* (DTAP) Program. (2003). National Center on Addiction and Substance Abuse at Columbia University.

94 King's County, NY District Attorney's Office. (2008). *Drug Treatment Alternative-to-Prison Annual Report.*

95 King's County, NY District Attorney's Office. (2008). *Drug Treatment Alternative-to-Prison Annual Report.*

96 King's County, NY District Attorney's Office. (2008). *Drug Treatment Alternative-to-Prison Annual Report.*

97 King's County, NY District Attorney's Office. (2008). *Drug Treatment Alternative-to-Prison Annual Report.*

98 King's County, NY District Attorney's Office. (2008). *Drug Treatment Alternative-to-Prison Annual Report.*

99 *Process Evaluation of the Brooklyn Treatment Court and Network of Services.* (1999). The Urban Institute.

100 National Drug Court Institute. *Painting the Current Picture: A National Report Card on Drug Courts and Other Problem-Solving Court Programs in the United States.* (2008). Volume II.

101 National Drug Court Institute. *Painting the Current Picture: A National Report Card on Drug Courts and Other Problem-Solving Court Programs in the United States.* (2008). Volume II.

102 National Drug Court Institute. *Painting the Current Picture: A National Report Card on Drug Courts and Other Problem-Solving Court Programs in the United States.* (2008). Volume II.

103 National Drug Court Institute. *Painting the Current Picture: A National Report Card on Drug Courts and Other Problem-Solving Court Programs in the United States.* (2008). Volume II.

104 National Drug Court Institute. *Painting the Current Picture: A National Report Card on Drug Courts and Other Problem-Solving Court Programs in the United States.* (2008). Volume II. (Citing Manlowe, D.B., DeMattero, D.S., & Festinger, D.S. (2003). A sober assessment of drug of drug courts. Federal Sentencing Reporter, 16(2), 153-157.)

105 National Drug Court Institute. *Painting the Current Picture: A National Report Card on Drug Courts and Other Problem-Solving Court Programs in the United States.* (2008). Volume II. (Citing Carey, S.M., Finigan, M., Crumpton, D., & Welles, M. (2006). California drug courts: Outcomes, Costs and Promising Practices: An overview of phase II in a statewide study. Journal of Psychoactive Drugs, SARC Supplement 3, 345-356.)

106 National Drug Court Institute. *Painting the Current Picture: A National Report Card on Drug Courts and Other Problem-Solving Court Programs in the United States.* (2008). Volume II. (Citing Rhodes, W., Kling, R. & Shively, M. (2006). Suffolk County Court Evaluation. Cambridge, MA: Abt Associates.)

107 Government Accountability Office. (2005) *Adult drug courts: Evidence indicates recidivism reductions and mixed results for other outcomes.* Report to congressional committees. Washington, DC

108 Shelby County, Tennessee Drug Treatment Court.

109 Janikowski, R., Afflitto, F., Morrozoff, D., Terrell, M. (2000). *Process Evaluation of the Shelby County Drug Court.* Center for Community Criminology & Research, Department of Criminology & Criminal Justice, University of Memphis.

110 Ensuring Sustainability for Drug Courts: An Overview of Funding Strategies. (2008). *Monograph Series 8.* National Drug Court Institute.

111 Ensuring Sustainability for Drug Courts: An Overview of Funding Strategies. (2008). *Monograph Series 8.* National Drug Court Institute.

112 Kyle, A.D., Housel, B. (2005). *The meth epidemic in America: Two surveys of U.S. counties.* Washington, DC: National Association on Counties.

113 Kyle, A.D., Housel, B. (2005). *The meth epidemic in America: Two surveys of U.S. counties.* Washington, DC: National Association on Counties.

114 Ensuring Sustainability for Drug Courts: An Overview of Funding Strategies. (2008). *Monograph Series 8.* National Drug Court Institute.

115 National Association of Drug Count Professionals.

116 Wilson, J.Q., (2000, April 13). A New Strategy for the War on Drugs. *The Wall Street Journal*

117 Wilson, J.Q., (2000, April 13). A New Strategy for the War on Drugs. *The Wall Street Journal.*

118 Johnston, L. D., O'Malley, P. M., Bachman, J. G., & Schulenberg, J. E. (2006). *Monitoring the Future national results on adolescent drug use: Overview of key findings, 2005.* (NIH Publication No. 06-5882). Bethesda, MD: National Institute on Drug Abuse.

119 Stahl, A. (1998). *Drug Offense Cases in Juvenile Court 1986-1995*, OJJDP Fact Sheet #81. Washington, D.C.: U.S. Department of Justice, Office of Juvenile Justice and Delinquency Prevention.

120 Cooper, C. (2001). *Juvenile Drug Court Programs.* Washington, D.C.: U.S. Department of Justice, Office of Juvenile Justice and Delinquency Prevention, NCJ 184744.

121 Upper Cumberland Community Services Agency (Cookeville, TN).

122 Upper Cumberland Community Services Agency (Cookeville, TN).

123 National Drug Court Institute. *Painting the Current Picture: A National Report Card on Drug Courts and Other Problem-Solving Court Programs in the United States.* (2008). Volume II.

124 National Drug Court Institute. *Painting the Current Picture: A National Report Card on Drug Courts and Other Problem-Solving Court Programs in the United States.* (2008). Volume II. (Citing Aos, S., Miller, M., & Drake, E. (2006). Evidence-based public policy options to reduce future prison construction, criminal justice costs, and crime rates. Olympia: Washington State Institute for Public Policy.)

125 National Drug Court Institute. *Painting the Current Picture: A National Report Card on Drug Courts and Other Problem-Solving Court Programs in the United States.* (2008). Volume II. (Citing Carey, S.M., Firigum, M., Compton, D., & Walles, M. (2006) California drug courts: Outcomes, costs and promising practices: An overview of phase II in a statewide study. Journal of Psychoactive Drugs, SARC Supplement 3, 345-356.)

126 King's County, NY District Attorney's Office. (2008). *Drug Treatment Alternative-to-Prison Annual Report.*

127 Tennessee Governor's Task Force on Methamphetamine Abuse. (2004). *Final Report.*

128 Ensuring Sustainability for Drug Courts: An Overview of Funding Strategies. (2008). *Monograph Series 8.* National Drug Court Institute.

129 Ensuring Sustainability for Drug Courts: An Overview of Funding Strategies. (2008). *Monograph Series 8.* National Drug Court Institute.

130 Ensuring Sustainability for Drug Courts: An Overview of Funding Strategies. (2008). *Monograph Series 8.* National Drug Court Institute.

131 U.S. Department of Health and Human Services. Substance Abuse and Mental Health Services Administration. (2003). *National Survey on Drug Use and Health.* Washington, DC.

132 National Association of Counties.

133 U.S. Drug Enforcement Administration. (2005, July 11). *The New York Times.*

134 U.S. Drug Enforcement Administration. (2005, July 11). *The New York Times.*

135 National Association of Counties.

136 *Community Prosecution Interviews.* Center for Court Innovation. Retrieved from http://www.courtinnovation.org

137 Kelling, G, & Wilson, J. Q. (1982, March). Broken Windows. *The Atlantic.*

138 Kelling, G, & Wilson, J. Q. (1982, March). Broken Windows. *The Atlantic.*

139 Francis, D. (2003, March). What Reduced Crime in New York City. *The NBER* (National Bureau of Economic Research) *Digest.*

140 Francis, D. (2003, March). What Reduced Crime in New York City. *The NBER* (National Bureau of Economic Research) *Digest.*

141 Keizer, K, Lindenberg, L., & Steg, L. (2008, December 12). The Spreading of Disorder. *Science*

142 WMC-TV. (2002, February 27).

143 Shelby County, Tennessee District Attorney's Office. (2002). *Annual Report.*

144 Wolff, R.V., & Worrall, J.L. (2004). *Lessons from the Field – Ten Community Prosecution Leadership Profiles.* Center for Court Innovation & American Prosecutors Research Institute.

145 Wolff, R.V., & Worrall, J.L. (2004). *Lessons from the Field – Ten Community Prosecution Leadership Profiles.* Center for Court Innovation & American Prosecutors Research Institute.

146 *Community Prosecution Interviews.* Center for Court Innovation. Retrieved from http://www.courtinnovation.org

147 Bearman, G., & Anderson, D.C. (1999). *Engaging the Community.* Center for Court Innovation & U.S. Bureau of Justice Assistance.

148 Bearman, G., & Anderson, D.C. (1999). *Engaging the Community.* Center for Court Innovation & U.S. Bureau of Justice Assistance.

149 Bearman, G., & Anderson, D.C. (1999). *Engaging the Community.* Center for Court Innovation & U.S. Bureau of Justice Assistance.

150 Engaging Stakeholders in Your Project. Center for Court Innovation & U.S. Bureau of Justice Assistance. Retrieved from http://www.courtinnovation.org/_uploads/documents/Engaging_Stakeholders_in_Your_Project%5B1%5D.pdf

151 Engaging Stakeholders in Your Project. Center for Court Innovation & U.S. Bureau of Justice Assistance. Retrieved from http://www.courtinnovation.org/_uploads/documents/Engaging_Stakeholders_in_Your_Project%5B1%5D.pdf

152 Bearman, G., & Anderson, D.C. (1999). *Engaging the Community.* Center for Court Innovation & U.S. Bureau of Justice Assistance.

153 Bearman, G., & Anderson, D.C. (1999). *Engaging the Community.* Center for Court Innovation & U.S. Bureau of Justice Assistance.

154 *Key Principles of Community Prosecution.* (2009). National Center for Community Prosecution, National District Attorneys Association.

155 *Key Principles of Community Prosecution.* (2009). National Center for Community Prosecution, National District Attorneys Association.

156 *Key Principles of Community Prosecution.* (2009). National Center for Community Prosecution, National District Attorneys Association.

157 *Key Principles of Community Prosecution.* (2009). National Center for Community Prosecution, National District Attorneys Association.

158 *Key Principles of Community Prosecution.* (2009). National Center for Community Prosecution, National District Attorneys Association.

159 *Key Principles of Community Prosecution.* (2009). National Center for Community Prosecution, National District Attorneys Association.

160 *Key Principles of Community Prosecution.* (2009). National Center for Community Prosecution, National District Attorneys Association.

161 *Key Principles of Community Prosecution.* (2009). National Center for Community Prosecution, National District Attorneys Association.

162 *Community Prosecution Interviews.* Center for Court Innovation. Retrieved from http://www.courtinnovation.org

163 *Community Prosecution Interviews.* Center for Court Innovation. Retrieved from http://www.courtinnovation.org

164 Wolff, R.V., & Worrall, J.L. (2004). *Lessons from the Field – Ten Community Prosecution Leadership Profiles.* Center for Court Innovation & American Prosecutors Research Institute.

165 Wolff, R.V., & Worrall, J.L. (2004). *Lessons from the Field – Ten Community Prosecution Leadership Profiles.* Center for Court Innovation & American Prosecutors Research Institute.

166 Wolff, R.V., & Worrall, J.L. (2004). *Lessons from the Field – Ten Community Prosecution Leadership Profiles.* Center for Court Innovation & American Prosecutors Research Institute.

167 Wolff, R.V., & Worrall, J.L. (2004). *Lessons from the Field – Ten Community Prosecution Leadership Profiles.* Center for Court Innovation & American Prosecutors Research Institute.

168 Center for Court Innovation. *Community Court Overview.* (2009). Retrieved from http://www.courtinnovation.org

169 Center for Court Innovation. *Community Court Principles*. (2009). Retrieved from http://www.courtinnovation.org

170 Center for Court Innovation. *Community Court Principles*. (2009). Retrieved from http://www.courtinnovation.org

171 Center for Court Innovation. *Community Court Principles*. (2009). Retrieved from http://www.courtinnovation.org

172 Center for Court Innovation. *Community Court Principles*. (2009). Retrieved from http://www.courtinnovation.org

173 Center for Court Innovation. *Community Court Principles*. (2009). Retrieved from http://www.courtinnovation.org

174 Center for Court Innovation. *Community Court Principles*. (2009). Retrieved from http://www.courtinnovation.org

175 Center for Court Innovation. *Red Hook Community Justice Center*. (2009). Retrieved from http://www.courtinnovation.org

176 Jacksonville, Florida Sheriff's Office. (Through former state attorney Harry Shorstein).

177 Watkins, A., Huebner, B., & Decker, S. (2009). Patterns of gun acquisitions, carrying, and use among   juvenile and adult arrestees: evidence from a high crime city. *Juvenile Quarterly* 25: 674-700.

178 Watkins, A., Huebner, B., & Decker, S. (2009). Patterns of gun acquisitions, carrying, and use among   juvenile and adult arrestees: evidence from a high crime city. J*Juvenile Quarterly* 25: 674-700.

179 Watkins, A., Huebner, B., & Decker, S. (2009). Patterns of gun acquisitions, carrying, and use among   juvenile and adult arrestees: evidence from a high crime city. *Juvenile Quarterly* 25: 681.

180 Watkins, A., Huebner, B., & Decker, S. (2009). Patterns of gun acquisitions, carrying, and use among   juvenile and adult arrestees: evidence from a high crime city. *Juvenile Quarterly* 25: 682.

181 Watkins, A., Huebner, B., & Decker, S. (2009). Patterns of gun acquisitions, carrying, and use among   juvenile and adult arrestees: evidence from a high crime city. *Juvenile Quarterly* 25: 690.

182 Watkins, A., Huebner, B., & Decker, S. (2009). Patterns of gun acquisitions, carrying, and use among   juvenile and adult arrestees: evidence from a high crime city. *Juvenile Quarterly*. (Citing Wright, J.D., Rossi, P.H. (1994). *Armed and considered dangerous: A survey of felons and their firearms*. Expanded edition. New York: Aldine de Gruyten.)

183 Watkins, A., Huebner, B., & Decker, S. (2009). Patterns of gun acquisitions, carrying, and use among juvenile and adult arrestees: evidence from a high crime city. Juvenile Quarterly 25. (Citing Sheeley, J.F., & Wright, J.D. (1995). *In the line of fire: Youth, guns, and violence in urban America*. New York, Aldine de Gruyter.)

184 Watkins, A., Huebner, B., & Decker, S. (2009). Patterns of gun acquisitions, carrying, and use among juvenile and adult arrestees: evidence from a high crime city. *Juvenile Quarterly* 25. (Citing Harlow, C.W. (2001). Firearm use by offenders. Washington, D.C.: Bureau of Justice Statistics.)

185 Watkins, A., Huebner, B., & Decker, S. (2009). Patterns of gun acquisitions, carrying, and use among juvenile and adult arrestees: evidence from a high crime city. *Juvenile Quarterly* 25: 674.

186 Watkins, A., Huebner, B., & Decker, S. (2009). Patterns of gun acquisitions, carrying, and use among juvenile and adult arrestees: evidence from a high crime city. *Juvenile Quarterly* 25: 692.

187 Watkins, A., Huebner, B., & Decker, S. (2009). Patterns of gun acquisitions, carrying, and use among juvenile and adult arrestees: evidence from a high crime city. *Juvenile Quarterly* 25: 690.

188 Watkins, A., Huebner, B., & Decker, S. (2009). Patterns of gun acquisitions, carrying, and use among juvenile and adult arrestees: evidence from a high crime city. *Juvenile Quarterly* 25: 682-3.

189 Watkins, A., Huebner, B., & Decker, S. (2009). Patterns of gun acquisitions, carrying, and use among juvenile and adult arrestees: evidence from a high crime city. *Juvenile Quarterly* 25: at 679 (Citing Thornberry, T.P., Krohn, M.D., Lizotte, A.J., Smith, C.A., & Tobin, K. (2003). Gangs and delinquency in developmental perspective. New York. Cambridge University Press.)

190 Watkins, A., Huebner, B., & Decker, S. (2009). Patterns of gun acquisitions, carrying, and use among juvenile and adult arrestees: evidence from a high crime city. *Juvenile Quarterly* 25: 686.

191 Watkins, A., Huebner, B., & Decker, S. (2009). Patterns of gun acquisitions, carrying, and use among juvenile and adult arrestees: evidence from a high crime city. *Juvenile Quarterly* 25: 684.

192 Watkins, A., Huebner, B., & Decker, S. (2009). Patterns of gun acquisitions, carrying, and use among juvenile and adult arrestees: evidence from a high crime city. *Juvenile Quarterly* 25: 688.

193 Sam Vincent Meddis. Poll: Treat Juveniles the Same as Adult Offenders. (1993, October 29) *USA Today.*

194 Tennessee Code Annotated 37-1-137(a).

195 Tennessee Code Annotated 37-1-137(a).

196 Tennessee Code Annotated 37-1-134.

197 Tennessee Code Annotated 37-1-101(a)(2).

198 U.S. Department of Justice. Bureau of Justice Statistics. (2008, August). *OJJDP Juvenile Justice Bulletin.* Washington, DC.

199 Tennessee Code Annotated 37-1-134

200 U.S. Department of Justice. Bureau of Justice Statistics. (2008, August). *OJJDP Juvenile Justice Bulletin.* Washington, DC.

201 U.S. Department of Justice. Bureau of Justice Statistics. (2008, August). *OJJDP Juvenile Justice Bulletin.* Washington, DC

202 U.S. Department of Justice. Bureau of Justice Statistics. (2008, August). *OJJDP Juvenile Justice Bulletin.* Washington, DC

203 Griffin, P., (2003, October). Trying and sentencing juveniles as adults: an analysis of state transfers and blended sentencing laws. *Special Project Bulletin.* National Center for Juvenile Justice. Washington, DC.

204 Griffin, P., (2003, October). Trying and sentencing juveniles as adults: an analysis of state transfers and blended sentencing laws. *Special Project Bulletin.* National Center for Juvenile Justice. Washington, DC. (Citing Massachusetts General Laws, ch. 119, § 54.)

205 Griffin, P., (2003, October). Trying and sentencing juveniles as adults: an analysis of state transfers and blended sentencing laws. *Special Project Bulletin.* National Center for Juvenile Justice. Washington, DC.

206 Griffin, P., (2003, October). Trying and sentencing juveniles as adults: an analysis of state transfers and blended sentencing laws. *Special Project Bulletin.* National Center for Juvenile Justice. Washington, DC. (Citing Minnesota Statutes, §§ 260B. 125, 260B, 130.)

207 Griffin, P., (2003, October). Trying and sentencing juveniles as adults: an analysis of state transfers and blended sentencing laws. *Special Project Bulletin.* National Center for Juvenile Justice. Washington, DC. (Citing Alaska Statutes, § 47.12. 065, 47.12.120(j), 47.12.160 and 705 Illinois Compiled statutes 405/5-810.)

208 Griffin, P., (2003, October). Trying and sentencing juveniles as adults: an analysis of state transfers and blended sentencing laws. *Special Project Bulletin.* National Center for Juvenile Justice. Washington, DC.

209 Griffin, P., (2003, October). Trying and sentencing juveniles as adults: an analysis of state transfers and blended sentencing laws. *Special Project Bulletin*. National Center for Juvenile Justice. Washington, DC. (Citing Missouri Statutes § 211.073.)

210 Griffin, P., (2003, October). Trying and sentencing juveniles as adults: an analysis of state transfers and blended sentencing laws. *Special Project Bulletin*. National Center for Juvenile Justice. Washington, DC. (Citing Levitt, S.D. 1998. Juvenile crime and punishment. *Journal of Political Economy* 106:1156-85.)

211 Griffin, P., (2003, October). Trying and sentencing juveniles as adults: an analysis of state transfers and blended sentencing laws. *Special Project Bulletin*. National Center for Juvenile Justice. Washington, DC.

212 Griffin, P., (2003, October). Trying and sentencing juveniles as adults: an analysis of state transfers and blended sentencing laws. *Special Project Bulletin*. National Center for Juvenile Justice. Washington, DC. (Citing Glassner, B., Ksander, M., Berg, B., and Johnson, B.D. A note on the deterrent effect of juvenile versus adult jurisdiction. *Social Problems*. 31: 219-21.

213 Griffin, P., (2003, October). Trying and sentencing juveniles as adults: an analysis of state transfers and blended sentencing laws. *Special Project Bulletin*. National Center for Juvenile Justice. Washington, DC. (Citing Lee, D.S., and McCrary, J. 2005. *Crime, punishment, and myopia*. Working paper 11491. Cambridge, MA: National Bureau of Economic Research.

214 Griffin, P., (2003, October). Trying and sentencing juveniles as adults: an analysis of state transfers and blended sentencing laws. *Special Project Bulletin*. National Center for Juvenile Justice. Washington, DC. (Citing Steiner, B., and Wright, E. 2006. Assessing the relative effects of state direct file waiver laws on violent juvenile crime: Deterrence or irrelevance? *Journal of Criminal Law and Criminology* 96: 1451-77.

215 Griffin, P., (2003, October). Trying and sentencing juveniles as adults: an analysis of state transfers and blended sentencing laws. *Special Project Bulletin*. National Center for Juvenile Justice. Washington, DC. (Citing Redding, R.E., and Fuller, E.J. 2004 (summer). What do juvenile offenders know about being tried as adults? : Implications for deterrence. Juvenile and Family Court Journal 35-45.

216 Griffin, P., (2003, October). Trying and sentencing juveniles as adults: an analysis of state transfers and blended sentencing laws. *Special Project Bulletin*. National Center for Juvenile Justice. Washington, DC.

217 Griffin, P., (2003, October). Trying and sentencing juveniles as adults: an analysis of state transfers and blended sentencing laws. *Special Project Bulletin*. National Center for Juvenile Justice. Washington, DC.

218 Griffin, P., (2003, October). Trying and sentencing juveniles as adults: an analysis of state transfers and blended sentencing laws. *Special Project Bulletin*. National Center for Juvenile Justice. Washington, DC. (Citing Von Hirsch, A., Bottoms, A.E., Burney, E., and Wikstrom P.O. 1999. *Criminal deterrence and sentence severity: An analysis of recent research*. Oxford, England: Hart.

219 Griffin, P., (2003, October). Trying and sentencing juveniles as adults: an analysis of state transfers and blended sentencing laws. *Special Project Bulletin*. National Center for Juvenile Justice. Washington, DC.

220 Withers, A., Huebner, B., and Decker, S. (2008). Patterns of gun acquisitions, carrying, and use among juvenile and adult arrestees: evidence from a high crime city. *Justice Quarterly* 25: 674-700.

221 Withers, A., Huebner, B., and Decker, S. (2008). Patterns of gun acquisitions, carrying, and use among juvenile and adult arrestees: evidence from a high crime city. *Justice Quarterly* 25: 691.

222 Withers, A., Huebner, B., and Decker, S. (2008). Patterns of gun acquisitions, carrying, and use among juvenile and adult arrestees: evidence from a high crime city. *Justice Quarterly* 25: 691 (Citing Pogarsky, G., 2007. Deterrence and individual differences among convicted offenders. Journal of Quantitative Criminology, 23, 59-74.)

223 Withers, A., Huebner, B., and Decker, S. (2008). Patterns of gun acquisitions, carrying, and use among juvenile and adult arrestees: evidence from a high crime city. *Justice Quarterly* 25: 693-4.

224 Withers, A., Huebner, B., and Decker, S. (2008). Patterns of gun acquisitions, carrying, and use among juvenile and adult arrestees: evidence from a high crime city. *Justice Quarterly* 25: 694.

225 Withers, A., Huebner, B., and Decker, S. (2008). Patterns of gun acquisitions, carrying, and use among juvenile and adult arrestees: evidence from a high crime city. *Justice Quarterly* 25: 674-700.

226 Pima County, Arizona Attorney's Office, Juvenile Arrests for Part I and Part II Crimes, 1995-2007

227 Snyder, H.N., & Sickmund, M. (2006). *Juvenile Offenders and Victims: 2006 National Report.* Department of Justice, Office of Justice Programs, Office of Juvenile Justice and Delinquency Prevention. Washington, D.C.

228 Ratio of youth coming into contact with Memphis-Shelby County Juvenile Court vs. those entering into the custody of the court due to serious and chronic offenses.

229 U.S. Department of Justice. Office of Justice Programs. (2001, September). *OJJDP Juvenile Justice Bulletin.* (Citing Baker, M.L. (2000). *Evaluation of the truancy reduction demonstration program: interim report.* Denver, CO: Colorado Foundation for Families and Children.)

230 U.S. Department of Justice. Office of Justice Programs. (2001, September). *OJJDP Juvenile Justice Bulletin.* (Citing Baker, M.L. (2000). *Evaluation of the truancy reduction demonstration program: interim report.* Denver, CO: Colorado Foundation for Families and Children.)

231 U.S. Department of Justice. Office of Justice Programs. (2001, September). *OJJDP Juvenile Justice Bulletin.* (Citing Kelley, B.T., Loeber, R., Keenan, K., and Delamante, M. 1997. *Developmental Pathways in Boys' Disruptive and Delinquent Behavior.* Washington, D.C. U.S. Department of Justice, Office of Justice Programs, Office of Juvenile Justice and Delinquency Prevention.)

232 U.S. Department of Justice. Office of Justice Programs. (2001, September). *OJJDP Juvenile Justice Bulletin.* (Citing Bell, A.J., Rosen, L.A., and Dynlacht, D. (1994). Truancy Intervention. *The Journal of Research Development in Education* 57(3): 2003-211.)

233 U.S. Department of Justice. Office of Justice Programs. (2001, September). *OJJDP Juvenile Justice Bulletin.* (Citing Bell, A.J., Rosen, L.A., and Dynlacht, D. (1994). Truancy Intervention. *The Journal of Research Development in Education* 57(3): 2003-211.).

234 U.S. Department of Justice. Office of Justice Programs. (2001, September). *OJJDP Juvenile Justice Bulletin.* (Citing Bell, A.J., Rosen, L.A., and Dynlacht, D. (1994). Truancy Intervention. *The Journal of Research Development in Education* 57(3): 2003-211.)

235 U.S. Department of Justice. Office of Justice Programs. (2001, September). *OJJDP Juvenile Justice Bulletin.* (Citing Snyder, H.N. and Sickmund, M. (1995). Juvenile Offenders and Victims: A National Report. Washington, D.C. U.S. Department of Justice, Office of Justice Programs. Office of Juvenile Justice and Delinquency Prevention.)

236 U.S. Department of Justice. Office of Justice Programs. (2001, September). *OJJDP Juvenile Justice Bulletin.* (Citing Garry, E.M. (1996). Truancy: First Step to a Lifetime of Problems. *Bulletin.* Washington, D.C. Department of Justice. Office of Justice Programs. Office of Juvenile Justice and Delinquency Prevention; Also citing Roderick, M. Chlong, J., Arney, M., DaCosta, K., Stone, M., Villarreal-Sosa, L., and Waxman, E. (1997). Habits Hard to Break. A New Look at Truancy in Chicago's Public High Schools. *Research in Brief.* Chicago, IL. University of Chicago, School of Social Service Administration.

237 U.S. Department of Justice. Office of Justice Programs. (2001, September). *OJJDP Juvenile Justice Bulletin.* (Citing Heaviside, S., Roward, C., Williams, C., and Farris, E. 1998. *Violence and Discipline Problems in U.S. Public Schools: 1996-1997.* Washington, D.C. U.S. Department of Education, Office of Educational Research and Improvement. National Center for Education Statistics.

Index

Symbols